I0819077

WILD WONDERS

The Untamed and Enigmatic Animals that Inhabit Yellowstone National Park

JULIA COOK

Foreword by Trevor Cook

EPIC INK

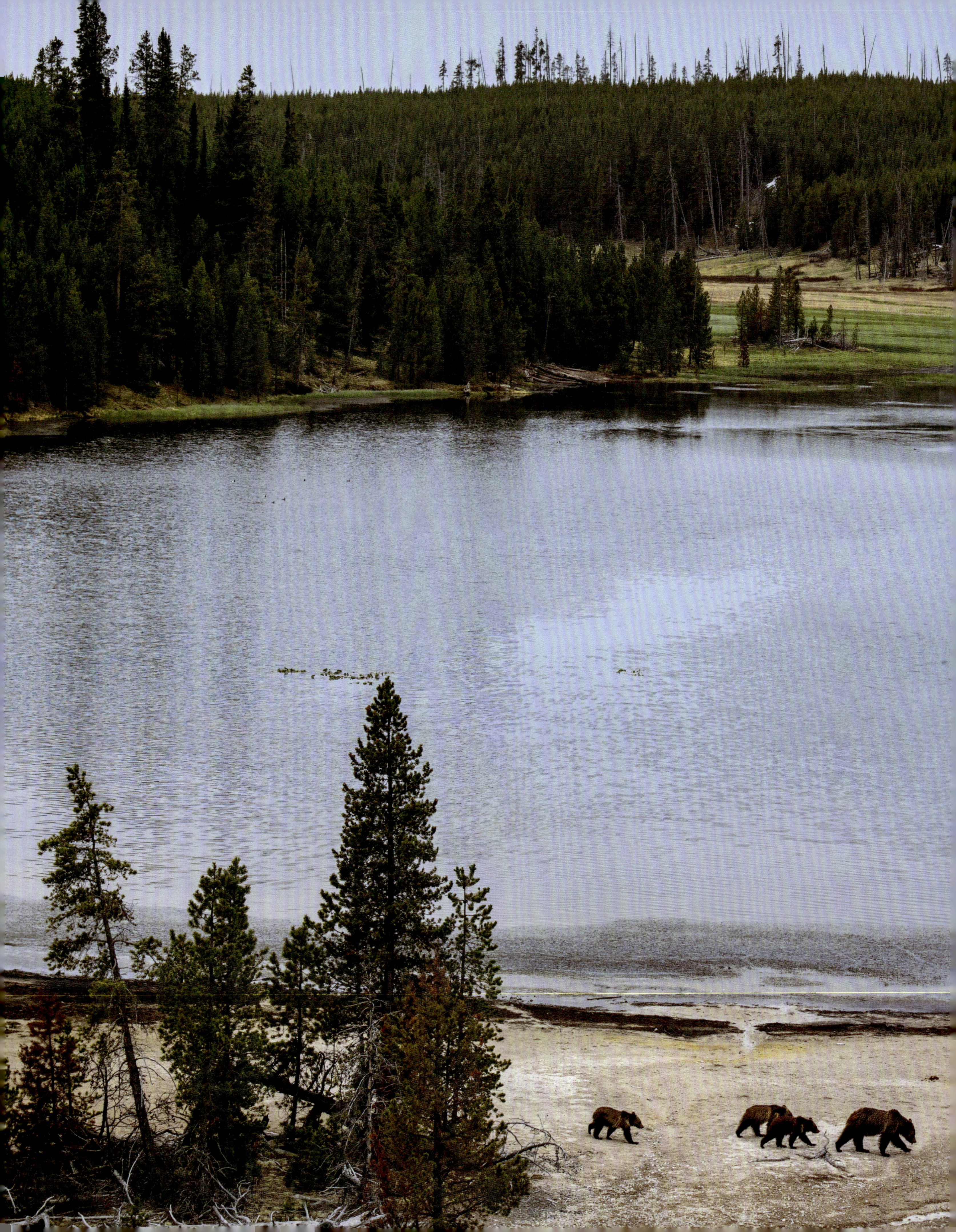

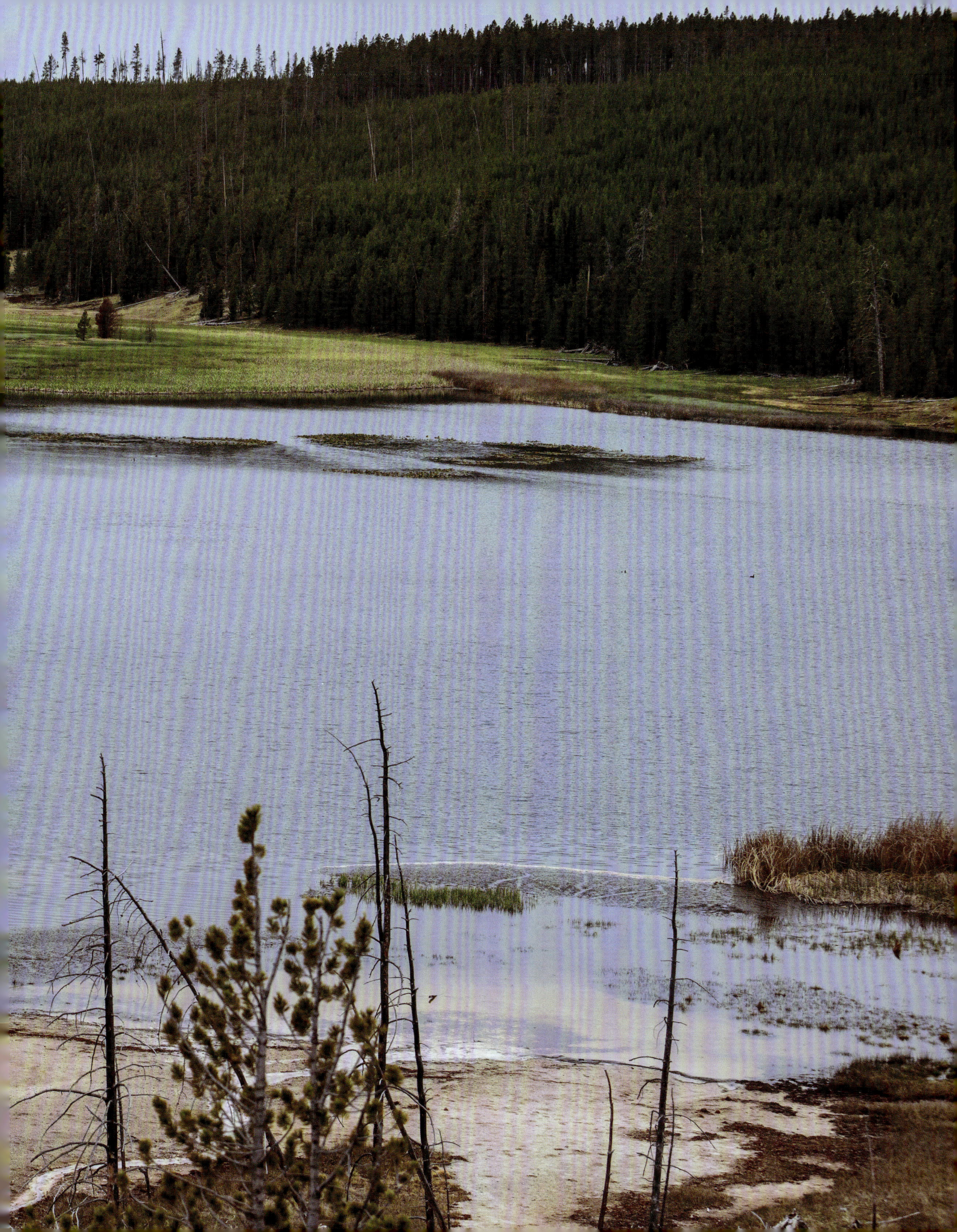

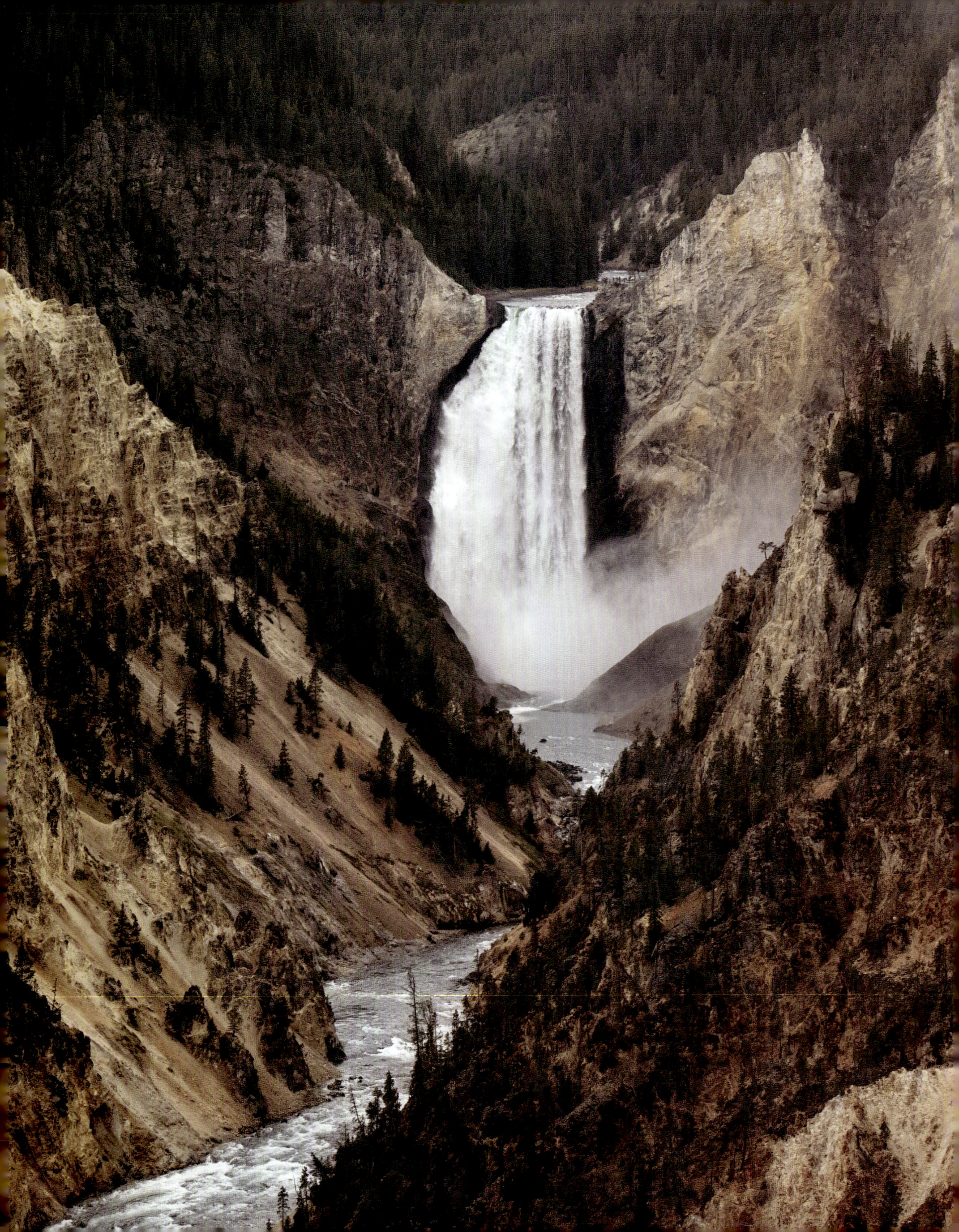

CONTENTS

◀ Lower Falls and the Grand Canyon of the Yellowstone.

▲ *Previous*: A mother grizzly and her triplets stroll along a small thermal lake in Yellowstone.

Foreword

Growing up, I never knew how lucky I was to be from Cody, Wyoming. We had one of the crown jewels of the American wilderness in our own backyard: Yellowstone National Park. As a little kid, I didn't feel the weight of having the world's first national park in my own backyard. In fact, I would ask my mom when we could go to the park, and I wouldn't be referring to the one down the street.

It wasn't until I began traveling the world that I realized just how many people not only knew of Yellowstone but had visited and deeply loved it, as people shared their fond memories with me of seeing their first grizzly bear or watching Old Faithful erupt. I would get blank stares when I said I was from Cody, Wyoming, but once I threw in our family's famous tagline—"fifty miles from Yellowstone"—immediately people from England to New Zealand could locate the part of the world that I call home.

I come from a family of Yellowstone enthusiasts. My great-great-grandparents homesteaded in southern Montana and would take month-long trips into the park on horseback. My grandparents would camp with us on the outskirts of Yellowstone as kids, my dad would take

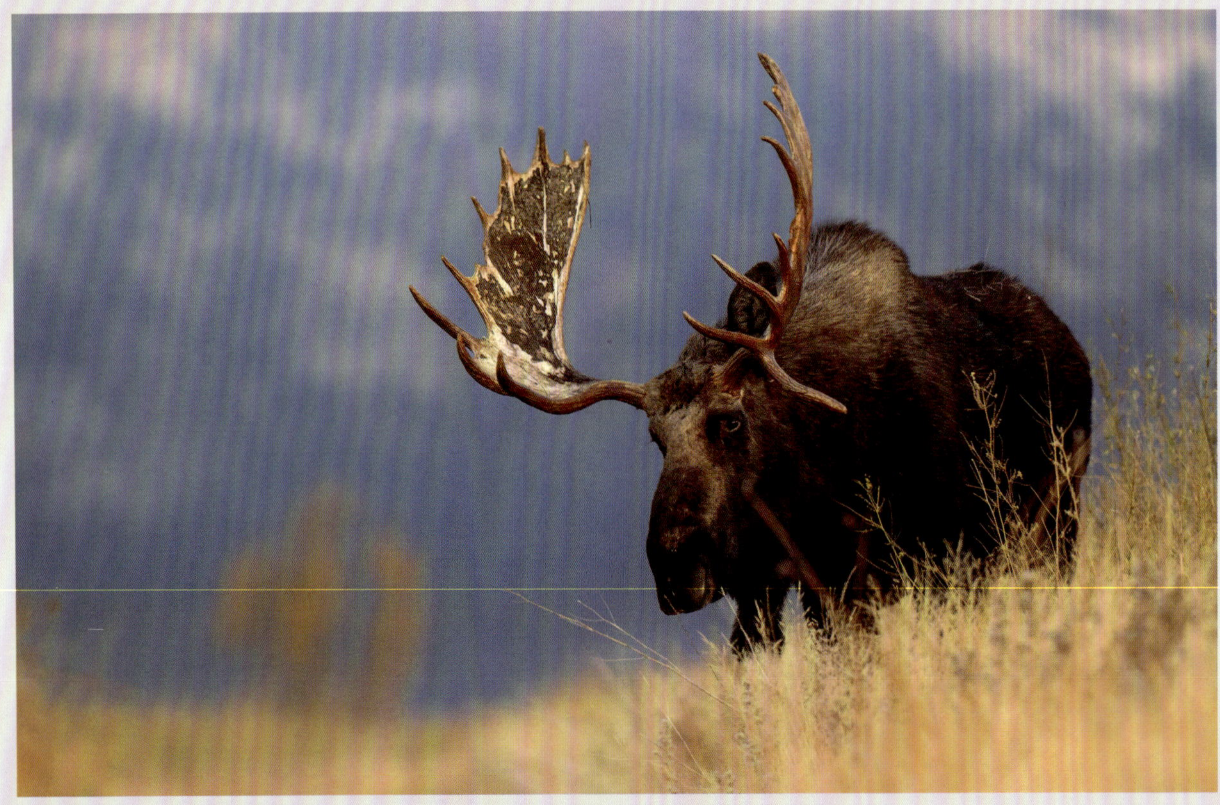

us fishing on Yellowstone Lake, and many special family dogs over the years joined us on our outings. It is my sister Julia, though, who anchors the love of Yellowstone in our family, causing us to see the park in deeper and more exquisite ways with each passing year.

This book offers a beautiful glimpse into Julia's Yellowstone via her eyes and her camera lens. Blending her love of history and science with storytelling and photography, Julia offers an interdisciplinary window into some of her favorite four-legged subjects of the Greater Yellowstone Ecosystem. Each image comes to life as she sets the scene, making us feel as if we were right there with her and her trusty dog Sylvan with each camera click.

One of the most beautiful things about Yellowstone is that it changes with every physical and metaphorical season, just as we do. Yet it acts as a familiar friend, welcoming us with its untamed majesty whether it is our first or our hundredth visit. As a dancer and choreographer, I have traded the pine trees of Wyoming for the skyscrapers of New York City. But it is the several trips home a year, back to the mountains and back to Yellowstone, that fuel me to keep doing life in a concrete jungle.

It is on these park trips with my sister that I feel immense pride—pride that only a big brother can have—for my sister and the incredible tenacity she has as a young, self-taught, strong female photographer, braving the elements to pursue her dream. Yellowstone has been many things for my sister: a friend, a refuge, a studio, and a home. It is a deeply personal and special place to her, but instead of keeping it for herself, she has chosen to share it with the world by educating people from every corner of the globe about the park and its wildlife. As artists, we can't keep our art to ourselves—we must put it out into the world to be seen and enjoyed. I hope you will follow along as my sister continues to do just that.

While Julia's front seat is not big enough to take all of you along for a day in Yellowstone with her (sometimes even I play second fiddle to Sylvan, who gets first dibs), I hope this book gives you a glimpse into Julia's Yellowstone. I hope it inspires you to take a trip to come see Yellowstone for yourselves. I hope it motivates you to protect our beautiful planet and champion conservation. But most of all, no matter where you live, I hope this book inspires you to get outside and enjoy the wonderful world we live in.

Trevor Cook is a dancer and choreographer born and raised in Cody, Wyoming, in the heart of Yellowstone country. Drawing inspiration from the beautiful natural settings of his upbringing, he blends theatre and dance to illustrate human experiences and tell redemptive stories lost to time.

◄ A bull moose walks through an autumn meadow.

Introduction

For me, Yellowstone is home. I grew up an hour away and spent many days of my childhood picnicking under lodgepole pines or catching cutthroat trout on Yellowstone Lake. I remember the thrill I felt when I saw a wolf for the first time. I have always loved the sulfuric smell of thermal areas, the smell of Yellowstone. Even as a little kid I eagerly awaited Yellowstone's opening weekend, when my family and I would drive over the still snow-covered Sylvan Pass, which remains my favorite place in the park to this day. Nothing compares to the rush of pure joy I feel when I drive the winding road up Sylvan Pass, the crisp, pine-scented air drifting through the windows and clouds hugging the peaks more often than not. I even named my dog Sylvan, a constant reminder of the place I love so much.

I have always had a deep connection to everything about Yellowstone, but its wildlife inspires me more than anything—especially grizzly bears. I don't remember seeing my first grizzly, though I wish I did. Watching bears, bison, or elk was a normal part of my childhood, but my first memorable encounter occurred when I was nine or ten, while peering out the back window of my dad's truck. We had driven into Yellowstone in the late afternoon, something we did often, and had come across a grizzly sow with two cubs in a large meadow filled with sagebrush. While the mother dug for roots, the two young cubs regularly stood up on their back legs, only their heads peeking above the tall sage. I felt such excitement watching their natural behavior as the cubs played together, completely unbothered that anyone was watching. We waited until the wild family disappeared into the forest. I still think about those bear cubs every time I pass that meadow. I wonder if I have crossed paths with either bear in adulthood, or if their bloodline continues in any of the bears I photograph regularly today. Regardless, I am forever thankful to the cubs for giving me a look into their lives and further sparking my love for all things wild.

Through each wildlife encounter I have, no matter how brief, I feel continually more connected to and in awe of our wild world, whether it's the first steps of a newborn bison calf or the last breath of an elk at the paws of a wolf pack. I feel drawn to the wildness held deep in a bear's eye and the secrets told in the howl of a wolf. It's that wildness that I try to capture in my photography.

I first started photography in the spring of 2020. The COVID-19 pandemic brought my normal college experience at the University of Wyoming to a halt, but Yellowstone remained a place of solitude and wildness. At first, photography was a creative outlet and a way to spend more time with wild animals, but it very quickly became all I thought about. By that fall, I had decided I wanted to become a full-time wildlife photographer; after graduating college, I was.

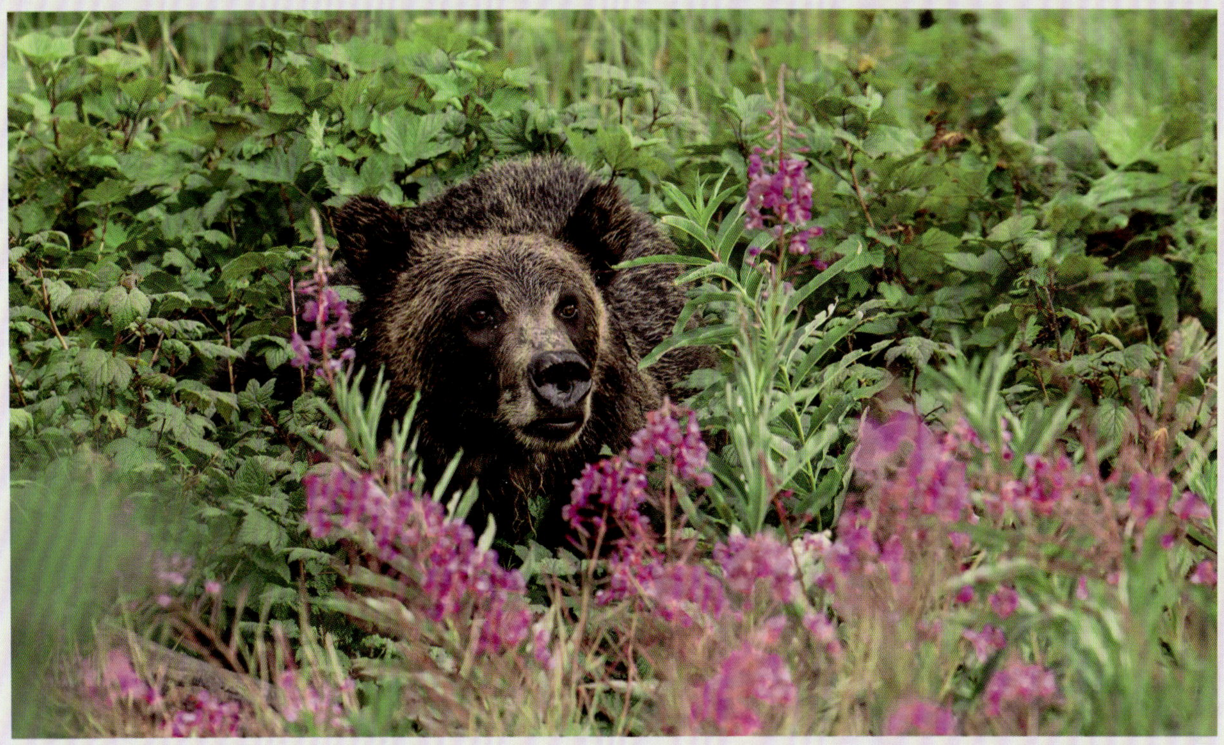

My goal as a photographer is to create impactful images of wildlife to inspire others to care about wildlife conservation. I am immensely grateful that I have been able to have such incredible encounters with wildlife and I wish everyone alive could for one second stare into the eyes of a wild bear; I think the world would be a different place if that were possible. Part of my passion for wildlife photography is in sharing my images with others so they may feel just a fraction of the same pure awe and wonder that I felt when capturing any given image. If even one person looks at one of my images and feels inspired to learn more about that species or to spend time in nature, I consider the image a success.

The following pages will serve as an introduction to the incredible mammals of Yellowstone, from the small red squirrel to the mighty grizzly. They are organized by habitat and elevation; as you progress through the book you will travel higher, through Yellowstone's changing landscape, beginning in the plains and ending atop a mountain in the alpine regions. You will learn about the ecology and life history of each species followed by a selection of images and the stories behind each encounter. Though an image will never compare to observing a wild animal in person, I hope the photos and stories in this book will inspire you to view wildlife differently and to love Yellowstone in the same way that I always have.

▲ A grizzly bear peeks through summer wildflowers.

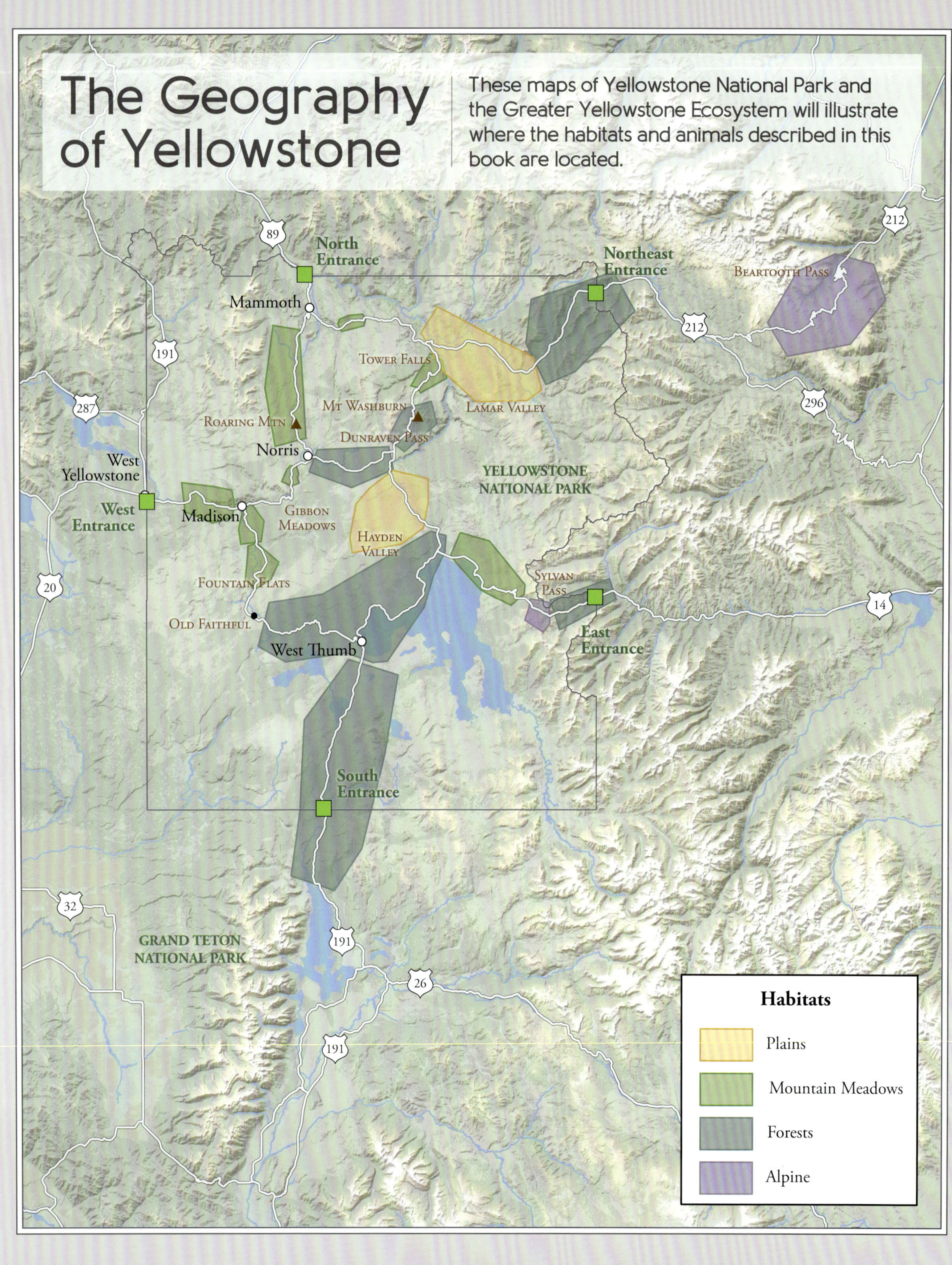

The Geography of Yellowstone
These maps of Yellowstone National Park and the Greater Yellowstone Ecosystem will illustrate where the habitats and animals described in this book are located.
North Entrance
Northeast Entrance
Beartooth Pass
Mammoth
Tower Falls
Lamar Valley
Mt Washburn
Roaring Mtn
Dunraven Pass
Norris
West Yellowstone
West Entrance
Madison
Gibbon Meadows
Yellowstone National Park
Hayden Valley
Sylvan Pass
Fountain Flats
Old Faithful
West Thumb
East Entrance
South Entrance
Grand Teton National Park
89
212
191
287
296
20
14
32
26
Habitats
Plains
Mountain Meadows
Forests
Alpine

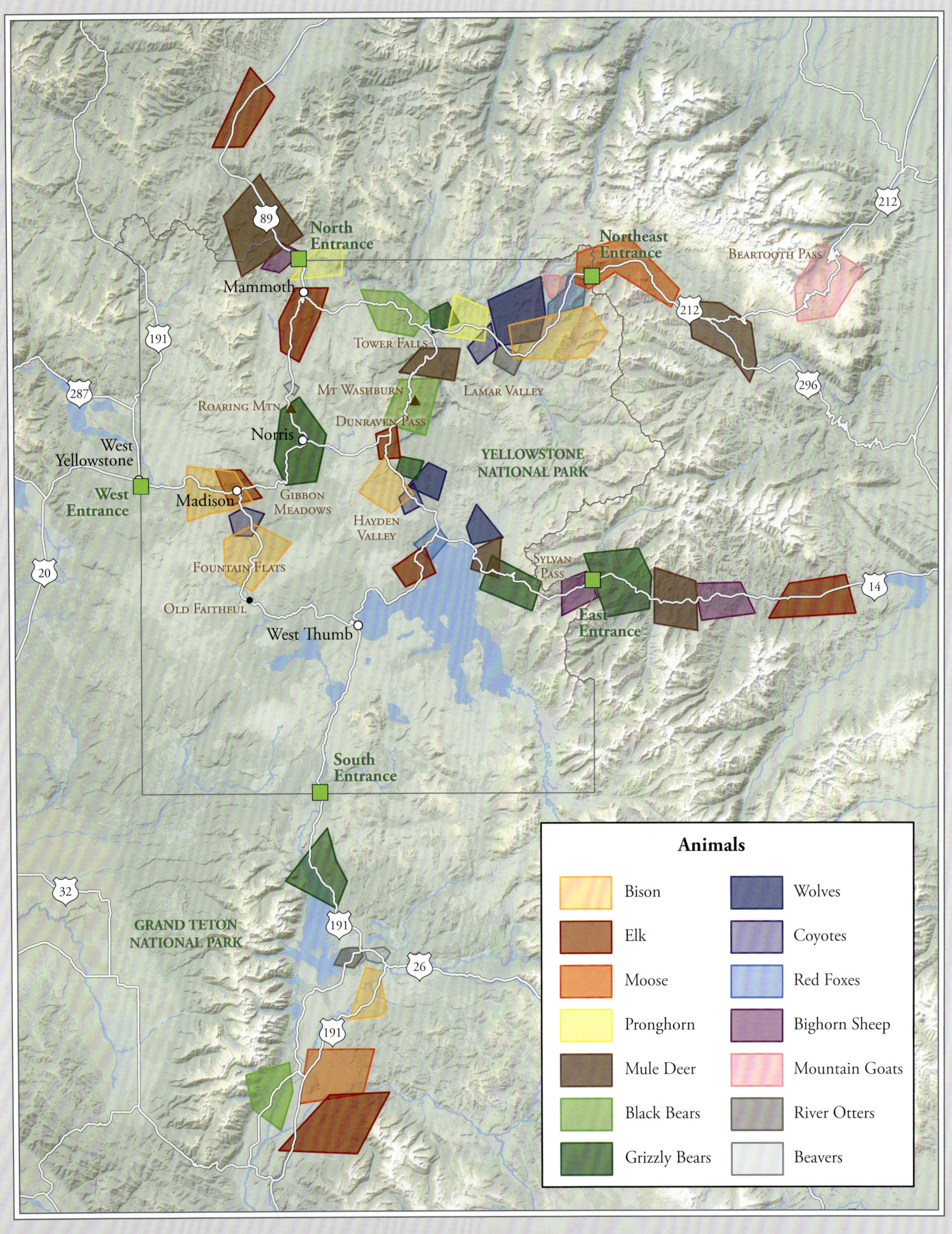

North Entrance
Mammoth
Northeast Entrance
Beartooth Pass
Tower Falls
Lamar Valley
Mt Washburn
Roaring Mtn
Dunraven Pass
Norris
West Yellowstone
West Entrance
Madison
Gibbon Meadows
Hayden Valley
Yellowstone National Park
Fountain Flats
Old Faithful
West Thumb
Sylvan Pass
East Entrance
South Entrance
Grand Teton National Park
89
191
287
20
212
296
14
32
26
Animals
Bison
Elk
Moose
Pronghorn
Mule Deer
Black Bears
Grizzly Bears
Wolves
Coyotes
Red Foxes
Bighorn Sheep
Mountain Goats
River Otters
Beavers

Yellowstone's History

The area that is now known as Yellowstone National Park carries an ancient history shaped by powerful natural forces over the last 150 million years. Glaciers grew and receded, shaping entire mountain ranges that stood in their paths. Rivers cut through the landscape, carving the impressive Grand Canyon of the Yellowstone over hundreds of thousands of years of uninterrupted flow. The park is the site of a dormant super volcano that last erupted over seventy thousand years ago, and geothermal activity beneath Yellowstone's surface has created a unique landscape unlike anywhere else on Earth. All the ancient forces that shaped Yellowstone still exist today, with thousands of thermal features serving as constant reminders of what lies just under the surface, and these forces will continue to shape Yellowstone far into the future.

Man has a long history in Yellowstone, with Indigenous peoples inhabiting the area for over ten thousand years. With abundant natural resources, Yellowstone provided everything for people to survive: bison and other game to hunt, trout to fish, numerous plants to gather, obsidian for arrowheads and other tools, and the thermal waters used for medicinal and religious purposes. Today, twenty-seven tribes have ancestral ties to the sacred land that is now Yellowstone. But everything changed when Yellowstone was established as a national park.

Yellowstone as we know it today became the world's first national park on March 1, 1872, through an act of Congress to preserve the natural wonders found there for the "benefit and enjoyment of the people." The act also established rules for the new national park, including bans on logging, mining, or settlement, including the clause that "all persons who shall locate or settle upon shall be considered trespassers and removed therefrom." As a result, all Indigenous peoples were forcibly removed from their ancestral homeland to create the illusion of an untouched and uninhabited wilderness.

Prior to its establishment as a national park, few people of European descent had ventured into what is now Yellowstone. Those who had, including fur trappers and mountain men, the famed John Colter among them, were laughed at and mocked for their seemingly fantastical stories of a wondrous landscape where steam rose from the earth and rivers of boiling water flowed. It remained one of the most remote and underexplored pieces of wilderness in the American West.

The first expedition into Yellowstone, in 1869, was the Folsom-Cook-Peterson expedition, organized by three Montana men: David Folsom, Charles Cook, and William Peterson. Despite attempting to explore the unknown and difficult terrain of Yellowstone alone and

► A grizzly bear stands up for a better look over tall vegetation.

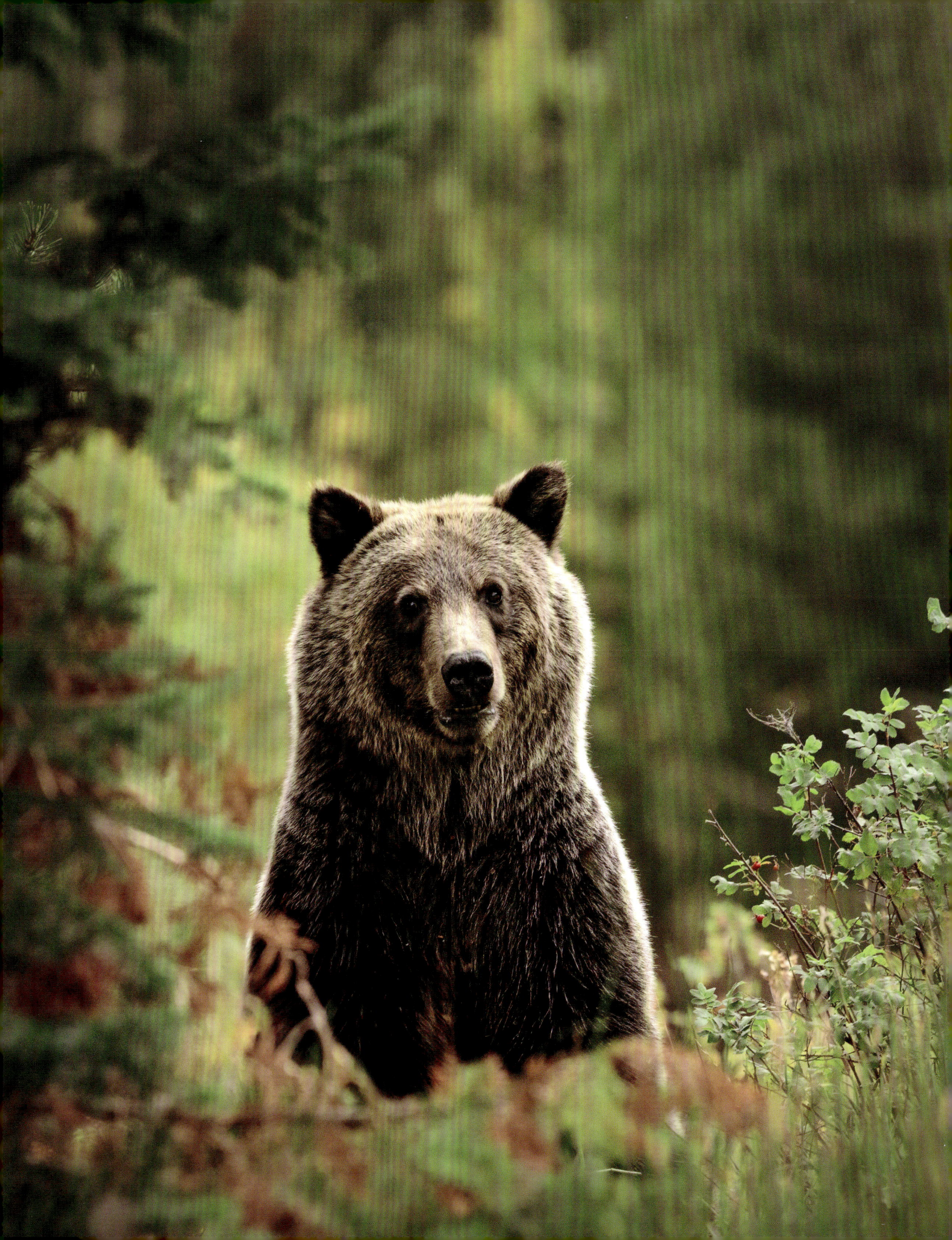

without military support, the three men were surprisingly successful in their endeavor. While the men were not expected to survive the wilderness of Yellowstone, they returned safely and published their descriptions of Yellowstone's strange landscape in early 1870. The publication was significant and confirmed accounts of a boiling landscape filled with springs, which, before being verified in a credible journal, had been regarded as nothing more than stories. The Folsom-Cook-Peterson expedition paved the way for later expeditions, and their publication launched Yellowstone into a new era of exploration.

Only a year after this mission, the first government-funded expedition entered what is now Yellowstone, beginning the first large-scale visitation to the area. Congress gave funding to an expedition led by Surveyor-General Henry Washburn and Montana businessman Nathaniel Langford, along with a military escort led by Lieutenant Gustavus Doane. The Washburn expedition was extremely successful in its endeavor to explore, survey, and document Yellowstone's landscape. Members of the party even made the first recorded descent into the Grand Canyon of the Yellowstone. The group eventually made their way to the west side of the park, to what is today the Upper and Lower Geyser Basins. While there, the men surveyed the area, noting the various steam vents, hot springs, and geysers. The most notable feature the party described was Old Faithful, which they named in honor of its regularity. The Washburn expedition also named various other features, though most were later renamed.

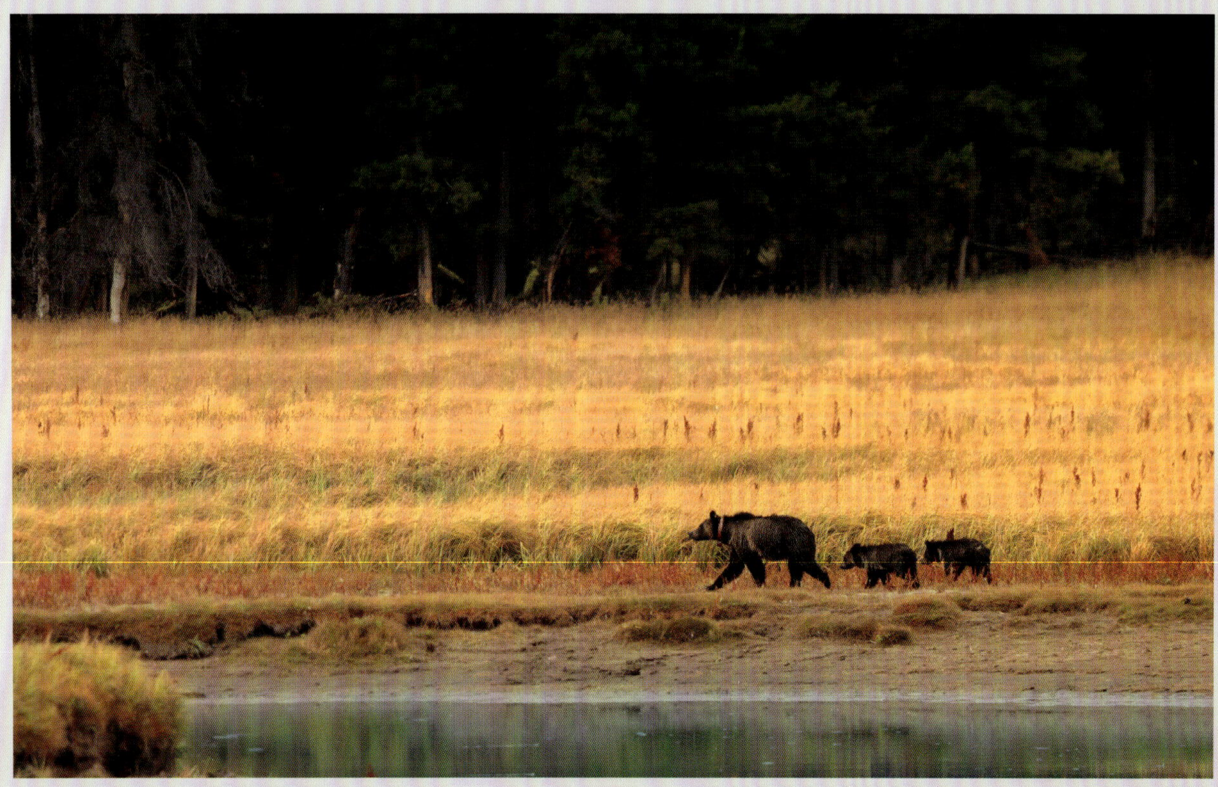

Following the success of the Washburn expedition, Congress was eager to send another group with even more specific goals in mind. The next expedition was led by Ferdinand Vandeveer Hayden, a geologist, with the overall goal of creating maps, collecting geological data, and capturing photographs of the area. The party covered much ground during their stay, making progress in Yellowstone's transition from unexplored wilderness to modern national park. Photographer William H. Jackson accompanied Hayden into Yellowstone and captured its unique natural beauty for the first time, including images of the Canyon and Lower Falls, Mammoth terraces, and various steaming geysers and hot springs, as well as the first image of Old Faithful's eruption. Jackson's photographs showed Congress the resources that lay within Yellowstone, emphasizing the need to protect the area. Within a year, Yellowstone would become the first national park.

During the early years of Yellowstone's status as a national park, travel within the park was limited to stagecoach or horseback, making travel slow. Hotels were built to accommodate travelers: first Lake Hotel in 1891, then Old Faithful Inn, built in the summers of 1903 and 1904 using raw materials harvested from the area. Designed as a rugged yet modern wilderness lodge, the lodgepole pine wood interior and the oversized fireplace gave visitors a comfortable place to stay that reflected Yellowstone's wildness.

Automobiles were introduced into Yellowstone in August 1916 and radically changed the way people visited and interacted with Yellowstone and its natural environment. Automobiles allowed people to visit Yellowstone more quickly and on their own schedule, no longer requiring guides, and the idea of the great American road trip developed throughout the 1920s and 1930s, bringing even more people to Yellowstone. With easy transportation, comfortable accommodations, new campgrounds, and family-friendly activities like fishing, sightseeing, and picnicking, Yellowstone became a place that could be enjoyed by anyone from anywhere.

Today, Yellowstone is one of the most visited national parks in the country. As the oldest, it also has a long history of attracting tourists from across the globe to enjoy its scenic landscapes, abundant wildlife, and unique geothermal features. Yellowstone and the nearby Grand Teton National Park, along with the surrounding national forests and wildlife refuges, are collectively known as the Greater Yellowstone Ecosystem and protect over fifteen million acres of pristine landscape and wilderness areas, representing a dense area of biodiversity with indescribable ecological importance. An island of conservation amid human development, the Greater Yellowstone Ecosystem is one of the few, and largest, truly wild places remaining in the lower forty-eight states. It has always and will continue to inspire all those who visit, remaining a place for the benefit and enjoyment of the people.

◀ A grizzly bear mother and her two cubs walk along a creek.

Ethical Photography

Wildlife photography is both an art and a science that is necessary to communicate the wild world to those who are disconnected from nature. In an ever-changing modern world, valuable pieces of nature are slipping away, and with green being replaced by gray in every way possible, meaningful connections within the natural world are rare but remain important.

Wildlife photography allows people a momentary glimpse into a world they may have never experienced before. Amid society's seemingly ever-shrinking attention span, an image provides enough context and power to inspire, evoke emotion, and convey meaning before the viewer is jolted back to reality. When words are too lengthy to communicate a message, it is the role of an image to encapsulate all those words with one glance.

Conservation photography has evolved as a new genre meant to show the conflicts between the human world and the natural world. Not all wildlife photography can be conservation photography, but there is a need for both; wildlife photography captures a viewer by presenting an entrancing or unique view within an animal's life, while conservation photography is meant to advocate for the specific species or environment, leaving a viewer with a sense of urgency and inspiration to support conservation.

Still, alongside the photographer's responsibility to create meaningful images, there is also a responsibility to keep wildlife wild. No single image is worth diminishing an animal's wildness to create, which is why ethical photography is at the forefront of my mind any time I am in the presence of a wild animal. There is no standardized ethical code of wildlife photography that photographers are required to follow, leaving ethics largely open for interpretation. For me, remaining ethical means avoiding anything that may change an animal's natural behavior, including baiting, using artificial calls, or approaching an animal too closely. As a photographer, I feel I have the responsibility to know when my presence is affecting an animal, and to remove myself before that occurs. Pinned back ears on a moose or a continued stare from a bear may seem insignificant, but both signal stress. Learning to read an animal's body language has helped me know how they feel and to leave them at peace if my presence is disruptive. I started wildlife photography not out of a love of photography, but out of a deep sense of love and awe for wildlife, and, as such, I feel responsible to do everything in my power to keep wildlife wild.

► A bull bison stands in a meadow as a summer storm blows in.

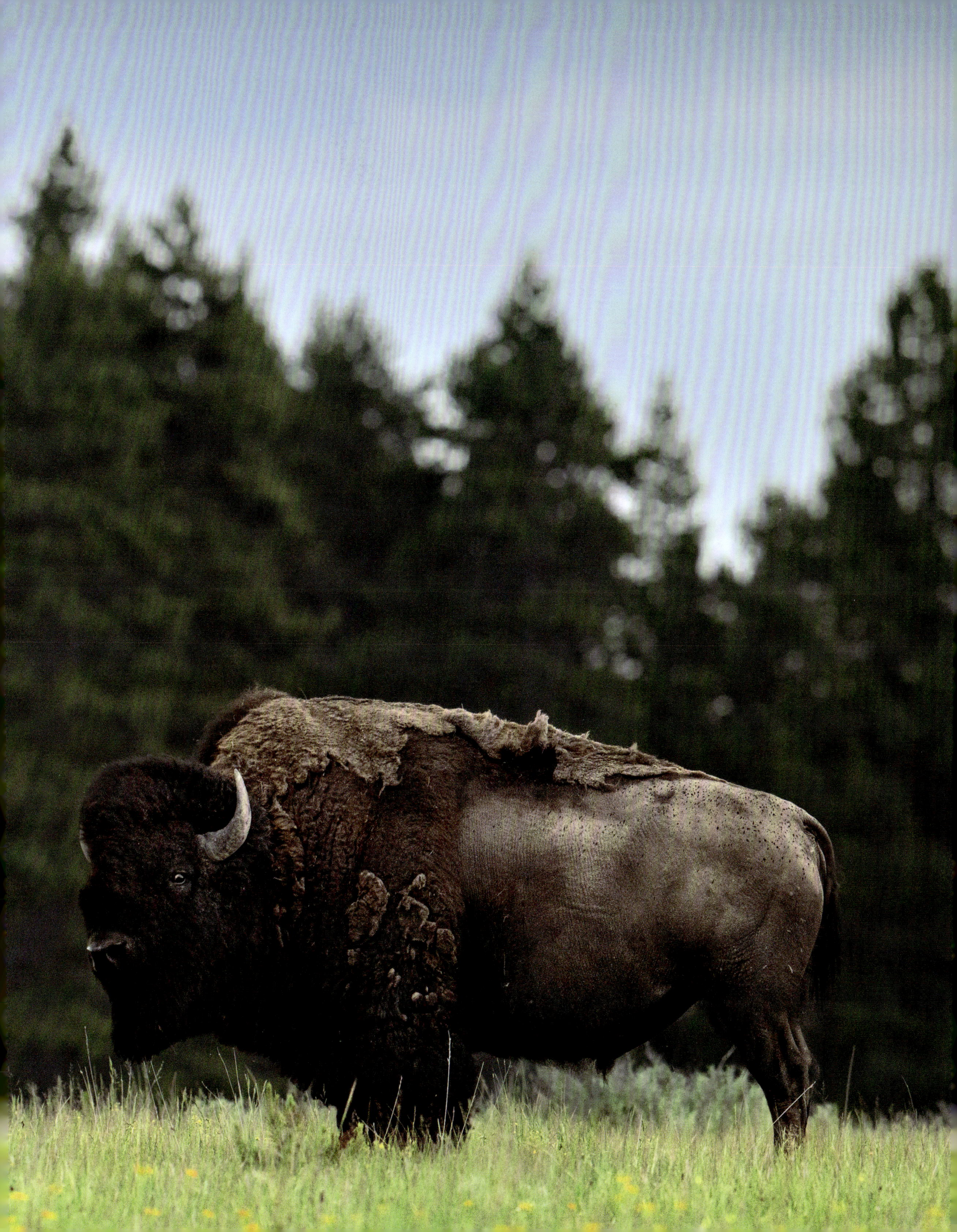

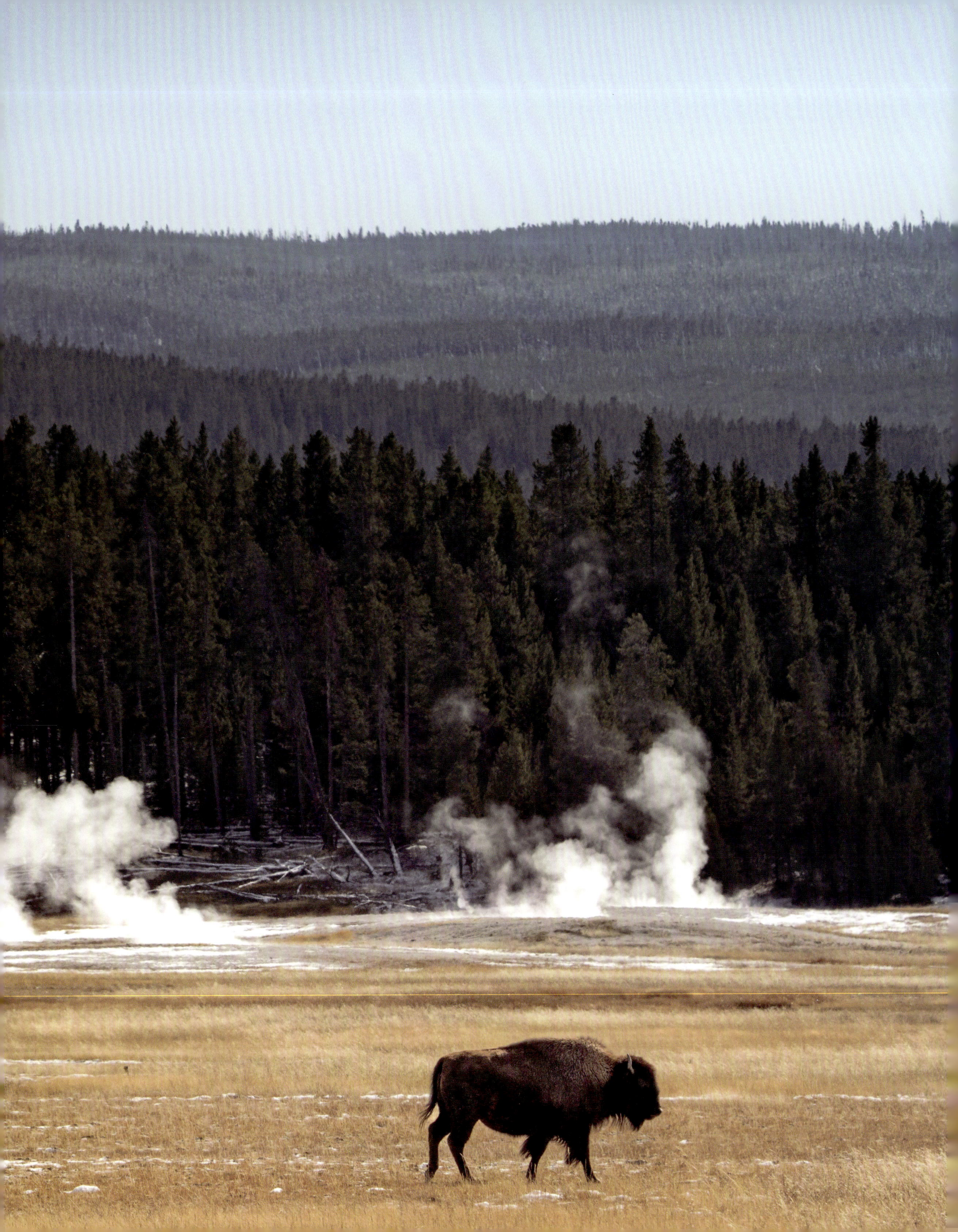

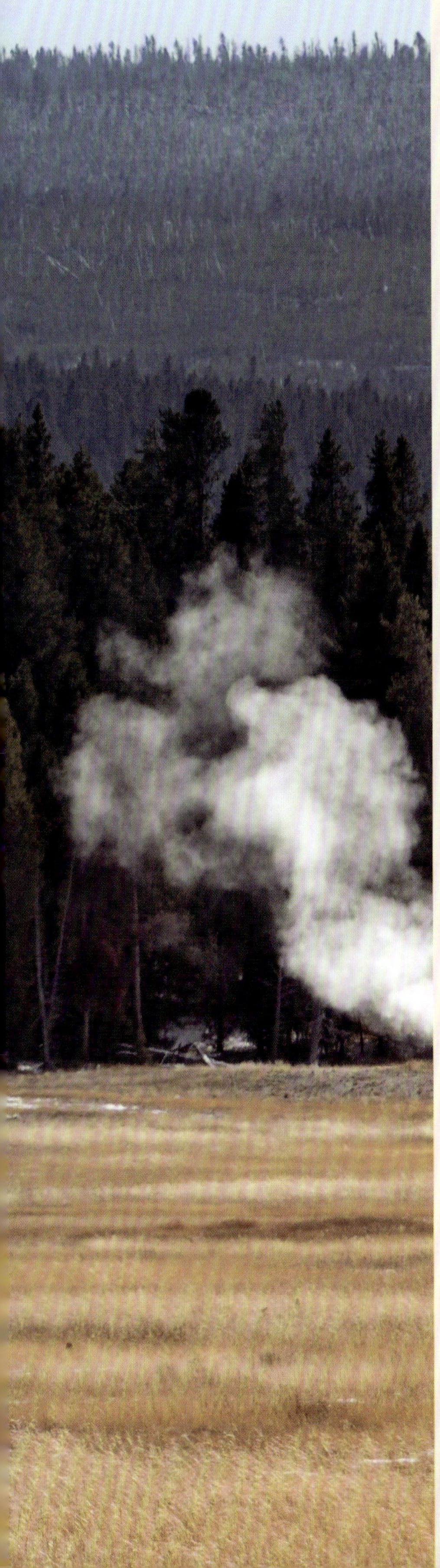

THE PLAINS

The plains of Yellowstone, teeming with life, are a remnant of the wild Great Plains that once spanned hundreds of miles from the slopes of the Rockies, bending to the will of no man. Here on the plains, extremes are further reaching and more severe: Winters are brutal, with wind whipping the ever-present snow into deep drifts that cover any vegetation, yet the spring brings a promise of rest. Snowmelt from the mountains carries water to the low valleys, bringing new life and turning the landscape countless shades of green. After the harshness of winter and without a healthy snowpack, the plains become dusty with drought; too much snowmelt can bring floods, reshaping the rivers and forever changing the landscape.

While the plains' vegetation may appear to lack diversity, numerous species of grasses, wildflowers, and shrubs actually cover the landscape, with mountain sagebrush one of the most plentiful. Wildflowers, including lupine, Indian paintbrush, and balsamroot, decorate the landscape, adding color to the vibrant green hills during their bloom from June through August.

The plains habitat is scattered across Yellowstone, with Lamar Valley being the most expansive. Lower in elevation than most of the park, spring arrives here first. Lamar Valley provides an excellent opportunity to view a range of wildlife, even in the winter months, as one of the few places that remains accessible year-round.

The wildlife that inhabits the plains are as resilient as the aged and weathered sagebrush dotting the area, perfectly suited to anything the wild can conjure. Bison are undoubtedly the most iconic species on the plains, but others thrive here, each carving out their niche in a balanced ecosystem. Welcome to the plains of Yellowstone.

◀ A lone bison traverses the plains of Yellowstone.

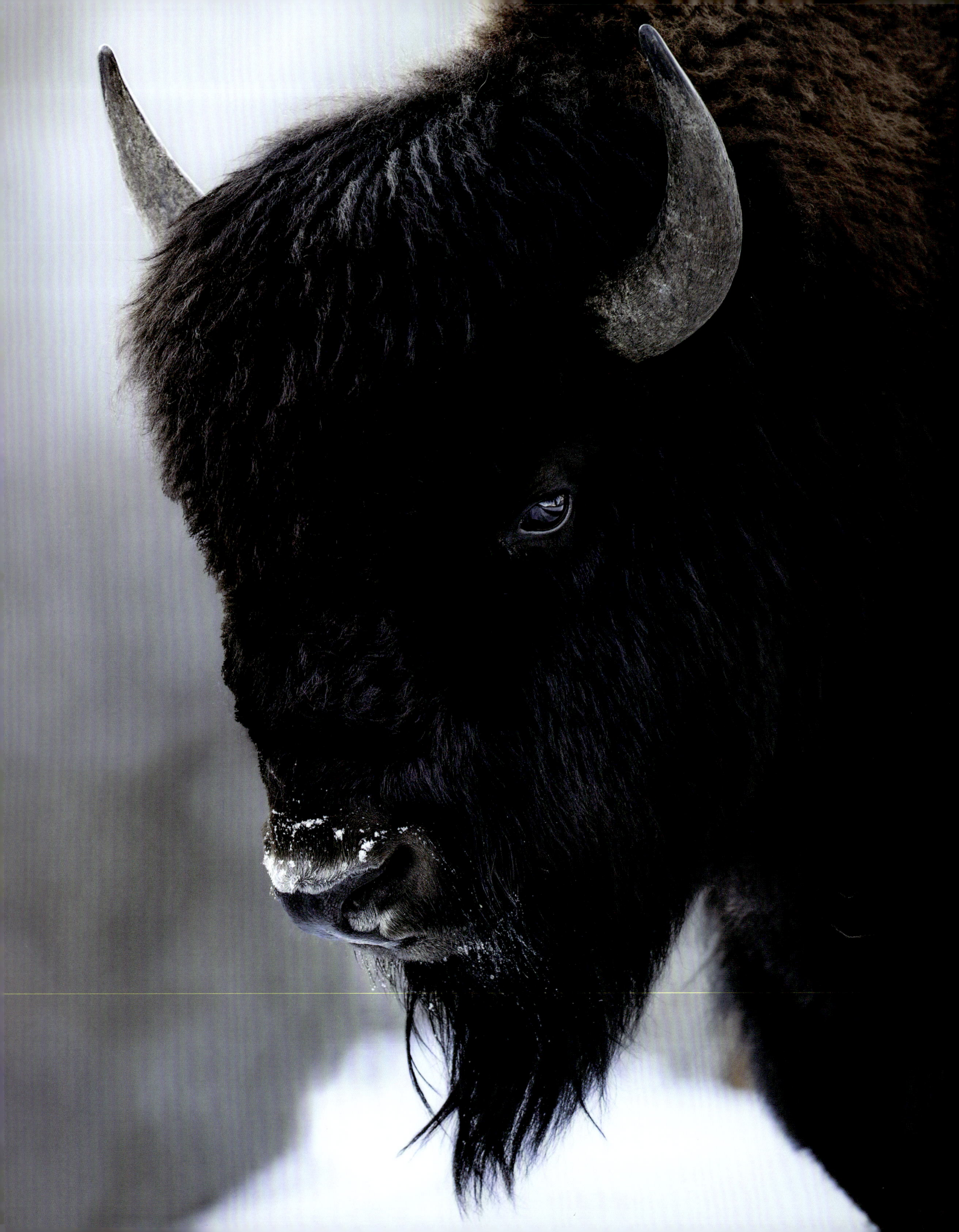

Bison

The American bison is an icon of the West. Today, the bison is the national mammal of the United States, a well-earned honor. Once numbering close to sixty million and roaming from coast to coast and as far south as Mexico, by the late nineteenth century, less than five hundred remained. Hunted by the thousands for their valuable hides and for the challenges they presented to western expansion, particularly to the railway, the once vast herds soon nearly disappeared forever—though not from Yellowstone.

A small population of roughly two hundred animals survived, protected from hunting by the still young national park. From the remaining population, a breeding program was developed to ensure their survival; today, more than five thousand bison roam freely throughout Yellowstone, the only place they have lived continuously since prehistoric times. They can be found in nearly every corner of the park, including near thermal areas where they seek the warmth of the ground, especially during winter. The largest herds will be found in Lamar Valley and Hayden Valley, occasionally even on the road, creating a unique form of traffic.

Bison are herd animals, often traveling in groups that range from just a few individuals to nearly one hundred. Herds congregate during the rut, or mating season, in August, as bulls fight for dominance and breeding rights. Their bellows ring out across the plains, and their dusty wallows dot the landscape.

Calves are born in spring, usually between late April and early June. Their red coats—which darken over their first few months—have earned them the nickname "red dogs." Bison calves begin walking with the herd just minutes after birth, reducing the time they are most vulnerable to predators like bears and wolves. Bison have an average life expectancy of between twelve and fifteen years, with few living to twenty.

◀ A bison in the snow during a Yellowstone winter.

I have always dreamed about what it would have been like to see bison by the thousands, stretching across the plains from horizon to horizon, in the time before they were hunted to the brink of extinction. While the days of the endless herds have long passed, on one summer morning, I was able to get a taste of what that may have been like.

Early in the morning, as the sun was just rising over the opposite hillside, a herd of bison began to move from the sagebrush slope into the green meadow below. Slowly at first, they meandered along in no rush at all, until the bison in front began to run. With each step, more and more bison picked up the pace, until the whole herd was running together in amazing unison, from the largest bulls to the young calves on wobbly legs. Instead of a cluster of individuals, the herd was one, moving in sync with each powerful step.

Hoofbeats sounded like distant thunder as the herd moved closer; I could almost feel the vibrations through the ground. The landscape had already dried from a rainstorm the previous afternoon, causing dust disrupted by pounding hooves to drift into the air, where sunlight caught the dust and gave it an almost fog-like appearance.

As the herd reached the bottom of the hill, they slowed to a steady lumber. Worn dirt trails crisscrossed the hillside, the exact path the bison had taken to enter the meadow. I wondered how long it had been since the first bison walked that same path, starting the pattern that would eventually wear a permanent path in the hillside. Creatures of habit, bison follow the same migration paths passed from generation to generation. In Yellowstone, the generational knowledge and instinct that survives within the herds could be traced back thousands of years. While the herds that exist today are only a fraction of what once was, the tiny calves on wobbly legs are the future of the herd, and a testament to the survival of their entire species.

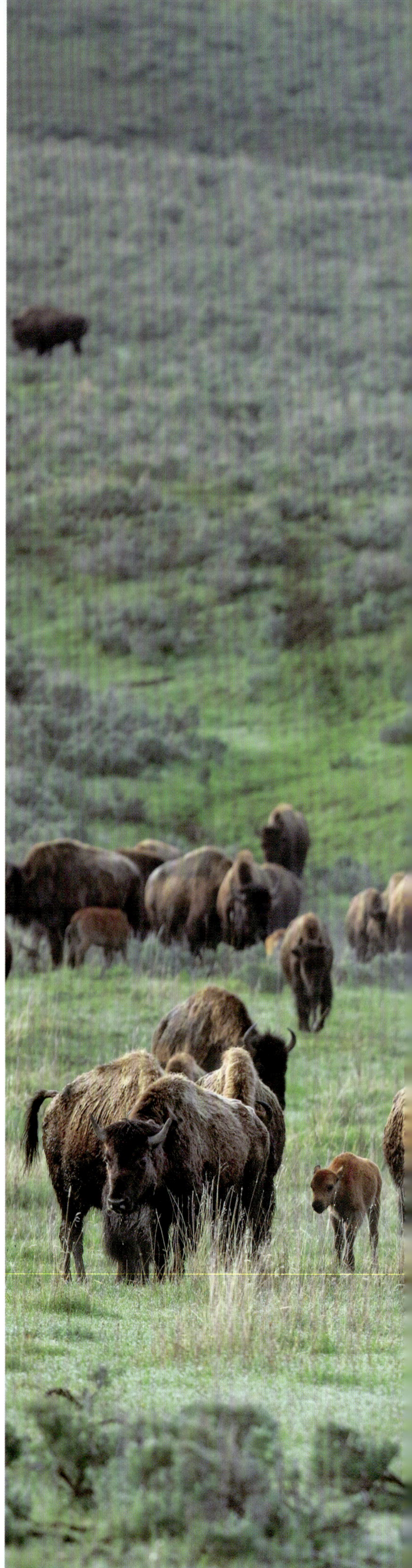

▶ A herd of bison move together though the sagebrush.

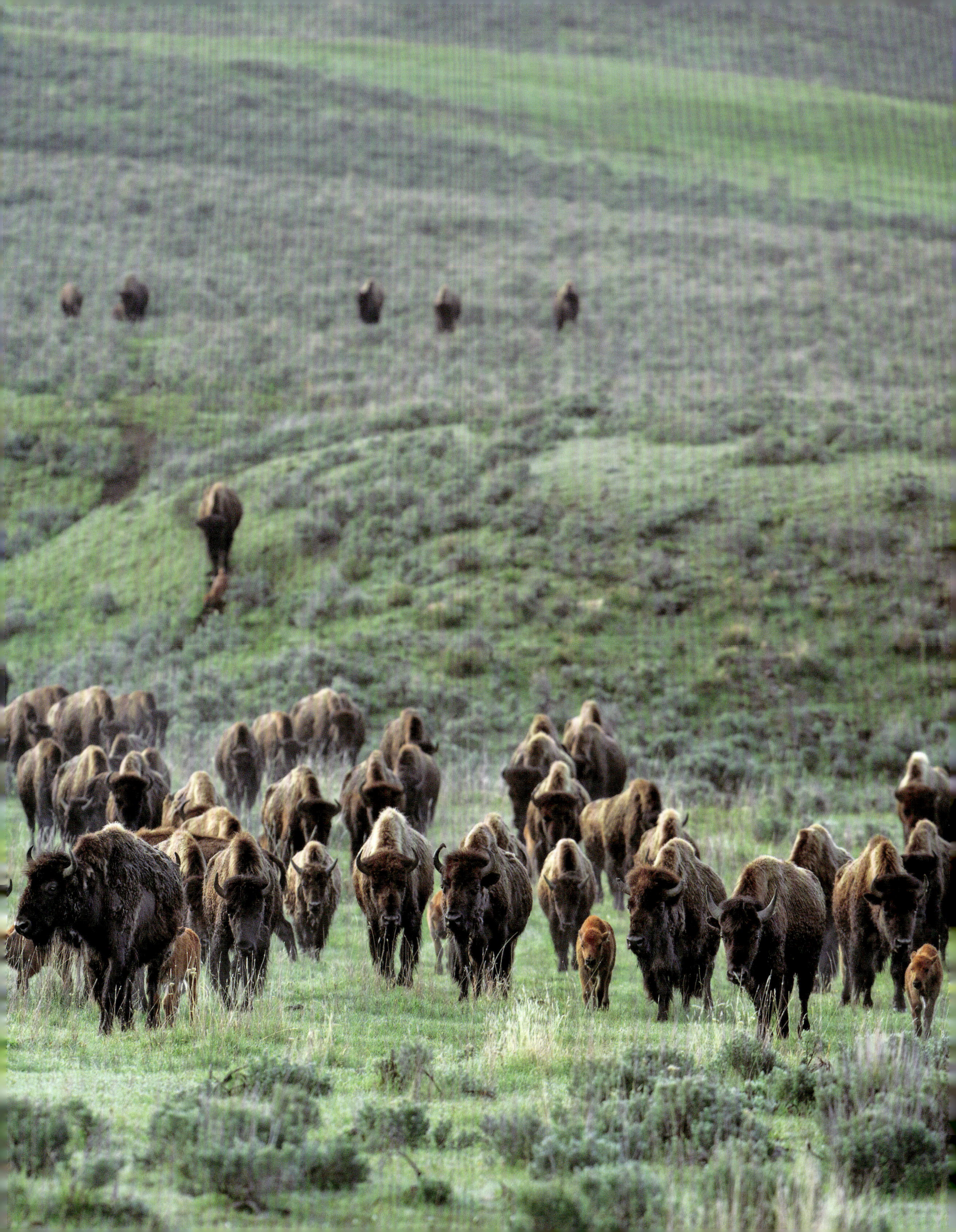

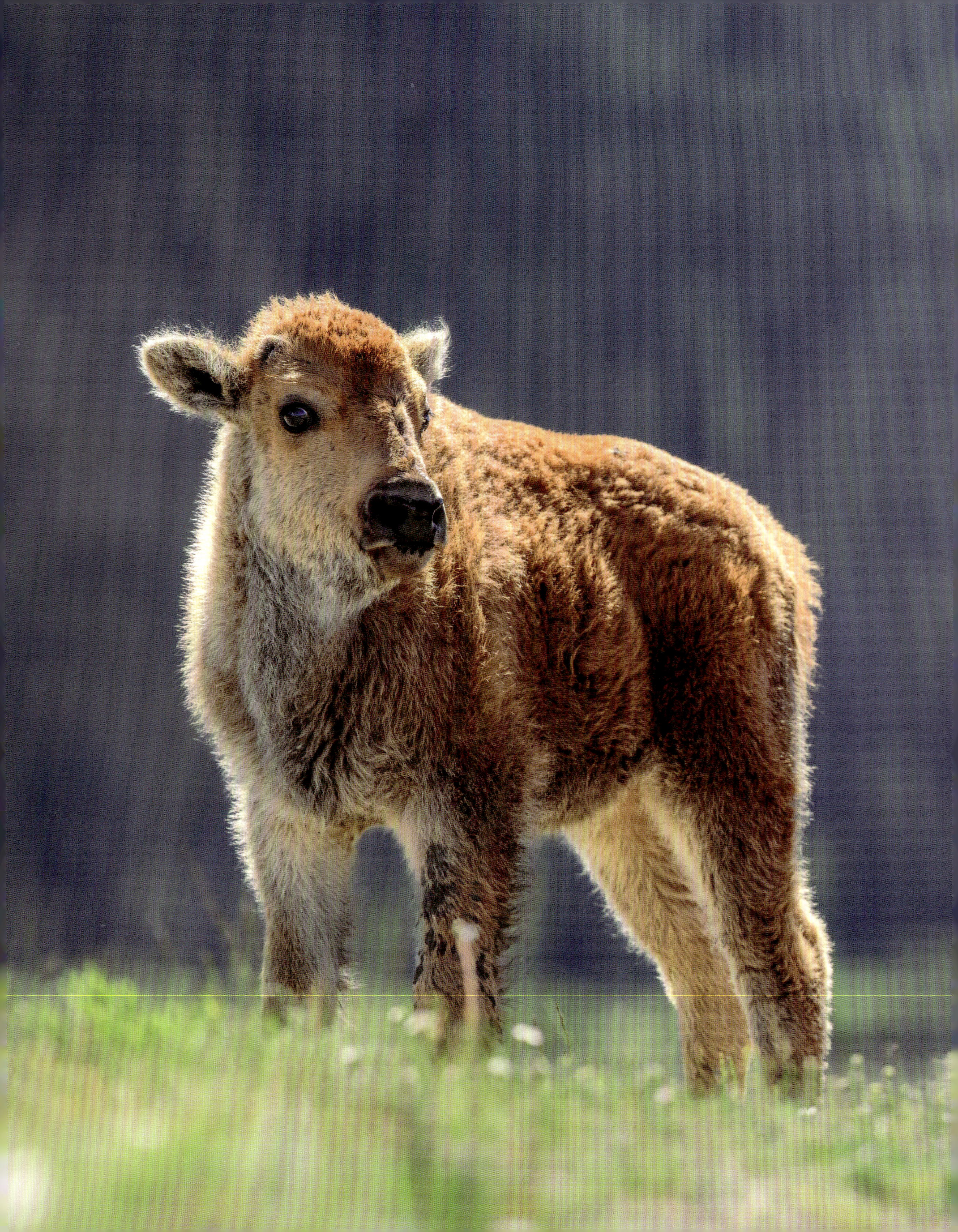

In late spring one year, I ventured into Lamar Valley specifically to photograph the new generation of Yellowstone's vast bison herd. Bison calves are full of spunk and wild curiosity, making them among the most fun animals to watch in the early spring and summer. Calves dotted the vast landscape, their red coats contrasting with the green valleys. Before long, I was almost surrounded by bison, their grunts and snorts filling the air along with their faint yet unmistakable smell. It isn't necessarily a bad smell—just familiar, instantly reminding me of my many summer days spent in Lamar.

Directly in front of me, a large herd was crossing the road. Only a few members crossed at a time, but at a steady pace, causing a traffic jam in either direction. Scanning the oncoming group for calves, I positioned myself near the bottom of a small rise, hoping one of the calves would walk over it before crossing. Four or five pairs of mothers and offspring crossed the road, none of which cooperated with my plan.

I was considering repositioning myself when a calf bounded to the top of the hill, a surprised and energetic expression on his face. He abruptly gave a small kick and a toss of his head before stopping and gazing across the meadow behind me where more of his herd were now grazing. He remained motionless for only a few seconds while I photographed him, taking in every detail.

The sun shone brilliantly on his frizzy red fur, making its edges glow. The smallest of horns barely peeked out from the wild curls. Mud was caked across his legs and belly, undoubtedly from running and playing after the morning rain. Like all bison calves, he appeared awkwardly disproportionate, with slightly too-long legs, though soon he would grow into his wildness. With another playful kick and head toss, the calf bounced across the road and rejoined the herd by his mother's side. As he left, I wondered if he would survive to grow into a dominant bull of Yellowstone, further carrying on the wild legacy of his species.

◀ A bison calf in Lamar Valley.

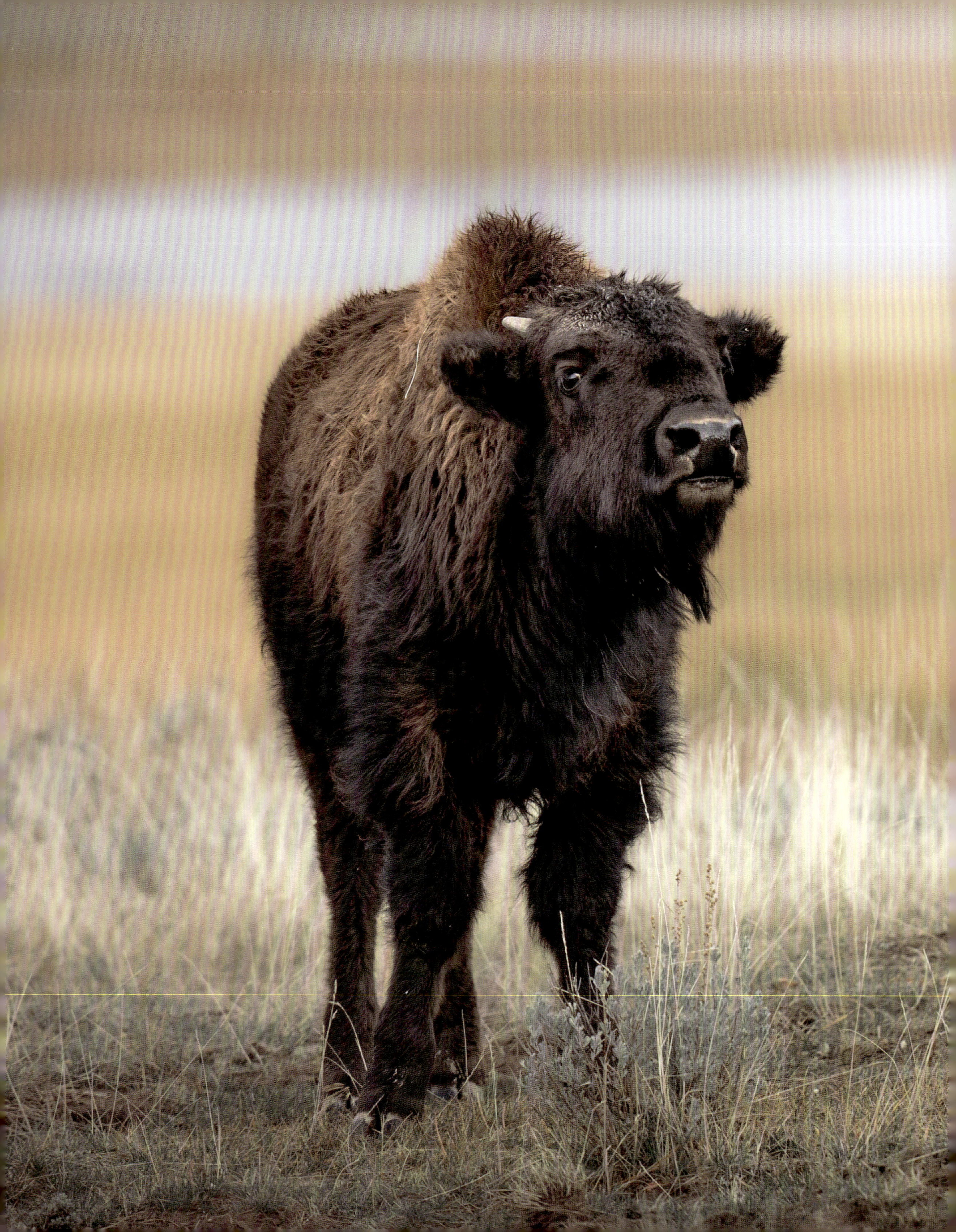

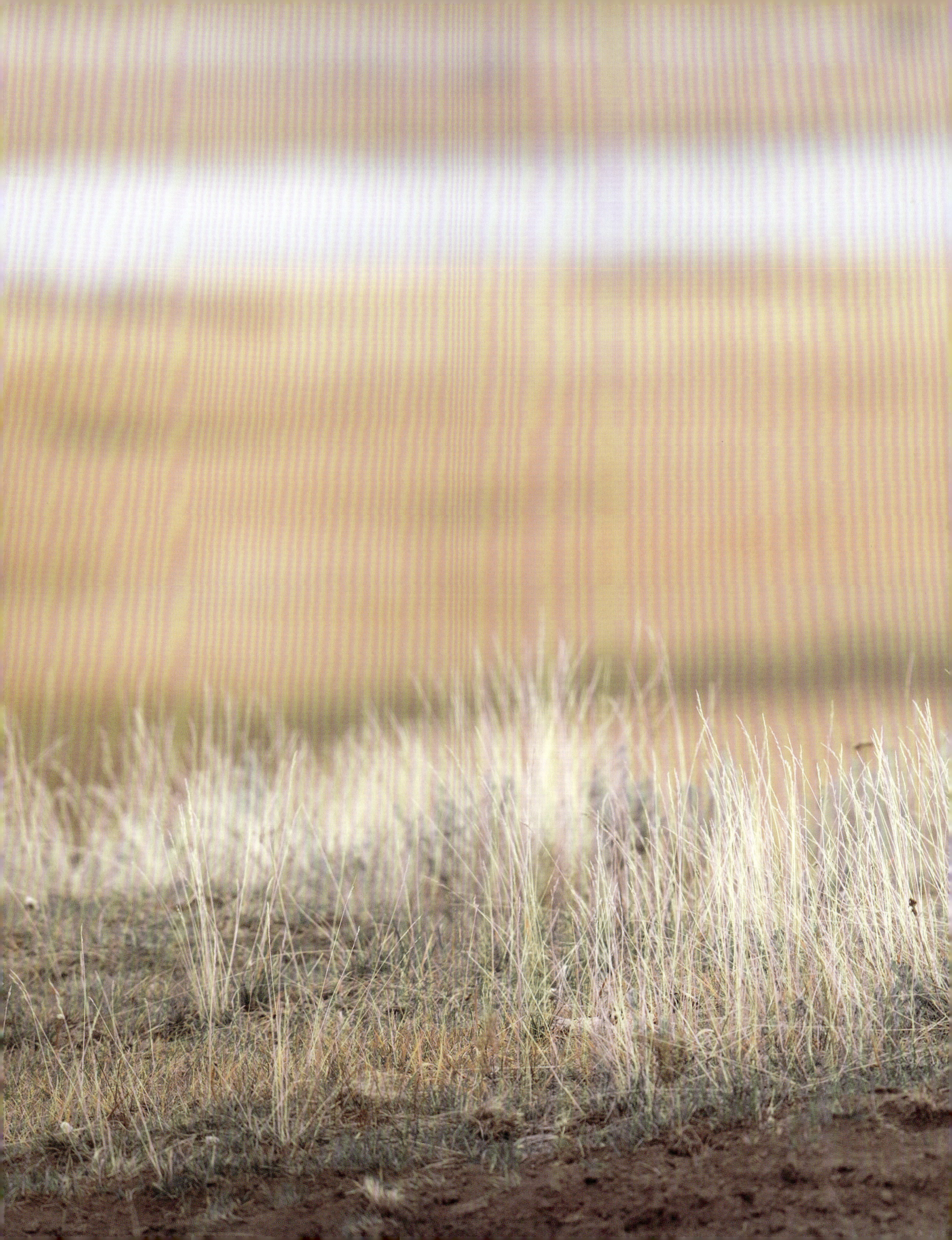

Bull bison are the most intimidating animal in Yellowstone; I'm far more scared of bison than even grizzly bears. Bison are unpredictable, aggressive, and extremely powerful animals, and they only become more unpredictable and aggressive at the end of summer during their mating season.

Late one summer, I ventured into Yellowstone to photograph the bison rut, when bulls battle each other for breeding rights. A large herd congregated in an open meadow, with numerous bulls vying for dominance. Deep bellows echoed across the meadow, each more unsettling and menacing than the last. Dust swept over the landscape, kicked up by the bulls as they rolled or stamped their hooves in frustration.

With bison on both sides of the road, it was overwhelming to decide what direction to point my camera—until I spotted a large, older bull walking through the meadow while pursuing a female. I decided to focus only on photographing him. With dulled horns and a few scars, the bull had obviously seen some intense battles during his prime. He lumbered closer, the fur on his legs swaying with each step until he abruptly stopped.

Swinging his head around, he glared at a nearby bull and let out a bellow so deep and powerful I could feel it in my chest. For a few seconds his eyes remained unwavering, watching the other bull slowly back away. Mud was caked around his eyes, which shone with fiery determination. I could see the beads of drool falling from the corners of his mouth, his deep flanks heaving with each breath. Letting out a grunt that blew up a cloud of dust, the bull took a few steps forward, his muscles clearly rippling with each movement as he went off to find another challenger to defeat.

▶ A battle-scarred bull during the bison rut.
▲ *Previous*: A young bison pauses atop an autumnal hill before following the rest of its herd.

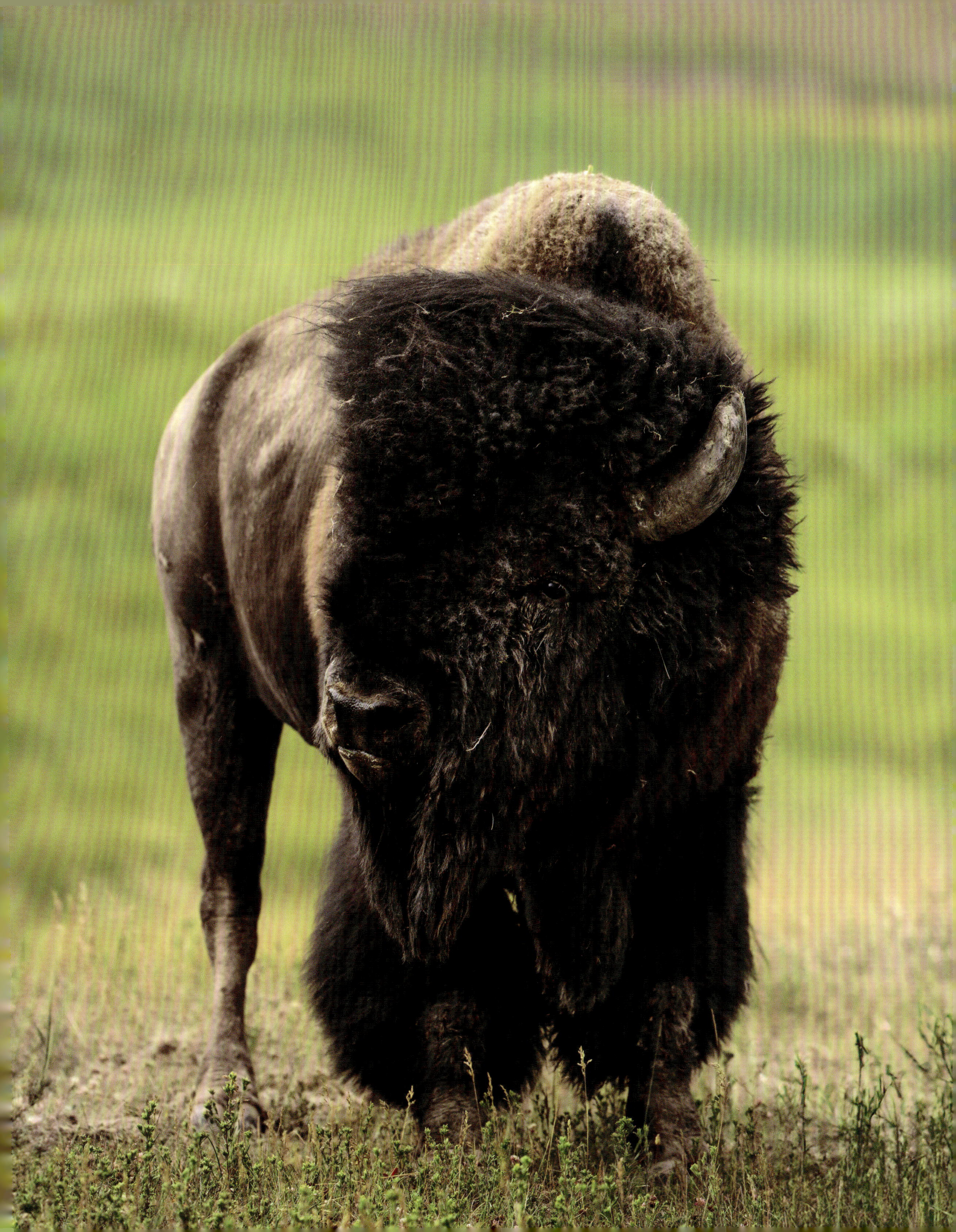

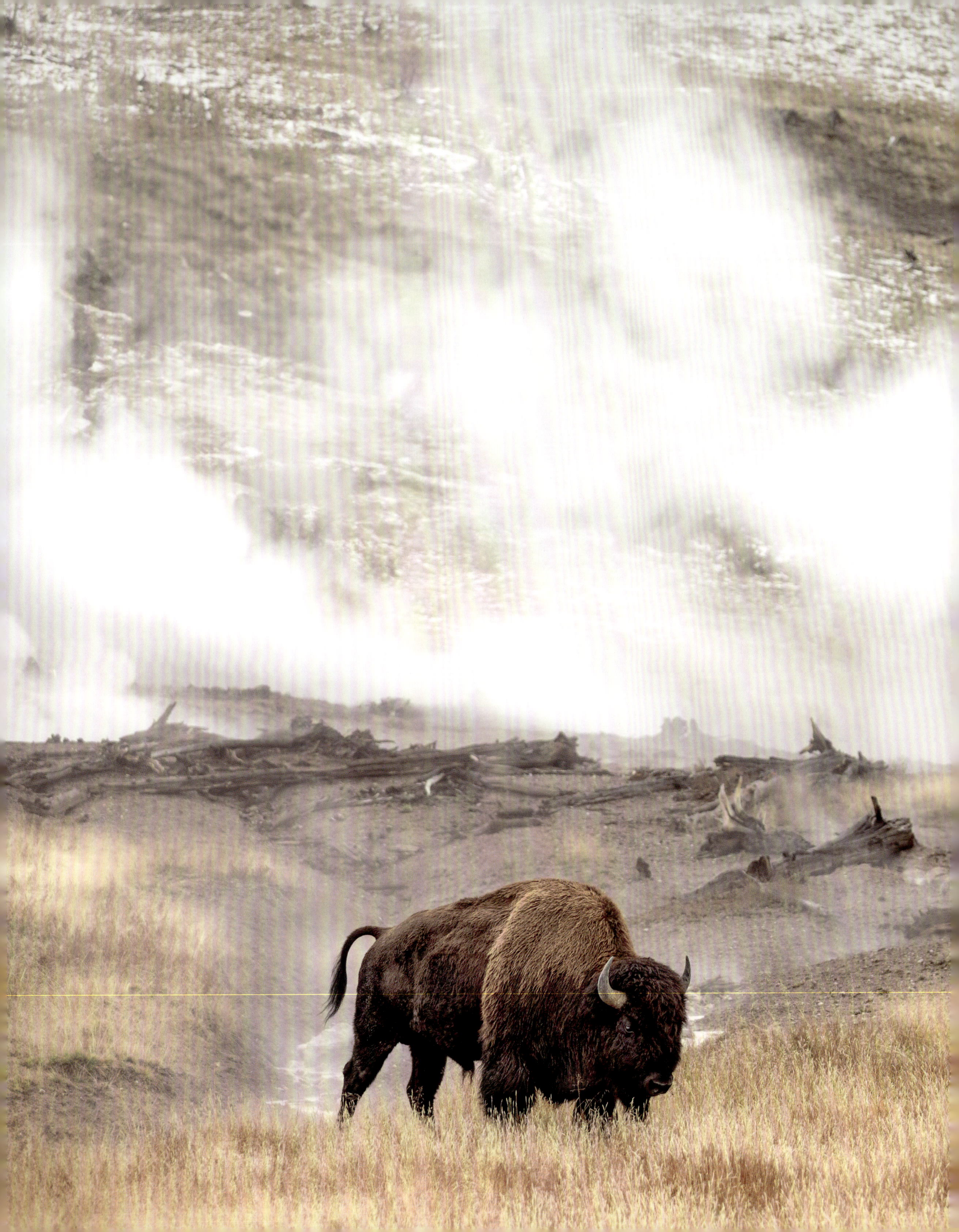

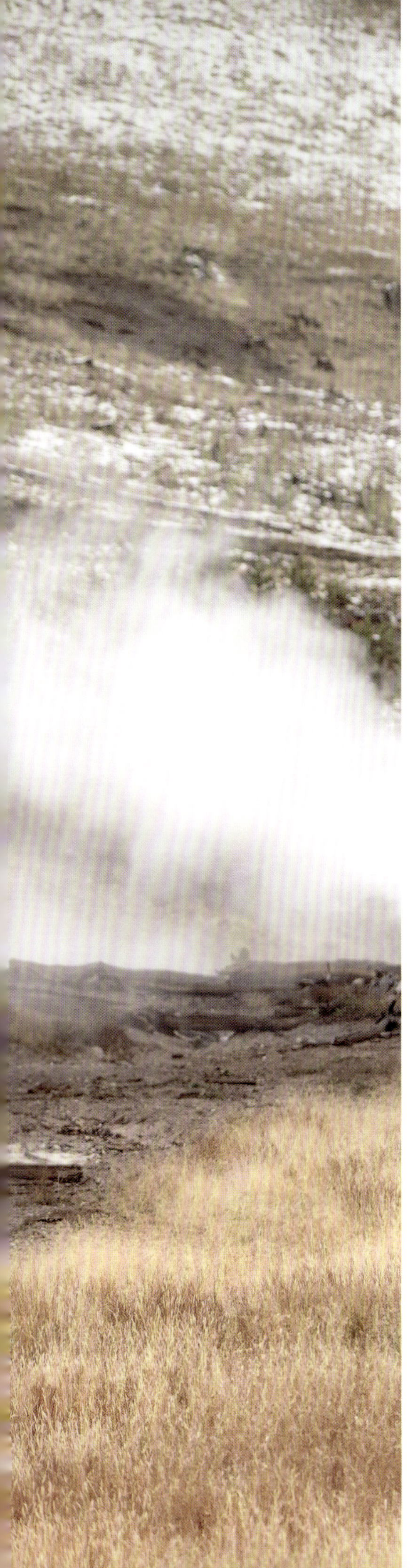

Yellowstone's dense concentration of thermal areas provides a unique landscape to explore, with vibrantly colored hot springs, billowing steam vents, and spewing geysers all fed by a vast system of underground volcanic activity. They also provide warmth to wildlife during cold weather, with bison frequenting thermal areas more than most other species.

During an overcast day in late fall, a herd of bison congregated at the base of some steam vents on a hillside near Yellowstone's Mud Volcano. With thermal activity heating the ground and nearby streams of warm water, the grassy clearing provided a comfortable resting place for the herd. Its members were scattered across the clearing while some calves, by now about six months old, bounced playfully nearby. Most of the cows were bedded down, but the herd's few large bulls remained standing, still vying for dominance at the end of their breeding season.

Nearby, the thermal vents of Mud Volcano sent plumes of steam into the air, carried gently by the light breeze. Some find the overpowering smell of the thermal areas to be pungent, almost like rotten eggs, but I personally love it. To me, the sulfuric smell is the smell of Yellowstone.

After close to an hour of watching the herd do little but rest, a few individuals stood up, then the rest of the herd followed suit. They proceeded in an unorganized cluster across the creek toward a larger meadow, never providing a good photographic opportunity. Once the cows and calves had left, the bulls began to follow in a single file, with the largest bringing up the rear. Anticipating the bull's movement, I framed my shot and waited until the bull walked in front of the steam vents, creating the quintessential Yellowstone photo.

◀ A bison bull warms up by the thermal vents near Mud Volcano.

Bison are survivors, something I am reminded of every winter. They boldly endure the harsh conditions of Yellowstone's coldest season, never surrendering or migrating to warmer areas. Winter in Yellowstone can drag on for eight months, but with a thick winter coat, bison persist.

During a winter trip into Yellowstone's northern range, I was swallowed by a snowstorm. Though elsewhere March is considered spring, winter weather still controlled the landscape, with snowdrifts covering entire valleys and trees standing eerily frozen under a blanket of snow. With decreased visibility, I parked my car to wait out the storm. Glancing out every window, I realized I was surrounded by white, the snowfall concealing everything from view.

Soon, a faint shape appeared through the storm. At first it was hardly distinguishable, but it gradually became larger and clearer: a bison was walking toward me. With lumbering intensity and a rhythmic, regular stride despite the deep snow, the bison seemed unphased by the snowstorm or the flakes accumulating on its thick fur.

Braving the cold, I stepped out of my car and began photographing the bison. The snow quickly collected on my camera and arms. The bison continued walking directly toward me, its head swaying slightly with each step. With the snow silencing the landscape, the only audible sounds were the bison's powerful and even breaths visibly billowing from its nostrils into the frozen air. Almost completely covered in snow, the bison appeared like an abstract shape moving through the white landscape, only its dark legs and horns clearly noticeable while the rest of its massive body faded to white in a perfect gradient.

As it got nearer, the bison veered to the left and lumbered up a steep hillside. It soon disappeared back into the snowy landscape just as quickly as it had appeared.

▶ A bison moves through the white landscape during a snowstorm.

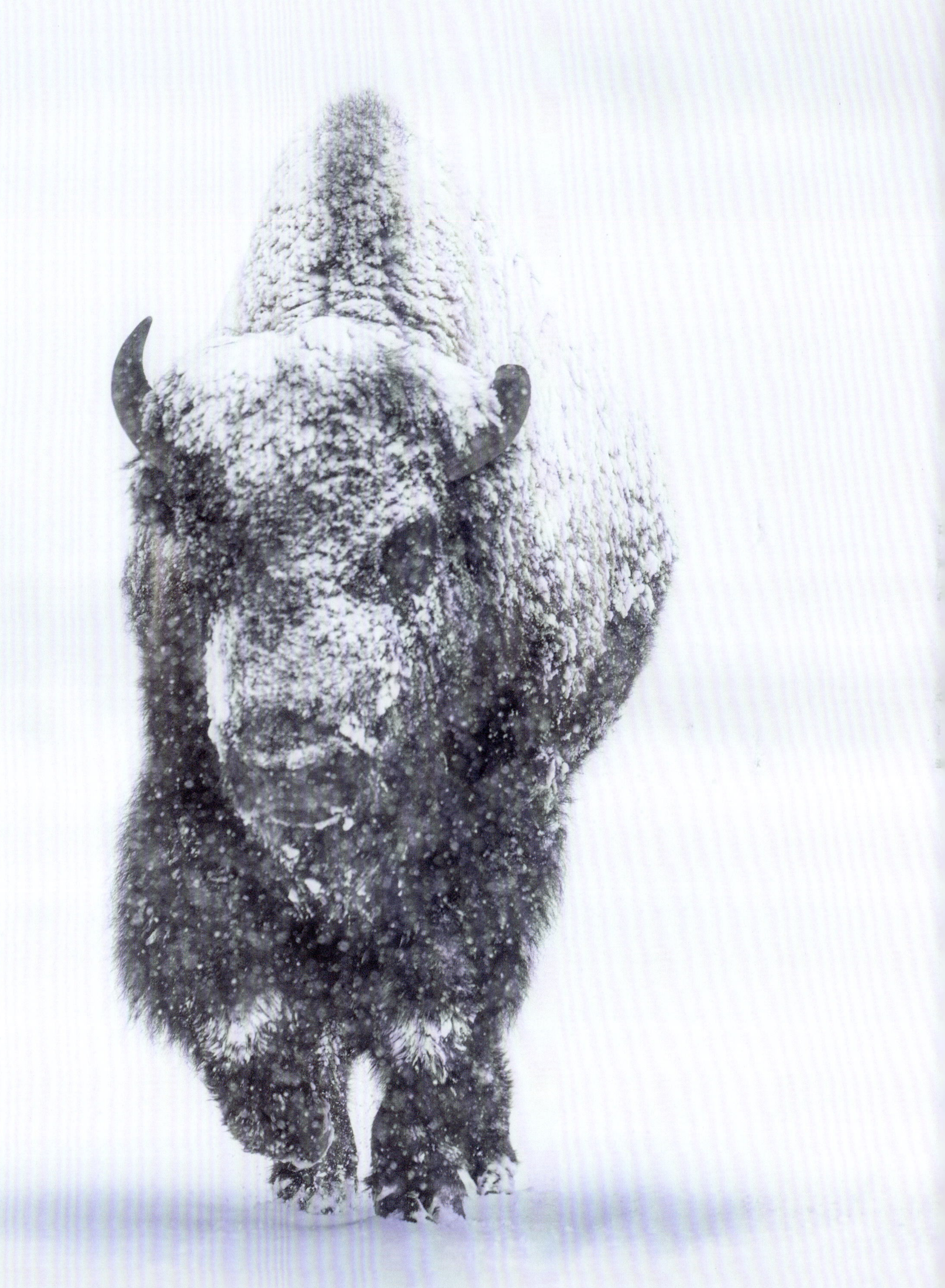

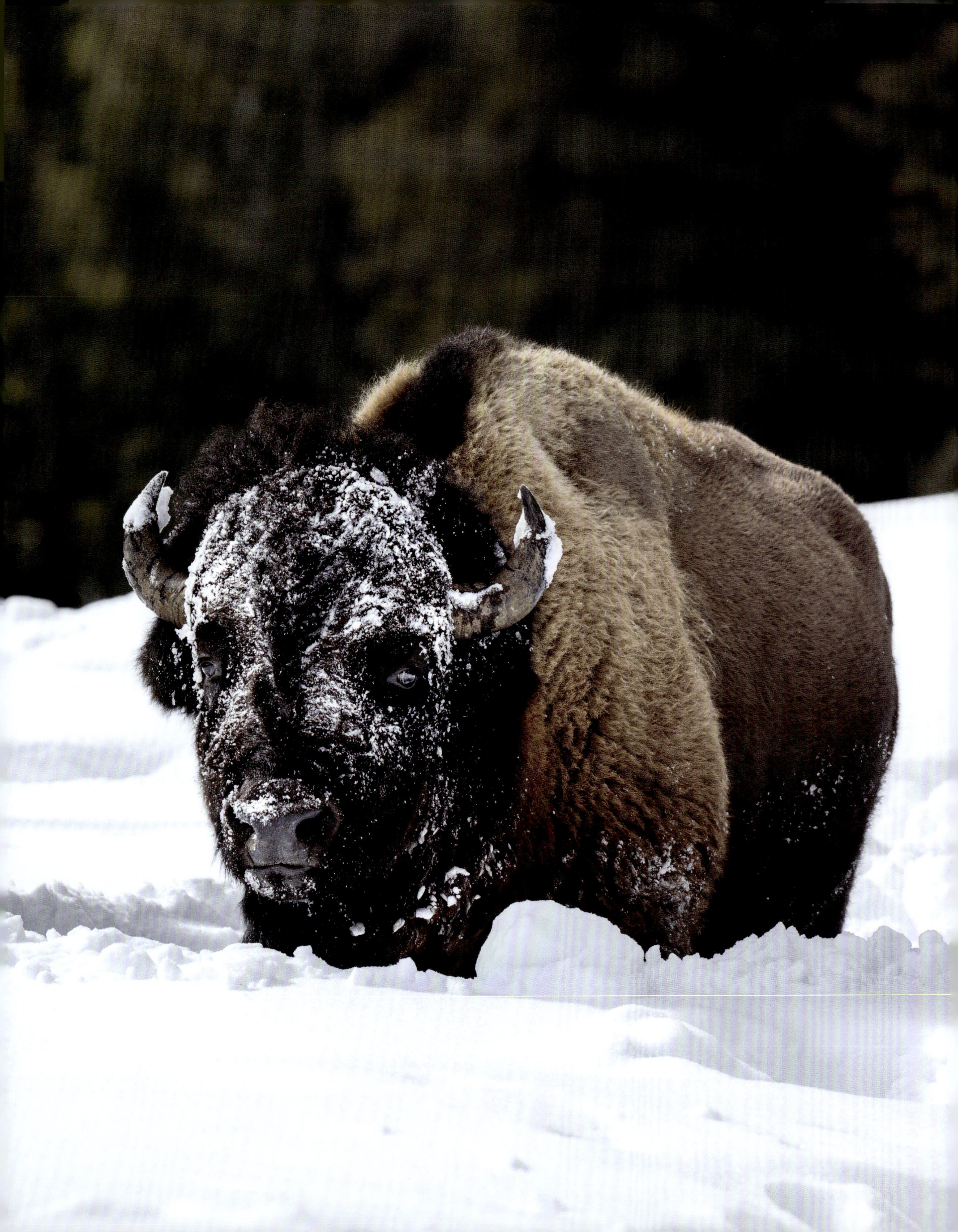

Bison are truly built for winter. Regardless of raging storms and howling blizzards, bison face winter head-on, doing whatever it takes to endure the long season.

I once ventured into Yellowstone near the end of a particularly harsh winter. Deep and constant snowfall had blanketed the valleys. One storm after another pummeled the landscape, causing trees to bend under the weight of snow and rivers to flow with ice. In Lamar Valley, bison dotted the white landscape, their backs facing the wind as they stood resolute against another incoming storm. Not wanting to brave the wind, I continued driving through the valley toward the forest in search of other wildlife.

In a small clearing at the forest's edge, I found a lone bull bison chest-deep in a snowdrift. I stepped out of my car and began photographing him, my boots crunching with each step as the wind gusts instantly penetrated my winter coat. A zigzag trench coiled through the clearing behind the bison. With brute force, he rhythmically shook his massive head through the snow, using it as a plow to clear a path and reach any remaining vegetation buried under the weight of winter. The muscles under his hump tensed with each pass. When he finally raised his head, the snow clung to the curly fur across his face like a mask. He didn't care.

I continued to watch as the bull repeated his plowing motion, pausing for only a few moments to graze upon whatever grasses he had uncovered. Although Yellowstone had been under winter's control for five months by that point, spring and the promise of new growth were still over a month away. Despite the harsh winter and the numerous bison who had already succumbed to the season's brutality, I had no doubt the bull in front of me would survive.

◀ A bison looks up from grazing beneath a blanket of snow.

Pronghorn

Pronghorn are one of the most unique species in the United States, with a fascinating evolutionary history. Though they're often referred to as antelope, the pronghorn's closest living relative is actually the giraffe. Though they once roamed across the West in numbers second only to the bison, today, about a million pronghorn remain throughout the grasslands and prairies. About four hundred reside in Yellowstone, where they can be seen throughout Lamar Valley or near the town of Gardiner. Pronghorn have long-ranging migration patterns across the American West, though barriers like fences and highways limit their movements and restrict migrations. Wildlife overpasses have been created in some locations to allow pronghorn to safely cross interstates and maintain their ancient migration paths.

The name pronghorn is derived from their characteristic horns, whose composition is unique. While all other horned animals have continuously growing horns made from keratin, the same material as our fingernails, pronghorns' horns are comprised of a keratin sheath that grows over a bony core. This sheath is shed each year before it regrows.

Both males and females have horns, though females' are significantly smaller. In addition to their horns, pronghorn are recognizable by their reddish-tan bodies with white undersides, long legs, and white rumps. Males also have thick black patches of fur along their cheeks. Fawns are born in the spring and can walk within thirty minutes of birth, an important skill to escape predators like wolves. Females and their fawns will come together to form nursery herds for protection against predators.

Pronghorn are incredibly fast, reaching speeds of 60 miles (96.5 km) per hour, making them the second-fastest land animal, only outpaced by the cheetah. Their speed developed as a strategy to evade their primary predator, the North American cheetah, and has remained even since the cat's extinction at the end of the last Ice Age. Today, their speed still helps them evade predators, though they lack stamina and can only run at top speeds for about half a mile. Often seen running across the plains, pronghorn are remarkable animals and truly unique among Yellowstone's other species.

▶ A pronghorn buck with its characteristic horns and black cheek patch.

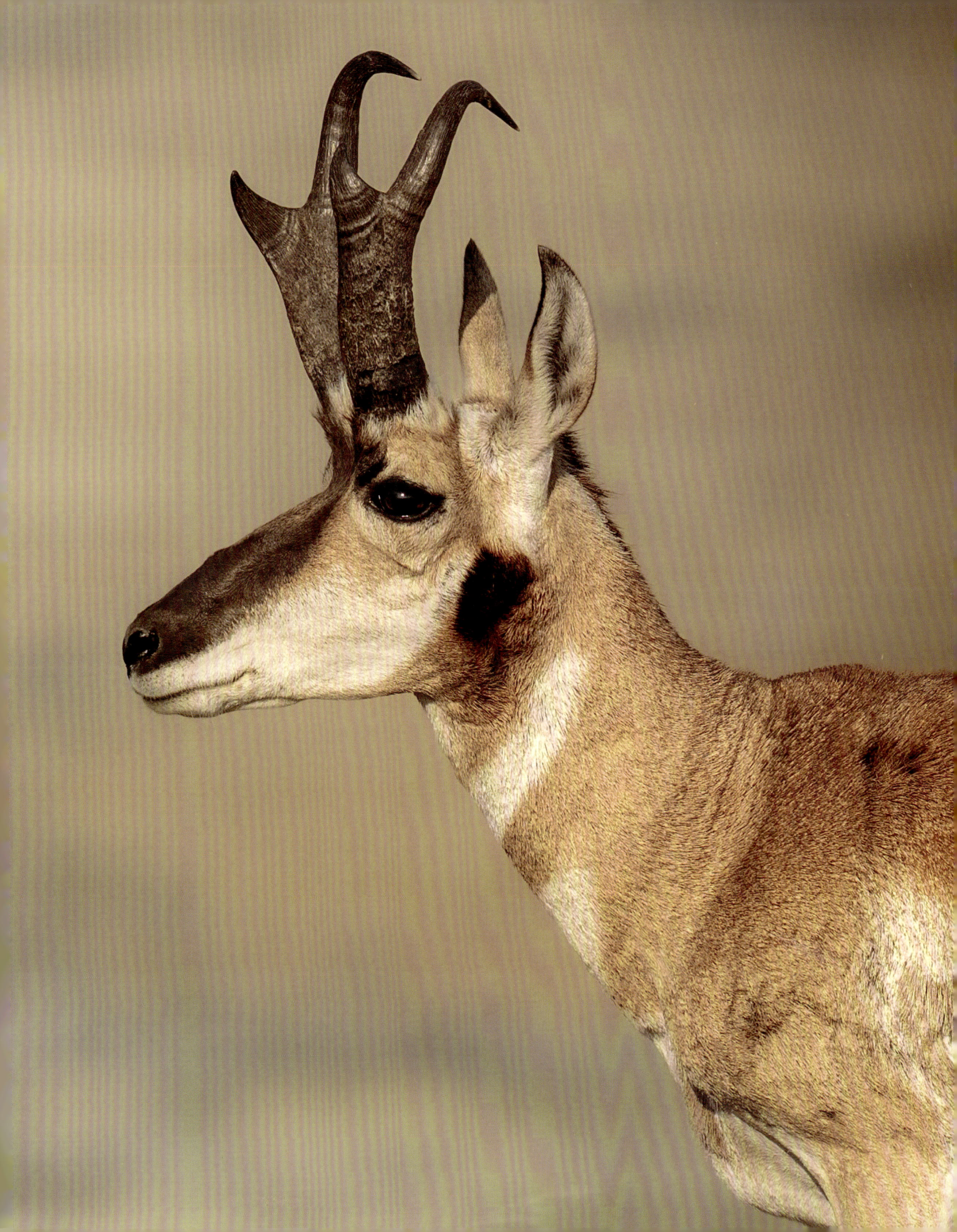

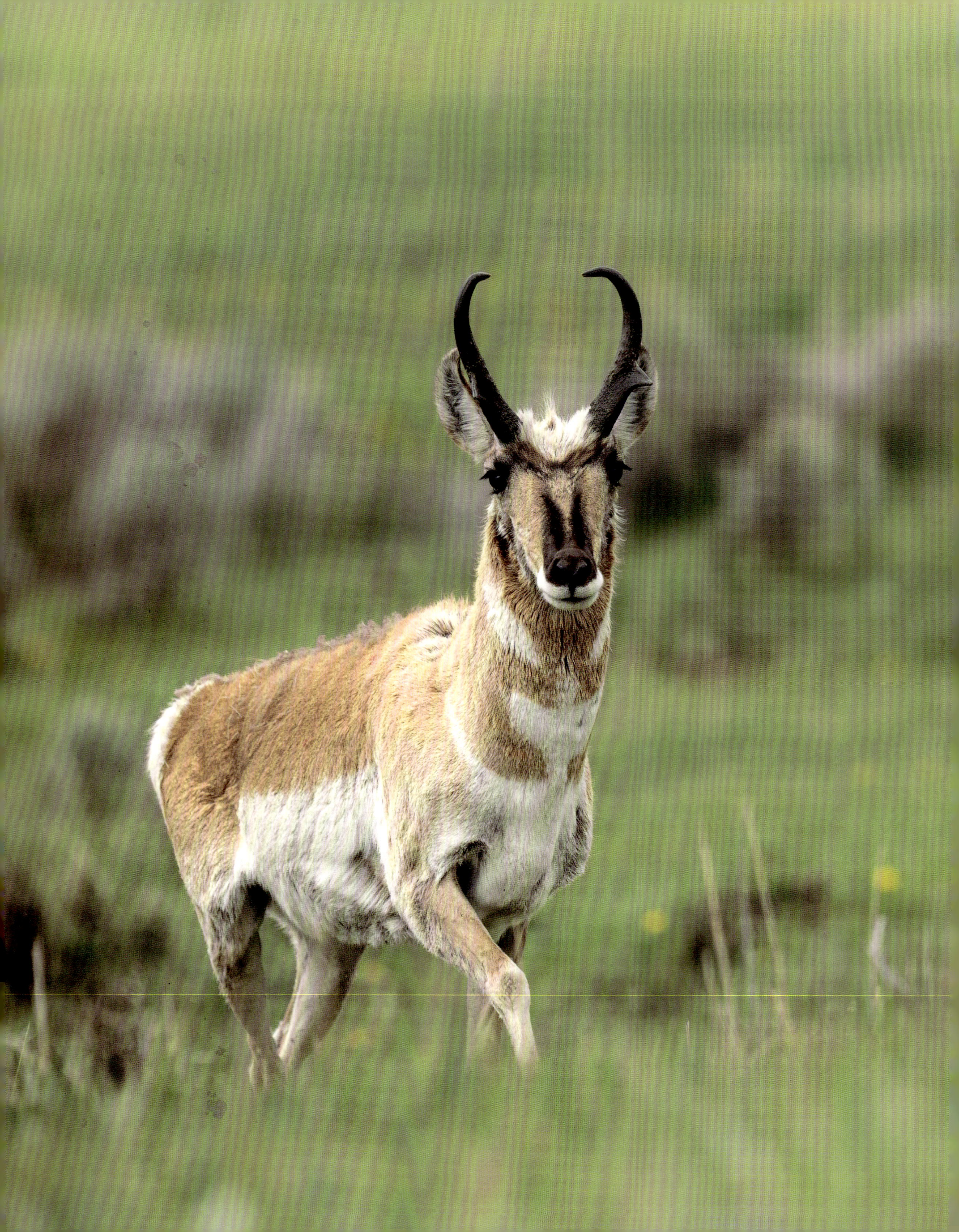

Pronghorn are exceptionally skittish, making them incredibly difficult to photograph at times. Once they detect movement, they usually turn and run in the opposite direction, spurred by instinct and thousands of years of being prey to larger animals. Yellowstone is one of the best places to photograph pronghorn, as here, people are not viewed as a threat like they might be outside the national park boundaries where pronghorn can be hunted. Being accustomed to people, Yellowstone pronghorn often graze peacefully near the road.

Early in the spring, I was driving through Yellowstone's Lamar Valley. Fed by snowmelt and spring thunderstorms, every hillside and meadow had transformed into vibrant hues of green with yellow flowers scattered throughout. The more subtle greenish gray of sagebrush provided a pleasant break from the almost overwhelming emerald and lime greens of other vegetation.

Noticing a small group of pronghorn grazing though the lush valley not far away, I stopped to photograph them. Cautiously approaching only a few steps at a time and avoiding sudden movements, I soon crept close enough to take my shot. A large and handsome buck grazed unbothered as I lifted my camera, the pale orange of his fur contrasted beautifully with the surrounding greens.

Before long, the buck began to walk up a small hill that rose between him and where I knelt, his head held high with pride while his eyes looked intently forward. Not wanting to startle him, I remained motionless while continuing to photograph him. When the buck crested the hilltop, he turned and walked broadside, no longer even looking in my direction, as if he had become bored of me. Awestruck by the buck's calm presence and his boldness in approaching me, I knew instantly I would love the images I had just captured.

◀ A pronghorn buck strolls through Lamar Valley in the spring.

I don't photograph pronghorn as often as I should, but they are incredible animals with their rugged, prehistoric look. They have remained unchanged by time or nature for thousands of years, perfectly suited for life on the plains. I am reminded of their uniqueness every time I am in their presence.

On a late fall day, I was standing in an open sagebrush valley and scanning the hills above with binoculars, looking for grizzly bears or wolves. Distracted by my search for other wildlife, I hadn't noticed a lone pronghorn buck moving through the valley slightly to my left. Finally, the movement caught my eye, momentarily startling me. Forgetting about bears or wolves, I eagerly grabbed my camera to begin photographing the pronghorn.

After capturing a few images of the buck calmly grazing, he suddenly burst into a run, gaining speed incredibly quickly. He was soon running close to top speed, and I was having a difficult time moving my camera fast enough to keep him in frame; instead, I lowered my camera to simply watch the sprint. His legs stretched easily, pushing him forward with powerful strides as if it took no effort whatsoever. The muscles bulged with each step, but his head remained surprisingly level despite his bounds. With nimble hooves, the buck dashed across the uneven plains, avoiding sagebrush hurdles and sidestepping prairie dog holes. He wasn't running; he was gliding.

With the valley's grasses a soft golden brown, the pronghorn's pale-orange fur almost faded into the surroundings. Only his underbelly was clearly visible, soon turning to a white flash as the buck sped through the valley. Equally quickly, the pronghorn's pace slowed first to a trot and then to a steady walk, before he put his head down to resume grazing.

▶ A pronghorn buck dashes across the plains.

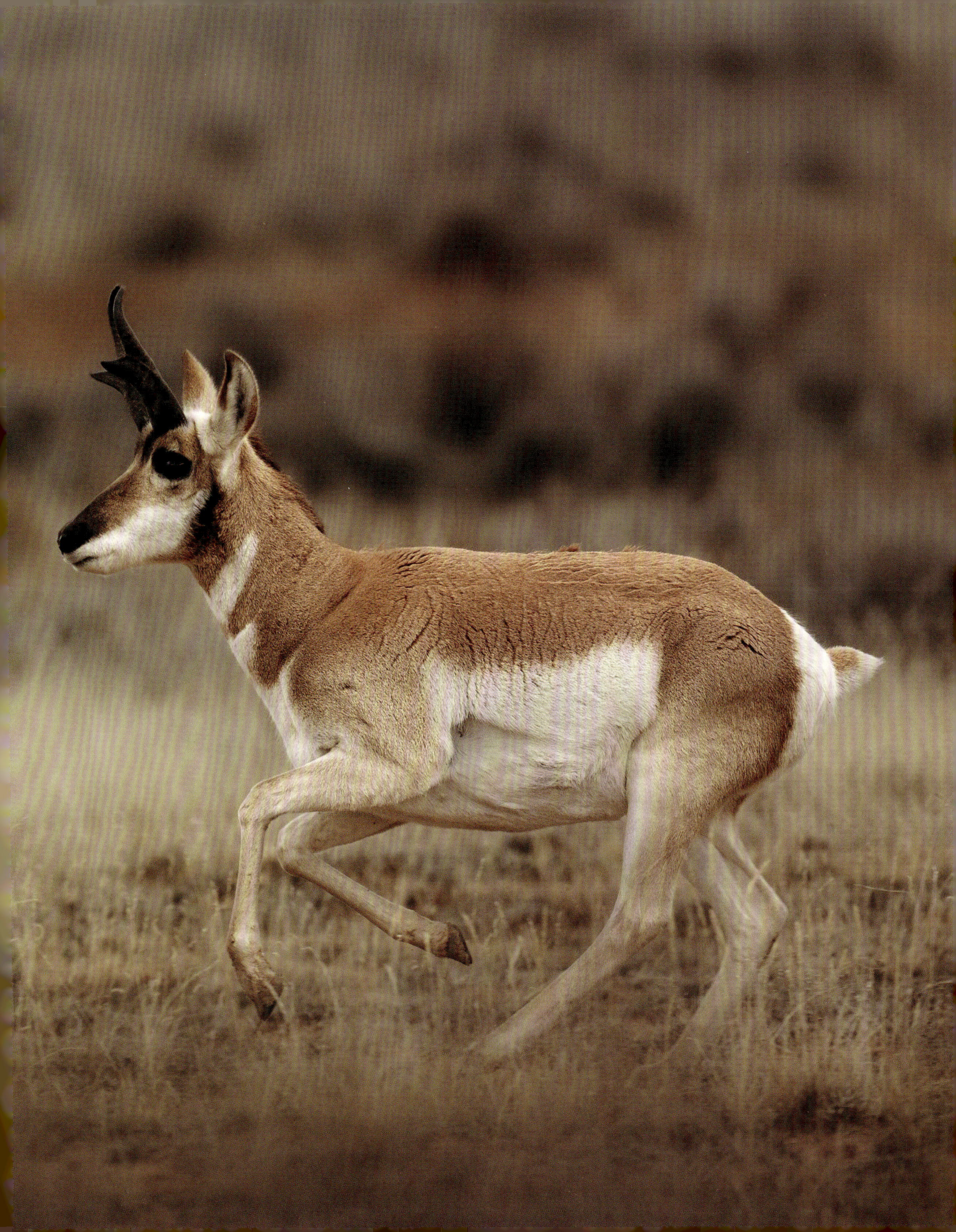

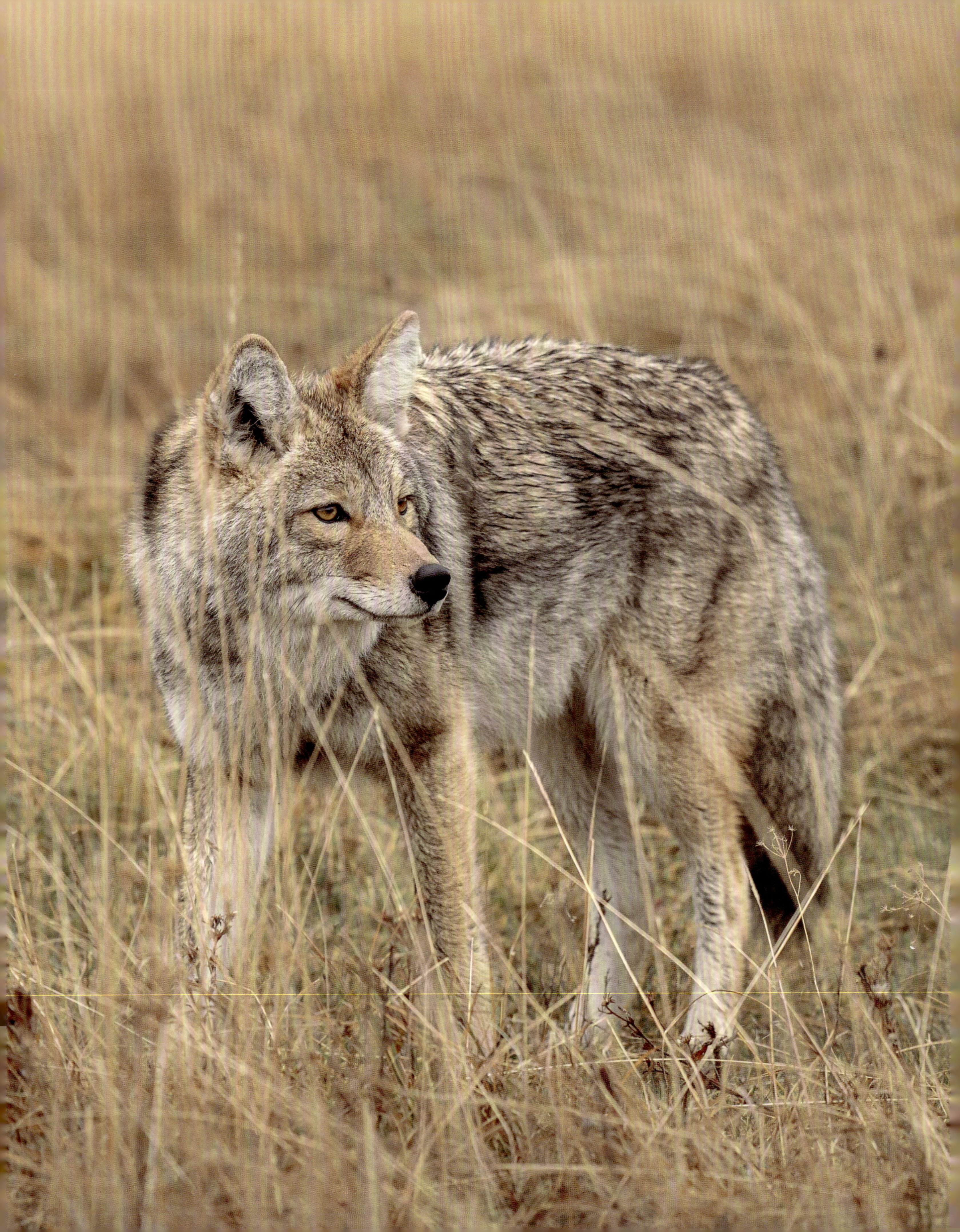

Coyote

Coyotes are often regarded as pests or nuisances, which is clear in the history of human interactions with the species. Intense hunting, trapping, and poisoning of coyotes began with westward expansion to eliminate their threat to livestock, and it persists to this day. Regardless of ongoing threats from humans, coyotes' ability to adapt to new environments allows them to thrive in almost any habitat, including throughout Yellowstone. Today, Yellowstone provides protection for coyotes, which can be seen in Hayden Valley, Lamar Valley, and various other open meadows throughout the park in every season.

Often mistaken for their larger wolf cousins, coyotes are identifiable by a few key traits. About one-third the size of wolves, coyotes also have a narrower build and a longer, more pointed nose. Ranging in color from light gray to tan, coyotes also typically have patches of orange fur, particularly near the ears and tail. They shed their thick winter coats during the summer months, giving them a sleeker appearance. With a variety of vocalizations including yips and shaky howls, coyotes are commonly referred to as song-dogs, most often heard near dawn and dusk.

Coyotes are typically solitary animals, apart from mated pairs and pups. Females give birth in the den in the early spring to anywhere from four to eight pups, which are cared for until late summer, when the pups disperse to live on their own. A coyote's average lifespan is roughly six years, or up to thirteen within Yellowstone.

Preying on small animals like mice, voles, and rabbits, coyotes display an interesting hunting strategy known as mousing. Using their keen sense of hearing to locate prey under grasses or snow in open meadows, a coyote will crouch down and use its powerful back legs to spring through the air, hopefully landing directly on top of its prey. Coyotes also scavenge off kills made by other predators like grizzly bears and wolves, though they must do so warily to avoid injury from those larger animals.

◀ A coyote pauses in the tall grasses of Yellowstone's plains.

Nothing compares to the few moments of early morning light just after sunrise. The first rays of the day cast a warm golden gleam across the landscape and chase away the chill of predawn. I'm always hoping to photograph animals at sunrise, though as the season progresses and Yellowstone's closing day looms, I become more content with every moment simply spent in the park.

On a cool morning in October, I pulled off the side of the road just before Yellowstone's Mud Volcano, my favorite thermal area in the park. The steam from the thermal vents left the cold air foggy, and hoarfrost clung to each individual blade of grass in the meadow. I stepped out of my car to watch the sunrise, the strong sulfur smell of the area hitting my nose. I leaned against my car, enjoying the moment and reflecting on the season's wildlife encounters, when I caught movement out of the corner of my eye. A coyote had trotted into the meadow.

I picked up my camera and kneeled in the frosty grass for a better angle. By now, the sun was just peeking over the top of the lodgepole pines, casting its warm glow across the meadow. The coyote stopped. Its ears were forward and alert, clearly listening for any prey beneath the tall grasses. In the morning light, the coyote's eyes were a bright amber, and its already golden fur seemed even brighter. Facing directly toward the rising sun, the coyote's head cast a dark shadow across its back while its face and chest were lit by the sunshine. The coyote remained there for a few moments as if in deep contemplation, admiring the sunrise just as I had done, before it trotted off and disappeared over a hill. The coyote was gone, and so was the morning light.

► A coyote soaks up an autumn sunrise.

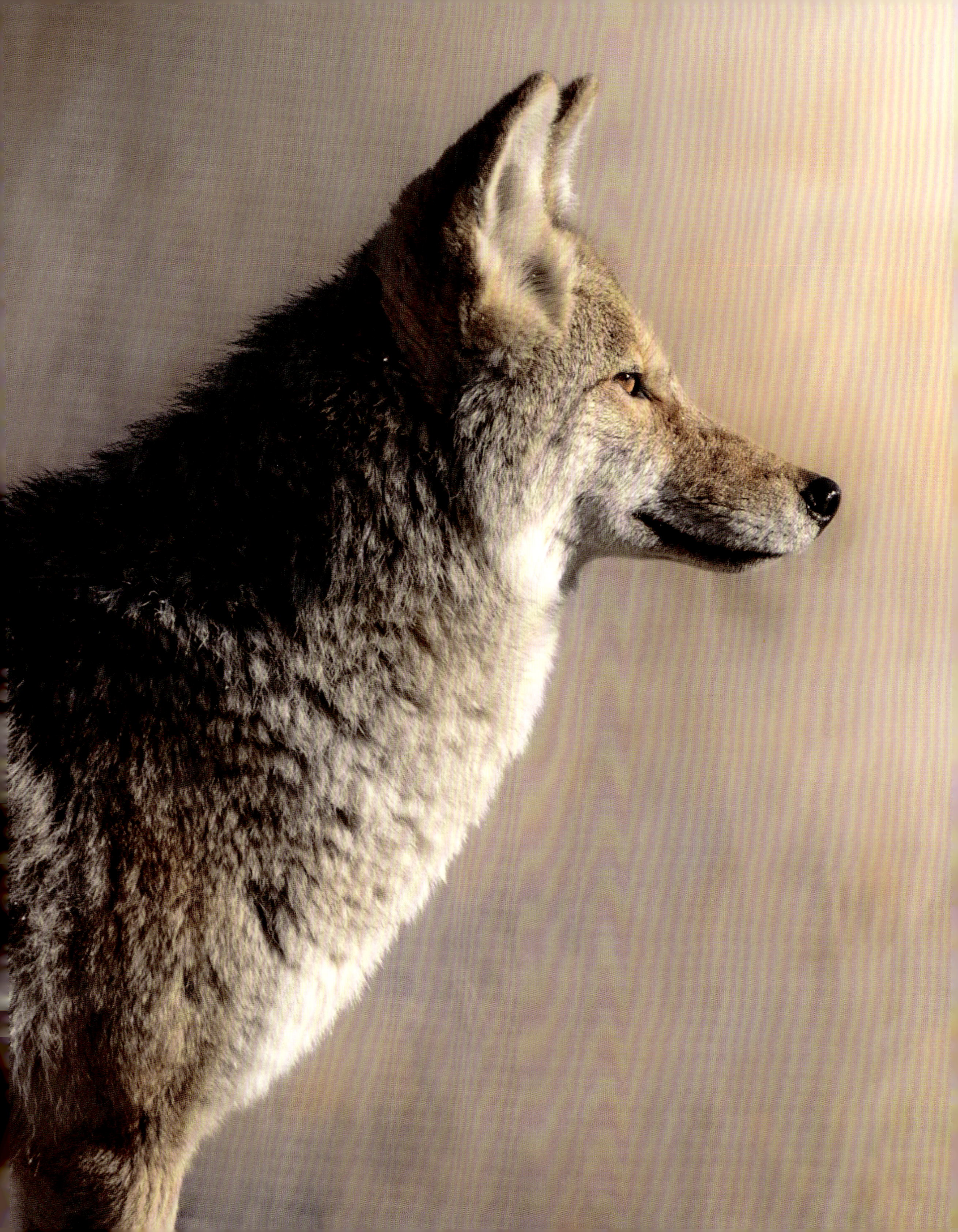

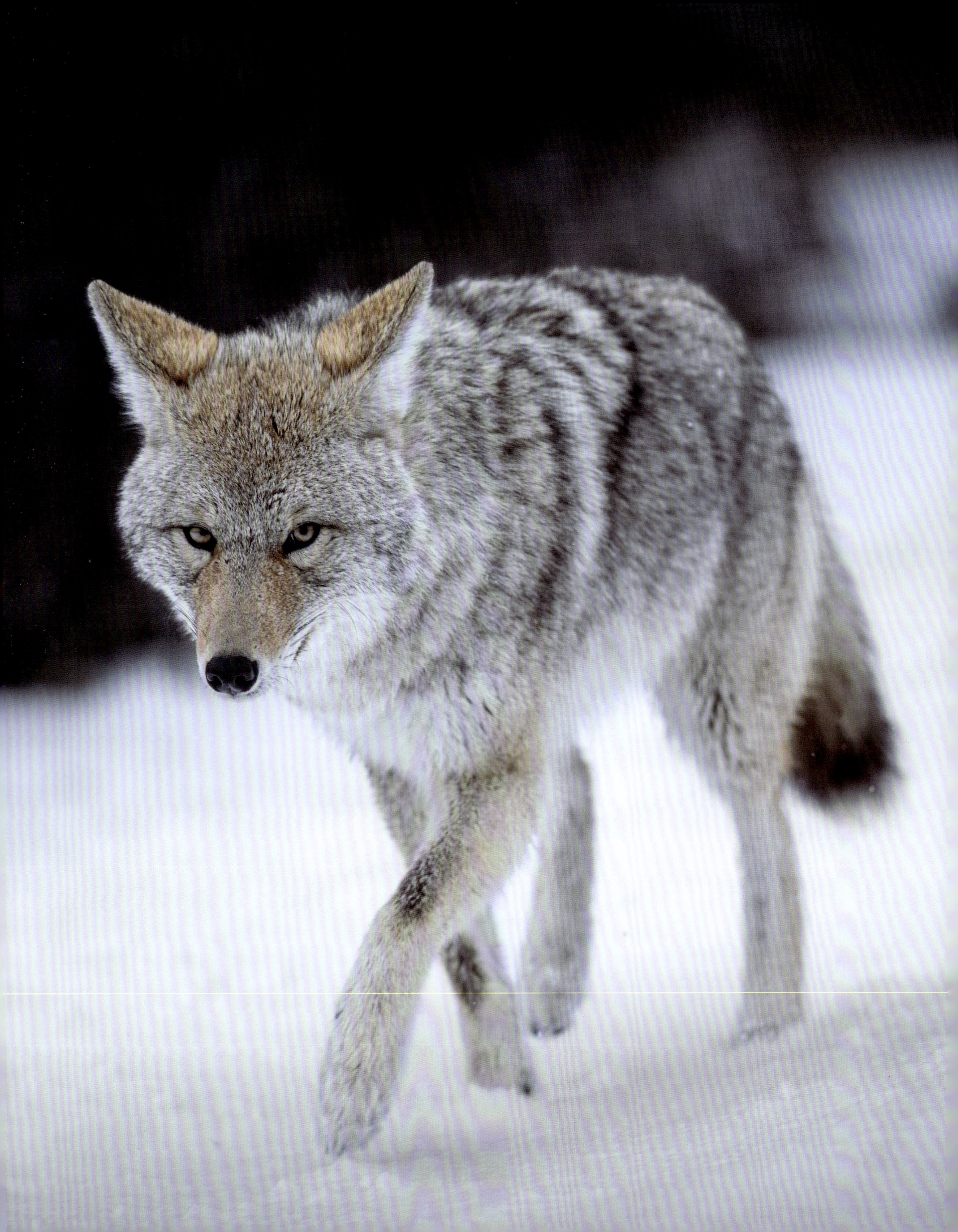

The morning after a snowstorm blew across Yellowstone's Northern Range, I ventured into the park on ice-covered roads in search of wildlife. With the temperature in the single digits, it was cold, though calm with the absence of wind. Everything was covered in fresh snow, which gave a tranquil stillness to the forests and meadows. It felt as though the entire landscape was resting.

Not expecting to see much wildlife, I continued on while simply enjoying the winter scenery. Despite the cold, I drove with my window rolled down so the sharp, fresh scent of winter could drift into my car. The only vegetation visible in the valley was the incredibly resilient sagebrush, though it glistened with a layer of frost. All else was buried under feet of snow. While thinking about how the now white landscape would transform to vibrant green in less than three short months, I noticed a coyote trotting down the road toward me.

Like humans, coyotes and other animals will often choose the easiest path; in winter, that path is usually the plowed road instead of the deep, drifted snowpack. I stopped my car and raised my camera to snap a few photos of the coyote. Its grayish coat matched the grayish sage, but its pale golden eyes and few tan patches of fur contrasted with the endless winter palette. A few clumps of snow clung to the coyote's lanky legs. Never blinking, the coyote stared at me with a mischievous and cunning expression as if it knew something I did not. Perhaps it knew of the coming storm that would hit by early afternoon, blanketing the valley with even more snow while strong winds concealed everything from sight. I would remain unaware of the storm's descent until just before it arrived in full force.

◀ An expressive coyote trots down a snow-covered road in Yellowstone's Northern Range.

Yellowstone becomes a wonderland of snow and ice during the winter months, but the majority of roads close for the season in late October, at least to cars. They stay accessible only by snowmobile through a limited permit, an incredible and wild way to explore Yellowstone.

I have gone into Yellowstone in the depths of winter on snowmobiles a few times, and each time it is an exciting endeavor, even if I don't see any wildlife. Familiar places are nearly unrecognizable under a blanket of deep snow, and the quiet hush over the landscape is unbelievably peaceful. On a January snowmobile trip with my family, we stopped in Hayden Valley where the snow drifted along hillsides and turned the entire valley a blinding white under the bright winter sun. With the machines turned off, the landscape was silent. We were the only people in the entire valley—something that would never happen any other time of the year.

While enjoying the blissful solitude around us, I noticed a dark spot across the valley. Taking a closer look with binoculars, I made out a lone coyote prancing across the top of the drifted snow. Even from a distance I could see the coyote's fluffy tail swaying back and forth with each step. Pulling my camera from my backpack, I began photographing the coyote, the only wildlife we had seen so far. It moved surprisingly quickly, leaving a line of tracks as it went. Soon the coyote arrived at the edge of an icy creek that meandered through the valley, its blue waters slowly flowing toward the Yellowstone River. Pausing at the shore, the coyote glanced in my direction, then stared at the creek for a few seconds as if debating whether it was worth crossing or not. The coyote and the creek added color, movement, and life to an otherwise colorless and empty landscape. Deciding not to cross the cold water, the coyote resumed its brisk trot and soon it was out of sight over a hillside, leaving the valley once again void of wildlife.

► A lone coyote stands out in a snow-covered Hayden Valley.

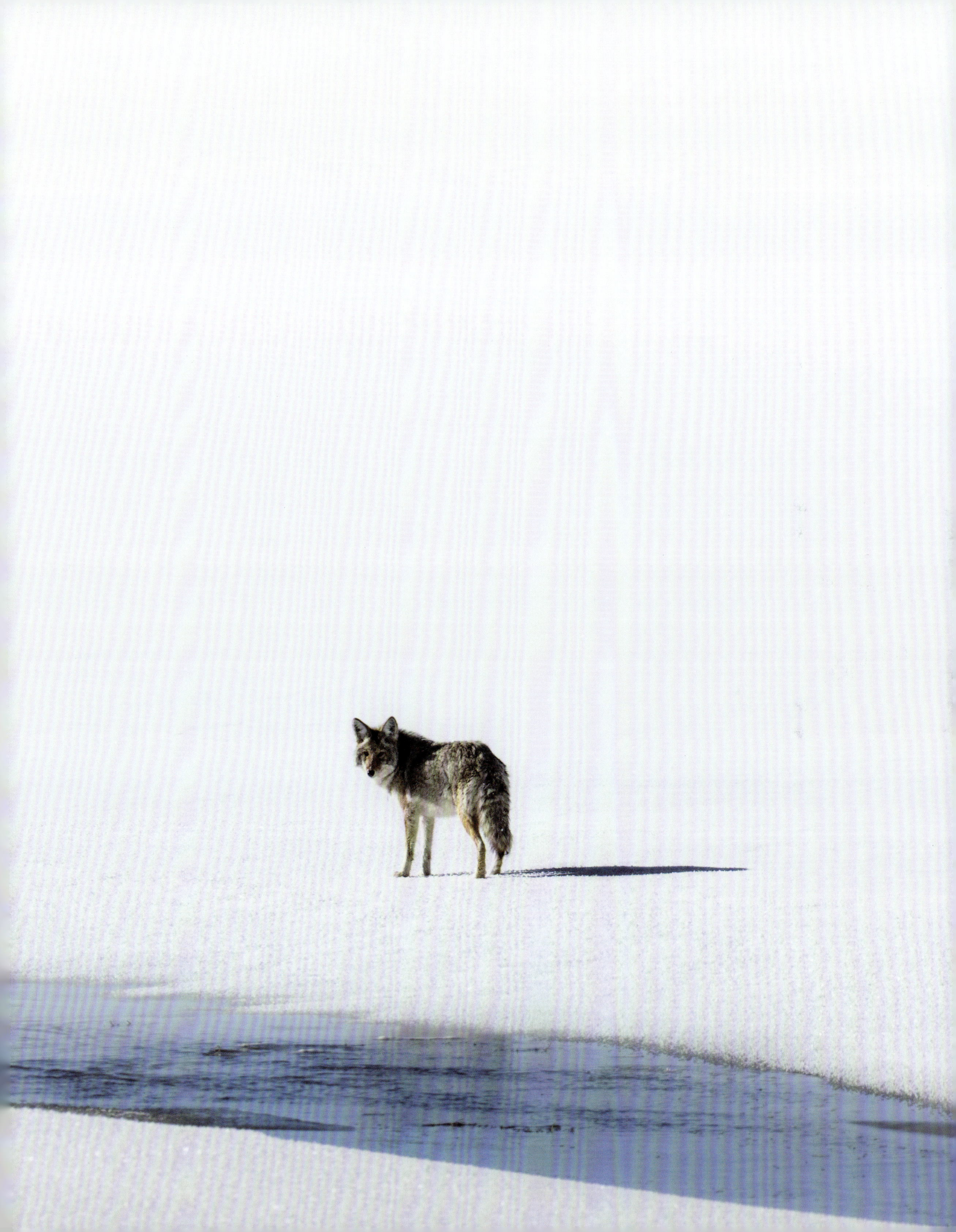

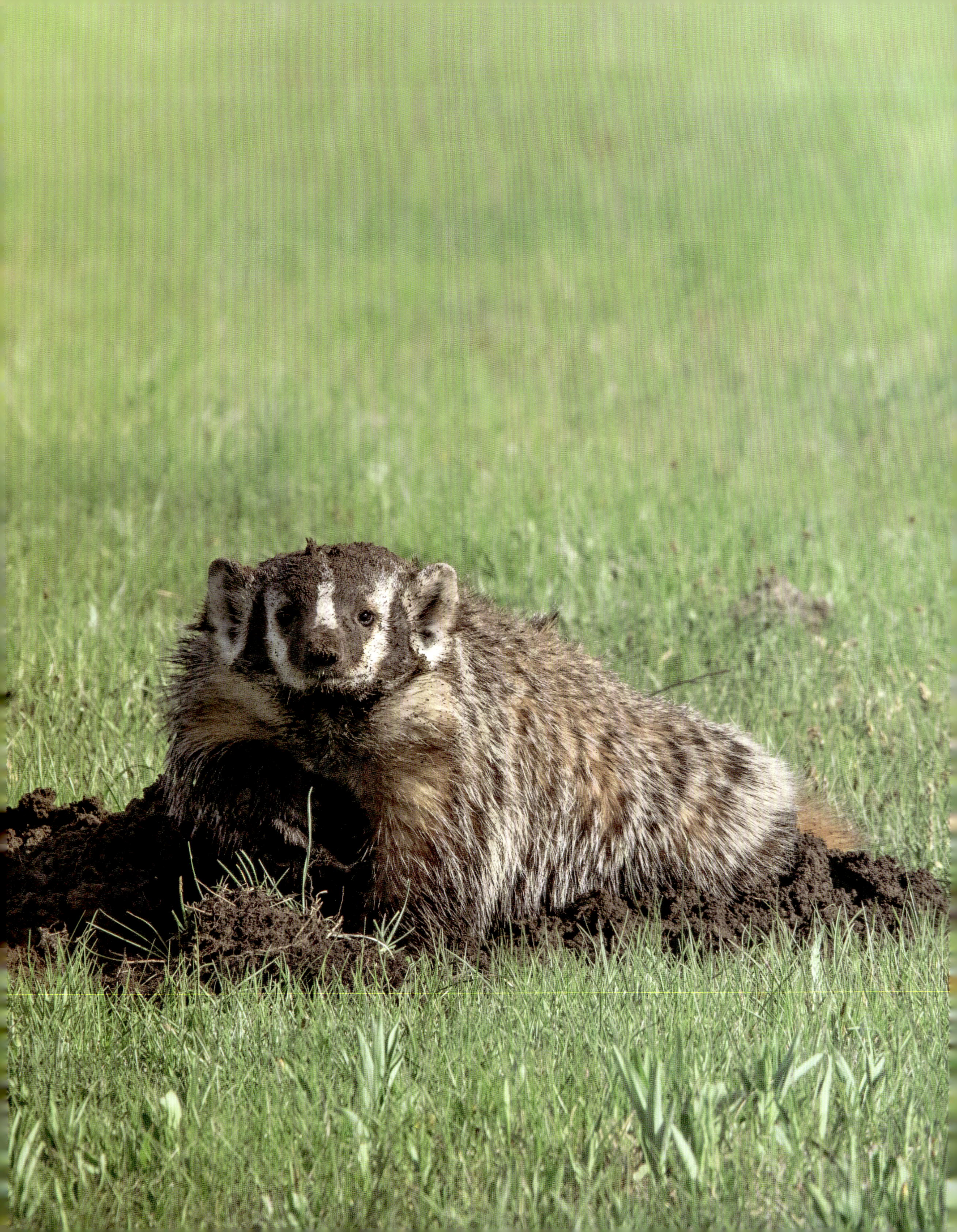

Badger

Badgers are one of the most fascinating and tenacious species in Yellowstone National Park. Known for their distinctive black and white facial markings and stocky, muscular builds, badgers are mostly solitary animals. Their powerful forelimbs and long claws allow them to excavate extensive burrow systems. Burrows are used for shelter, helping them easily evade larger predators like wolves, coyotes, eagles, and bears.

As primarily nocturnal animals, badgers emerge from their burrows at night to hunt and forage, though they can often be seen in the early mornings and evenings as they travel across open grasslands and sagebrush areas such as Lamar Valley. Despite their relatively small size, averaging 15 to 25 pounds (6.8 to 11.3 kg), badgers are fierce predators and will aggressively defend their territory. Their diet is diverse, including rodents, insects, birds, and even plants. In addition to digging burrows for shelter, badgers also use their digging skills to actively pursue prey like ground squirrels underground.

Mating occurs in the summer, though females have a unique reproductive strategy called delayed implantation that ensures cubs are born under optimal conditions. After an egg is fertilized during the mating season it will not implant into the uterine wall or become viable until much later, usually around February, and only if the mother is healthy. This ensures that cubs are born in the spring, when resources are more plentiful. Several other Yellowstone mammals also have delayed implantation, including bears and otters.

Female badgers give birth to litters of one to five cubs in the safety of their underground burrows. Cubs are born blind and helpless but grow quickly, emerging from the den with their mother after a few weeks. By late summer, they are ready to venture out on their own and establish their own territories. With an average lifespan of nine to ten years, badgers are adaptable and tough.

◀ A badger looks up from digging with a dirt-covered face.

I don't often photograph badgers; they frequently elude me. Since they're most easily found emerging from their burrows, I've spent numerous days scanning valleys and meadows for dirt piles, to no avail. Finally, in the early spring, I found a pile of dirt haphazardly strewn across a small hillside, a mess that could only be made by a badger.

Patiently—or impatiently—monitoring a mound of dirt began to feel crazy, but the clouds drifting overhead and bison grazing in the distance provided a pleasant level of entertainment to ward off boredom. Nearly an hour had passed before there were any signs of life. Eventually something moved at the top of the hill behind the den; the mother had returned from a hunt. Seconds after she arrived, three cubs emerged to greet her in a frenzy of tawny fur. With hungry mouths to satisfy, the mother was kept busy hunting.

Before long she lay down on the pile of dirt and sunned herself in the heat of the day. It wouldn't be difficult to mistake her for a small boulder, leading me to wonder how many badgers I had looked past but never seen. Looking more closely, I could see streaks of mud covering her snout, well hidden between the white stripes across her face. Her long and sharp claws were undoubtedly her most notable feature, perfectly suited for digging into the rugged ground.

As she relaxed, the cubs dove in and out of the den, kicking up clouds of dust as they came and went. One cub seemed to prefer spending more time in the den, where the shade and cool earth likely provided a comfortable retreat from the hot sun above. The other two cubs wrestled together at the edge of the den in a flurry of fur and claws. Once they became bored, they lay near mom, curiously looking toward the nearby hill where I sat. Other than being smaller, the cubs looked nearly identical to their mom. I suspected it would only be a couple of weeks before the cubs were sent out to find their own corner of the valley to call home; for now, they were enjoying the simple life of adolescence and returned to wrestling.

▶ A mother badger and her cubs relax near their den.

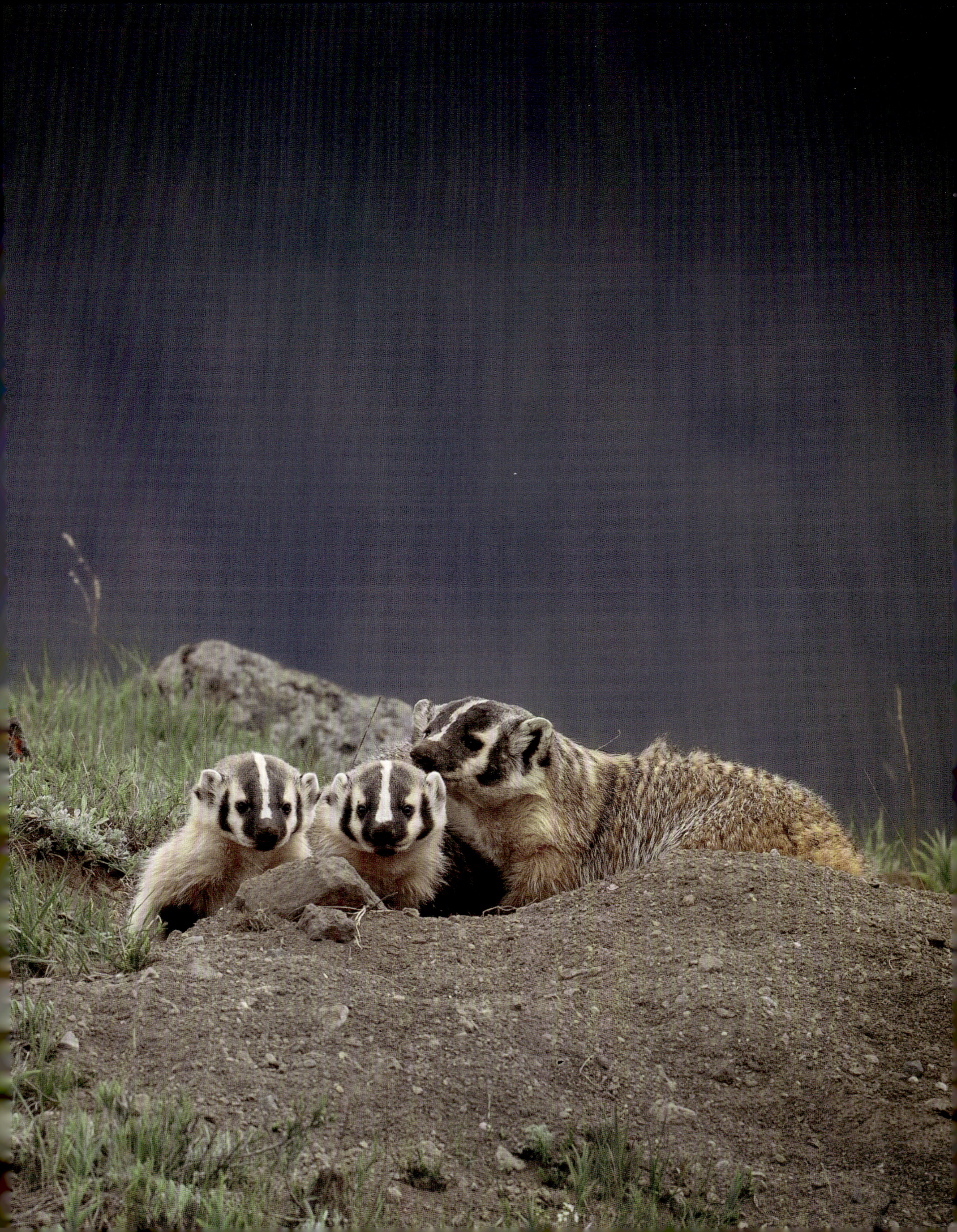

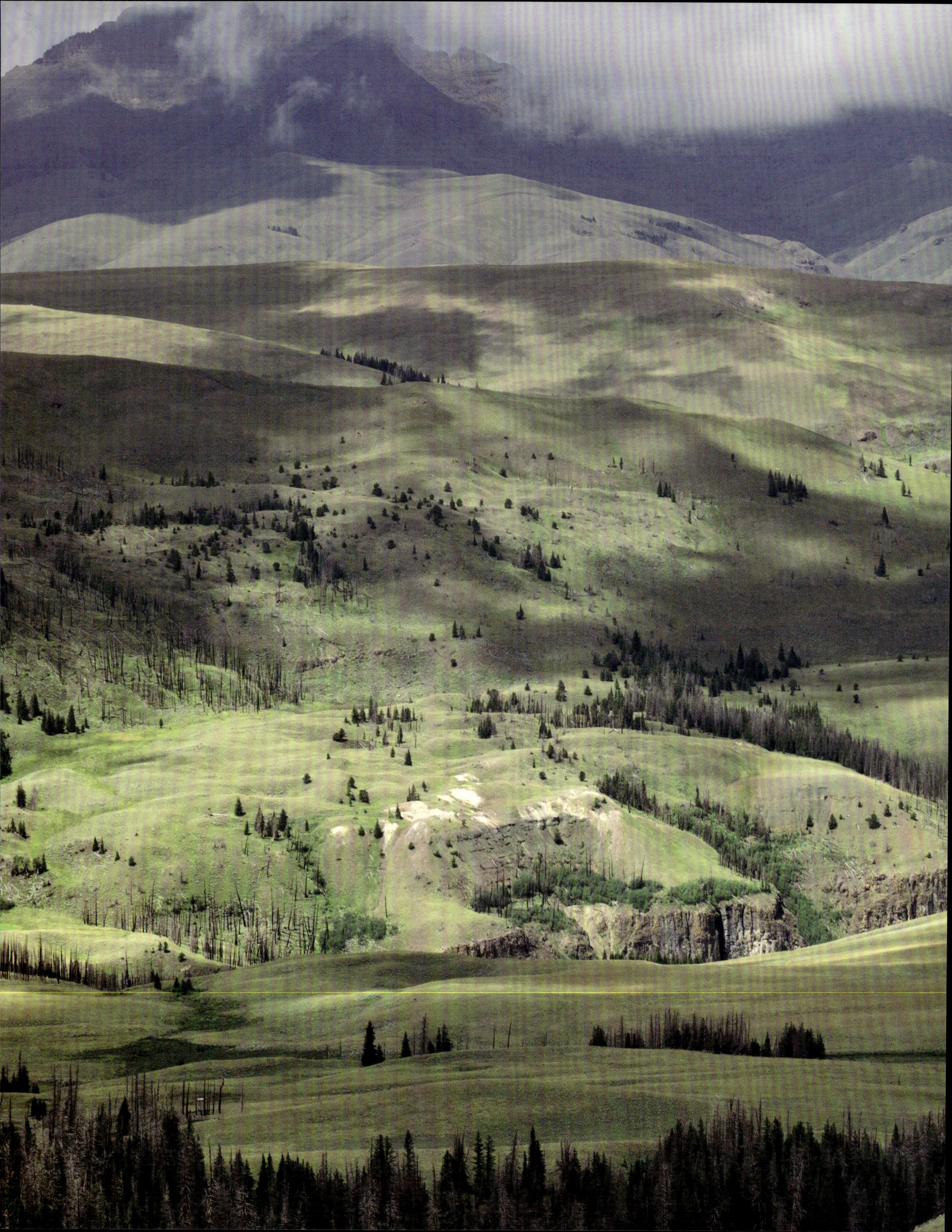

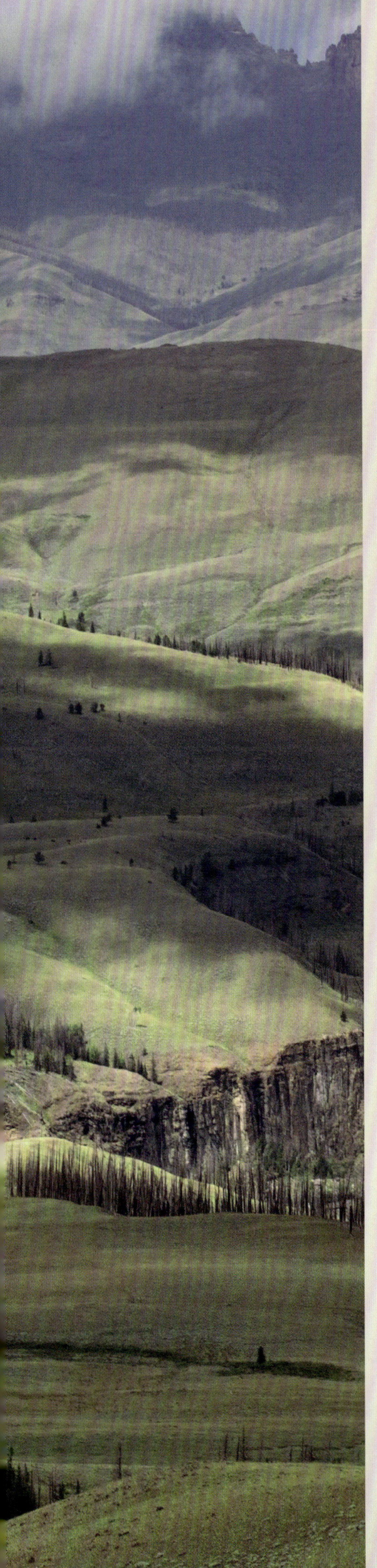

MOUNTAIN MEADOWS

Mountain meadows within Yellowstone are incredibly diverse. Without clear boundaries, it can be challenging to distinguish where the plains end and forests or alpine regions begin; the mountain meadows are where the three collide. Here, sagebrush gives way to trees along mountain slopes and the edges of forest clearings. Vegetation like grasses, roots, berries, and wildflowers thrives in mountain meadows. Streams and rivers create wetland habitats as they rush down to the plains below, providing habitats suitable for a wide variety of species.

Located at varying elevations, mountain meadows can be found scattered across all regions of the park. Some areas are sprawling, lush fields covering entire mountain slopes, while others are nothing more than small clearings, islands of grass amid towering pines. Dunraven Pass winds through both forests and mountain meadows, and the Madison and Firehole Rivers carve through many others. Some meadows are dotted with thermal features, particularly on the west side of Yellowstone in areas near Roaring Mountain or the Lower Geyser Basin. Between Yellowstone Lake and Sylvan Pass, charred trees remain from long-extinguished fires, crisscrossing the now rich meadows like pickup sticks.

The species that thrive in the mountain meadows are adaptable, conditioned for a variety of habitats and commonly seen elsewhere in Yellowstone as they move between areas—especially opportunistic feeders like the grizzly bear and gray wolf. The mountain meadows are a crossroads for many species, including those from the plains and forests like coyote, bison, and elk. Welcome to the mountain meadows of Yellowstone.

◀ A characteristic Yellowstone mountain meadow.

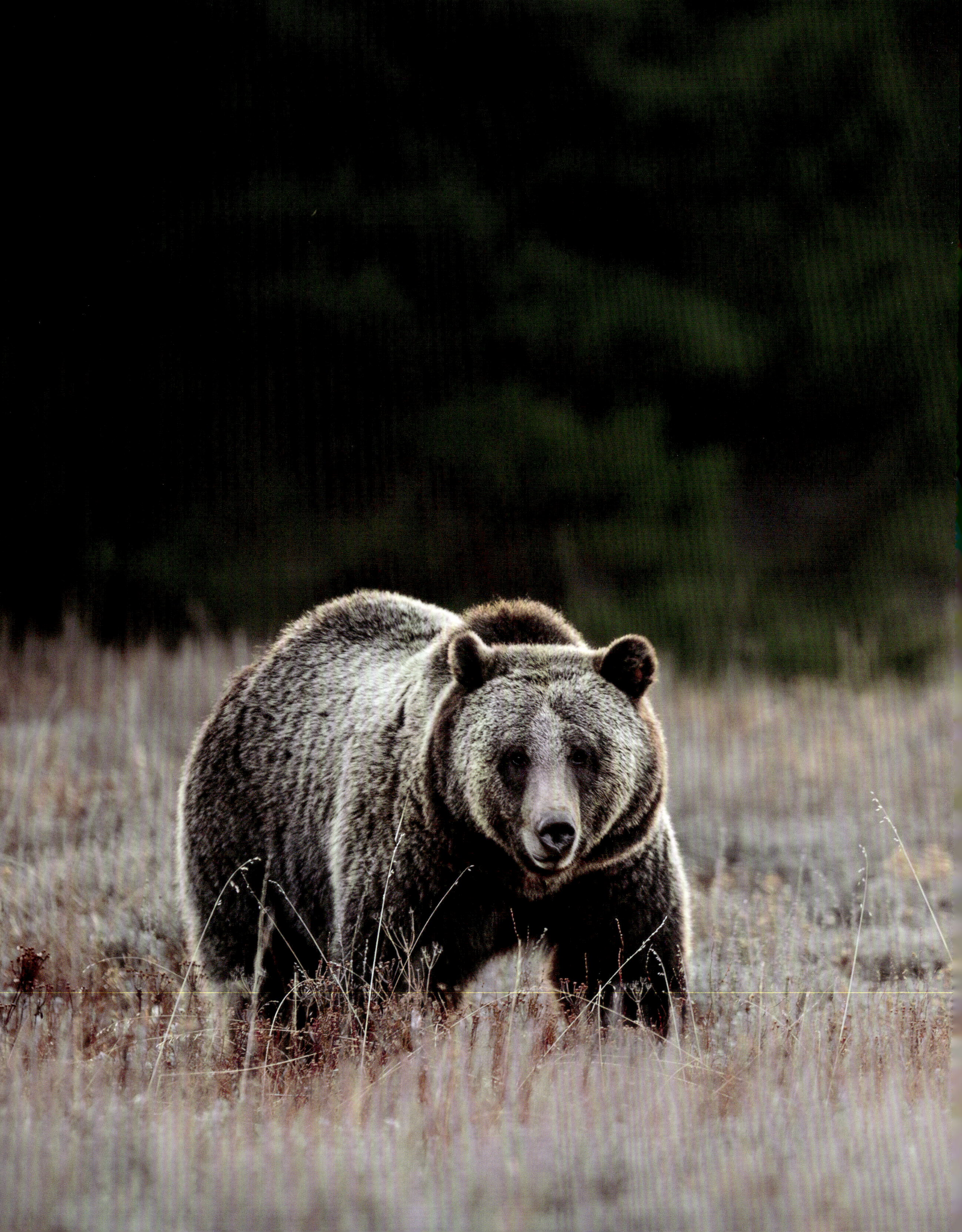

Grizzly Bears

Grizzly bears are Yellowstone's largest predators, weighing anywhere from 200 pounds to 700 pounds (90.7 to 317.5 kg) for the largest males. While many fear grizzlies, they are largely conflict-avoidant and can be safely observed from a distance along roadways throughout the park.

Grizzly bears can be a wide range of colors from light blond to nearly completely black. Some grizzly bears may wear radio tracking collars or ear tags for identification purposes as part of ongoing research. As extremely opportunistic eaters, grizzlies consume a wide variety of food, including large mammals, rodents, berries, roots, grasses, white bark pine nuts, and even moths. More than 60 percent of a Yellowstone grizzly bear's diet comes from the area's over 260 different species of plants. Long claws and powerful shoulder muscles, which form a characteristic hump, make grizzlies excellent and powerful diggers. Grizzlies spend most of their time feeding, packing in the calories in preparation for their winter hibernation.

By mid-November, most grizzlies will have gone to den, though some may remain active through December as long as food is still available. Males, called boars, will start to emerge in March, while females, or sows, might stay in the den with cubs until late May. During hibernation, a grizzly's heart rate will drop to only about ten to fifteen beats per minute.

Grizzly cubs are born in the den during late January and February; though they weigh only about a pound at birth, they grow quickly from drinking their mother's fatty milk. Most sows give birth to one to three cubs per litter, though quadruplets have been documented. Cubs typically stay with their mothers for two years before being chased off to live independently, allowing the mother to breed again. A major risk for young cubs is male bears, who will kill cubs that are not their own. As a result, some female bears have learned to stay close to developed areas as protection from males, who tend to avoid humans. These sows are known as roadside females.

Grizzlies live on average between twenty and twenty-five years, though they have been documented surviving into their thirties. Because of habitat fragmentation, the Yellowstone grizzly population is a genetic island not connected to any other grizzly population. This makes lack of genetic diversity a risk for the species. Other risks include conflicts with humans such as vehicle strikes.

◀ A grizzly bear strolls through a meadow shortly after sunrise.

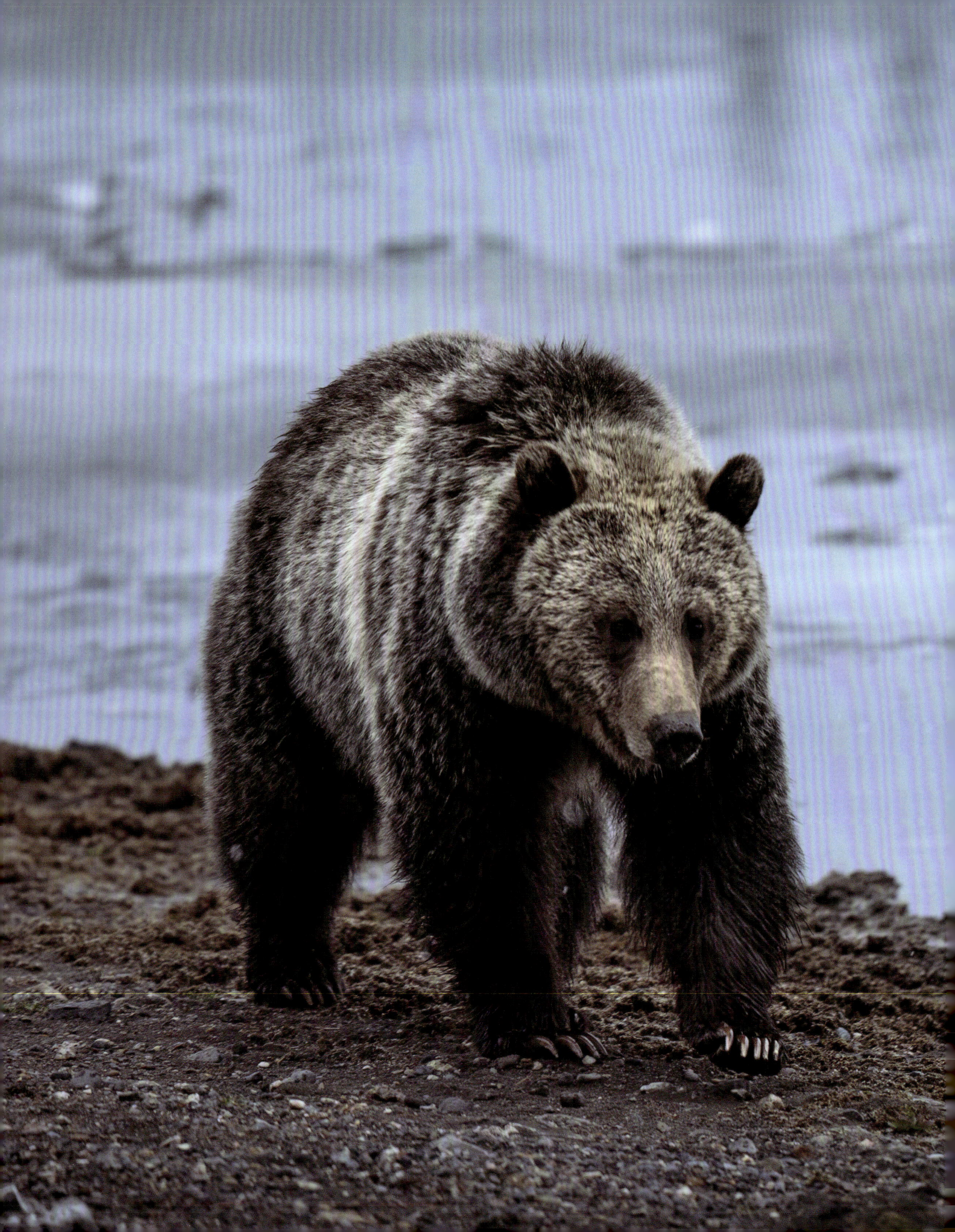

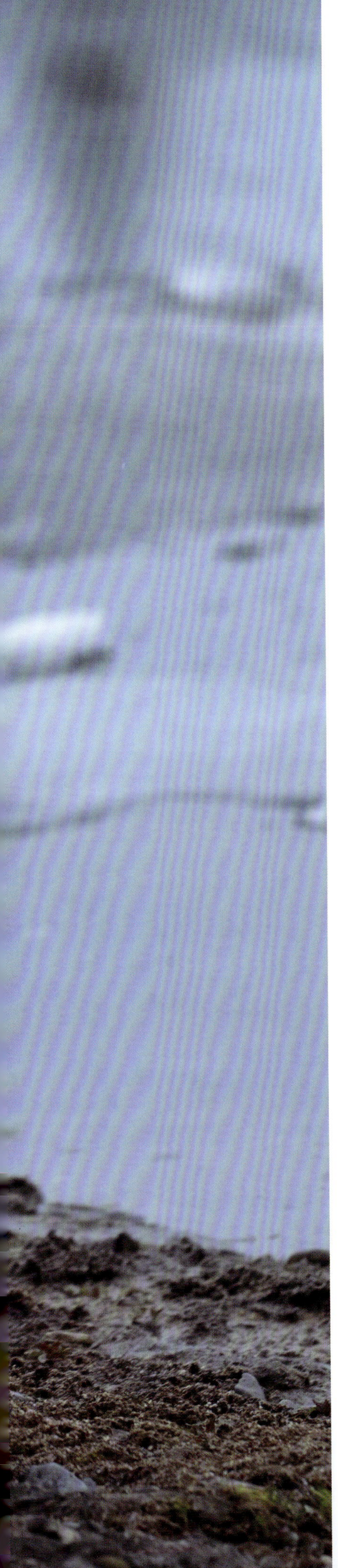

A part of me spends all year waiting for spring. It is my favorite season in Yellowstone for many reasons, but more than anything I love spring because of grizzly bears. The bears are the bloodline of the landscape. When they make their spring return, they bring a new sense of wildness that rejuvenates the land. I can't help but feel reenergized when spring, and the grizzlies, finally arrive.

It was mid-May, but patches of snow still covered the ground, its vital water already seeping into the soil and fueling the greens to come. By now, several bears had returned to their spring and summer homes in the low valleys. Yellowstone Lake had started to thaw, creating intricate lines and cracks as the ice broke apart. While looking toward a pile of ice forced against a rocky point by persistent wind, I noticed a dark shape in motion. I quickly identified it as a grizzly bear, and one I photograph often. In a split second of eagerness, I realized she was moving toward the beach, and the rocky shoreline would lead her directly toward where I waited in my car.

It doesn't happen often, but photographing a grizzly on the beach is something I constantly hope for. Trying to contain my excitement, I steadied myself and began the photo shoot. As she approached, I could hear pebbles shifting under her paws and her long claws scraping against larger stones. Her winter coat was still full, but soon it would begin to shed as the seasons continued to shift. The blond fur across her face and shoulders beautifully reflected the bleak light through storm clouds that carried spring snow. With the frozen lake behind her and snowflakes in the air, the scene was the perfect representation of all the reasons I love spring. The bear eventually passed my car and disappeared, leaving me with my heart racing. Spring had arrived in full force and I was once again walking where the bears walk.

◀ Newly emerged from winter hibernation, a female grizzly walks alongside the still-icy Yellowstone Lake.

During late January and early February my mind wanders to the mountain slopes, where deep in the protection of their den, grizzly cubs are being born. Despite the storms that may rage outside, the helpless cubs are safe against their mothers' warm bodies. They will grow there for a few months before emerging from their dens. Every year, I cannot wait to meet the new generation of grizzly bears.

June had begun, leaving the snow and desolate landscapes behind. Colors had returned; balsamroot wildflowers bloomed, and the morning skies were painted with the vibrance of summer sunrises. Before dawn, I ventured out in search of a grizzly I photograph often but hadn't had the privilege to see yet this season. She had just recently returned to the green meadows and hillsides of her summer home, a new cub at her side. Eager to photograph the youngster, I searched the hillsides in the morning gloom. The sun was rising quickly, and soon there was enough light for me to spot the pair cautiously moving downhill across fallen logs.

The mother continued with intense purpose until reaching a patch of cow parsnip, a favorite summertime food. While the mother bear fed, the curious young cub couldn't resist exploring his wild home. He had likely only been out of the den for a few weeks, making each new sight and smell a thrilling and educational experience. He enthusiastically leapt into the parsnip patch and disappeared under the cover of the broad leaves. His mother, unamused, continued feeding.

A few moments later the cub's head appeared through the leaves; he was looking directly at me. After clambering onto one of the many fallen logs in the area, the cub tilted his head. His tiny white claws shone in the morning light, and his wild, frizzy fur stuck out in all directions. My mind wandered to the past, when I had watched the cub's two older sisters at this young age (they were now both powerful and capable grizzlies in their own right). I couldn't suppress a sense of excitement at the thought of one day seeing the bear the small cub would become, joining his ancestors in a long and successful line of Yellowstone grizzlies.

▶ A grizzly cub poses atop a log in a patch of cow parsnip.

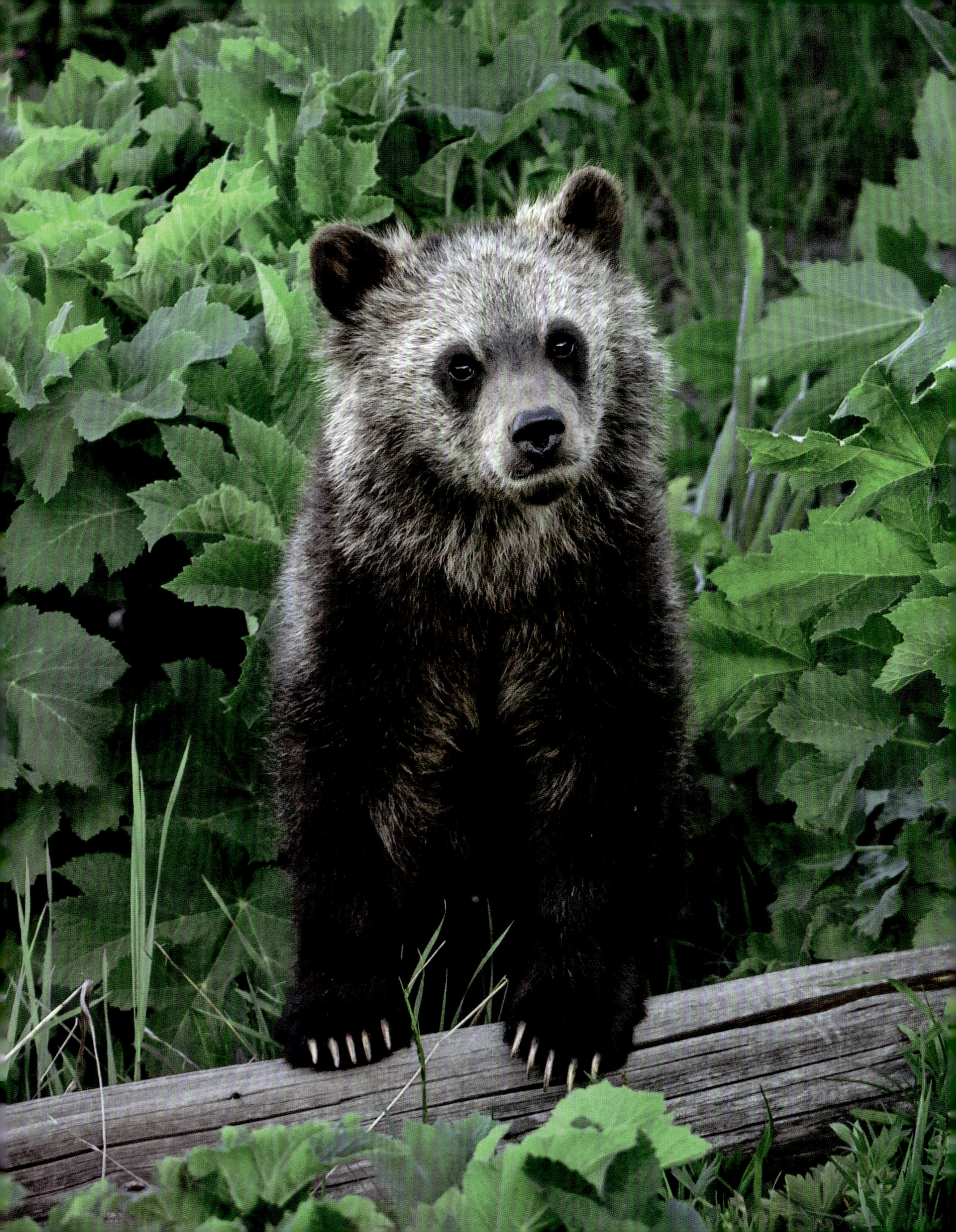

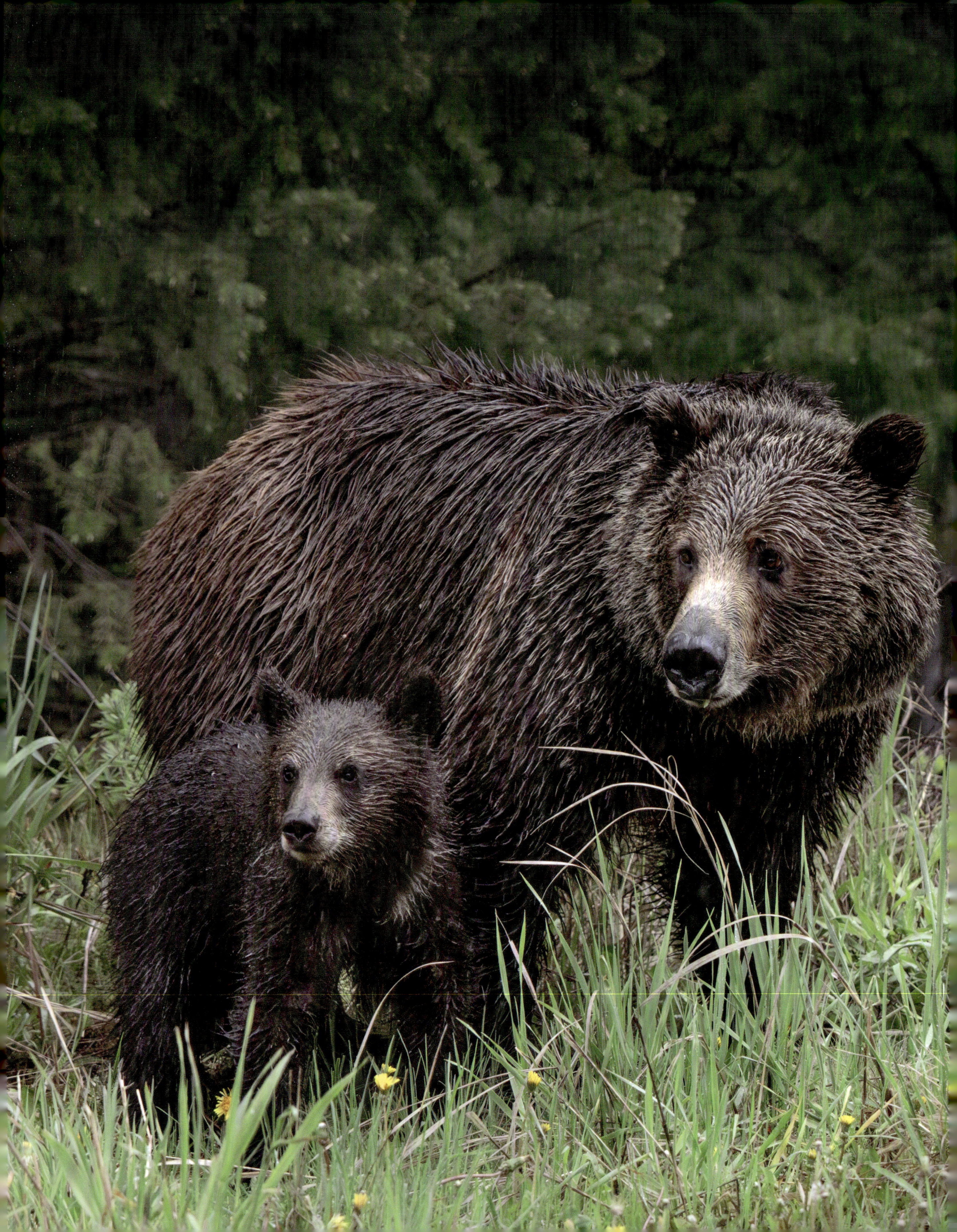

In a single year in the Yellowstone ecosystem, I usually see between forty and fifty different grizzly bears, each identifiable by a combination of their location, physical features like coloration or size, and the presence of any ear tags or radio collars. Some grizzlies I see nearly every day while others I may only cross paths with once and never spot again. I'm always equally excited by any grizzly sighting—a bear is a bear, after all—but the encounters that remain among the most special are the rare instances I am able to spend time alone with a bear. There is nothing else like it.

It was late June. Rainstorms had pelted the region almost nonstop for three days, and the rivers swelled with the spring runoff. I journeyed into the forest on an evening drive and came across a mother grizzly bear and her young cub. I had never seen this sow before, and she was beautiful. Rain clouds hung so low over the mountains behind the bears that their peaks were completely hidden among the white wisps. Without wind, raindrops fell straight down, collecting on pine boughs or falling directly into the streams and rivers. Everything in the forest was drenched, including the bears, but neither attempted to shake off their fur. Instead, the pair grazed calmly along the road, taking advantage of the lush roadside grasses. I photographed the two through my open car window and was soon equally soaked. Over the soft pitter-patter of raindrops, I could hear the bears chewing and snipping each blade of grass. No one else was around, allowing for a truly serene experience with the bears.

With a mixture of curiosity and caution, the cub occasionally looked my way with round eyes and an inquisitive expression. Only a few months old, the cub mimicked every move its mother made (the first of many vital steps in learning how to be a grizzly bear) and never strayed far from her side. I watched the pair for close to an hour while the light dwindled behind the cloud cover. As dusk approached, the mother turned and disappeared into the thick pine forest, her cub right on her heels. I mentally thanked them for the incredible encounter and wondered if I would ever see either bear again.

◀ A mother grizzly and her cub with soaked fur after a spring rainstorm.

By the time summer finally arrives in Yellowstone, it has been a long time coming. It gradually inches nearer throughout spring until all at once, and seemingly overnight, summer is back in full force. This season brings pros and cons for photographers: The warmer weather can decrease wildlife activity, but the brilliancy of summer vegetation and wildflowers provides colorful photo opportunities.

Bear activity usually declines as June nears its end and July begins, but one young grizzly was surprisingly active and visible during her first summer on her own. On a late summer evening I found her in a clearing as she foraged her way through the open forest. Her mother had chased her away just a month previously and she was still learning to navigate her wild world as an independent bear, evident by her wary demeanor. Finally, after pacing through the meadow as if unsure which direction she wanted to go, she plopped down among the pine trees.

From the road, I started photographing the young bear—a bear I had watched grow up from the time she was a tiny cub. The tall summer grasses swayed in the gentle breeze and rubbed against her chest and legs. Casting her head around, she turned and looked westward toward the evening sun. She was strikingly beautiful, her caramel-blond fur shining in the soft light that filtered through the trees overhead. Her eyes, though soulful and full of youthful energy, had a new sense of seriousness I had never noticed before that had likely developed through her time on her own. For the first time, I saw a true grizzly and not a cub. I couldn't help but stand in reverence for the exquisitely capable and gorgeous bear she had become.

► A newly independent female grizzly enjoys a summer evening.

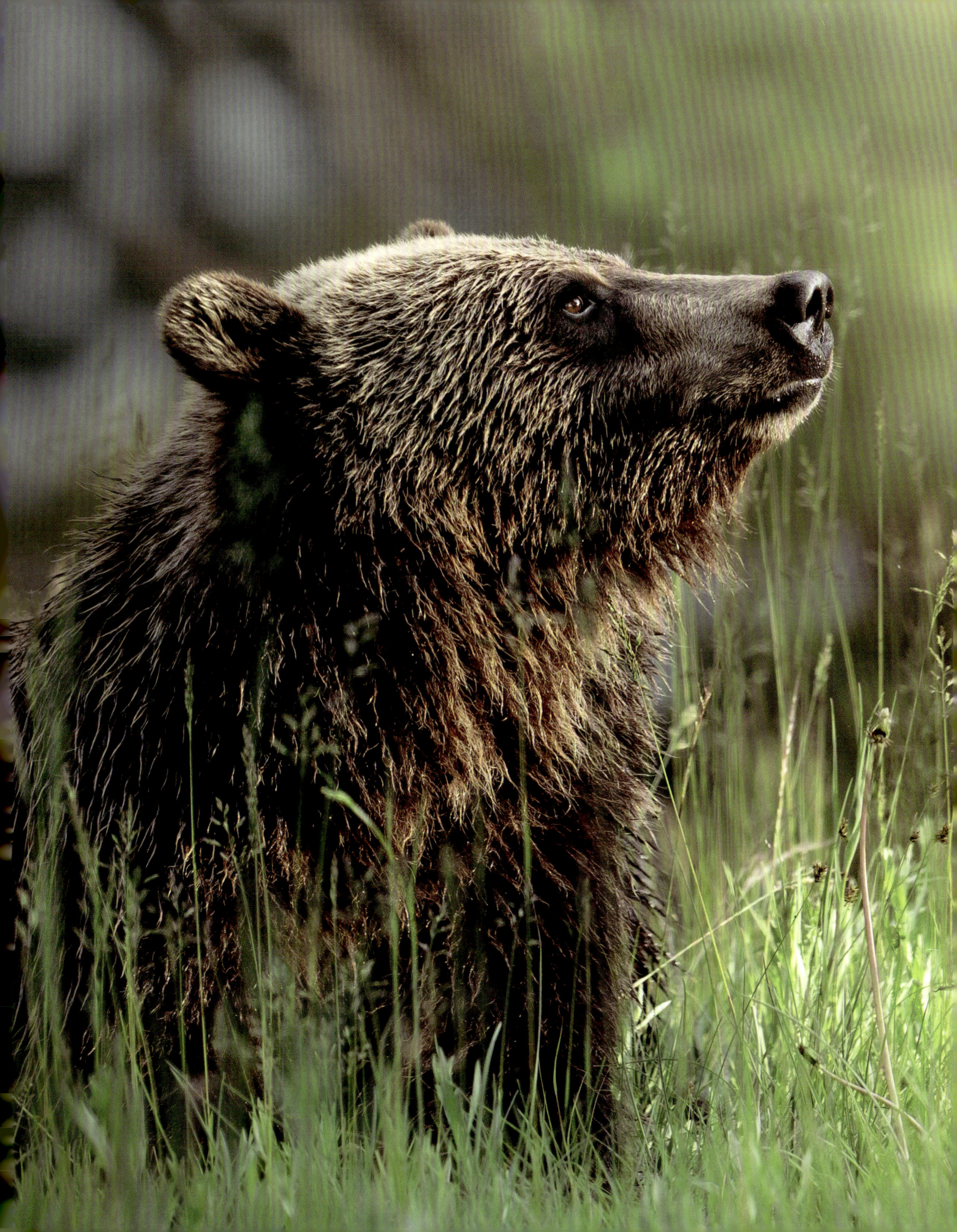

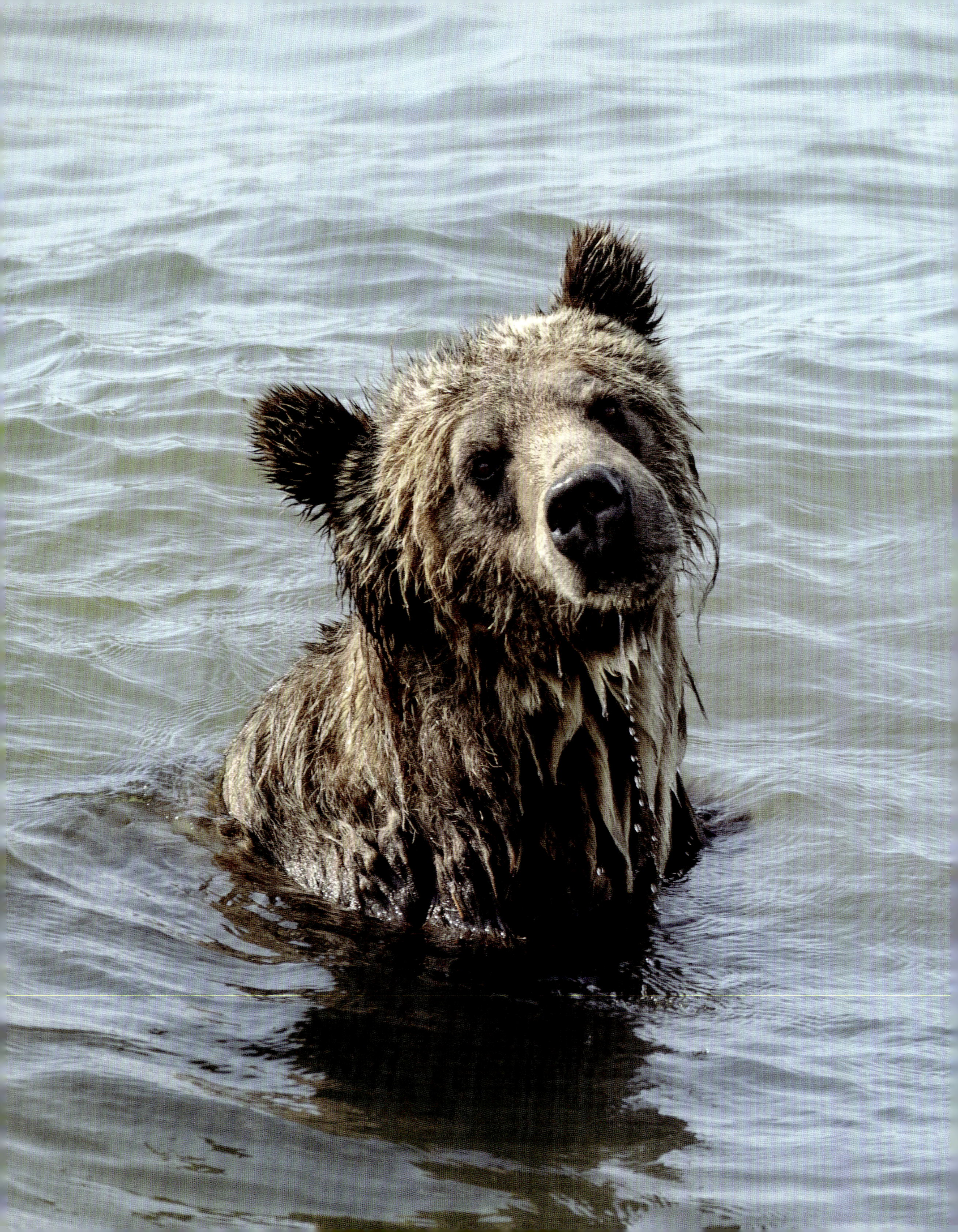

July tends to be a slow month for grizzly bears, as they search for food and seek refuge from the valleys' sweltering heat in the high country. Like grizzly bears, I am not particularly fond of hot summer days and would much rather spend a day outside under clouds and storms than a blue sky. Still, not even the heat of summer can prevent me from searching for grizzly bears, even if the odds are against me.

The temperature was in the high eighties when I entered the park for the afternoon, unusually hot for Yellowstone even in July. My hopes of seeing any wildlife plummeted. Heat haze radiated off the pavement as I drove. Without a cloud in sight, there would be no relief from the intense sun until it began to set. I continued down the road without any real plan, painfully aware the odds of seeing any animals were slim. But a pleasantly surprising sight met me as I rounded a curve along Yellowstone Lake: A grizzly bear was sitting in the water.

I had never seen a grizzly swimming in the lake, so I eagerly grabbed my camera and started photographing the bear, one I had never seen before. Only his head and shoulders were visible above the surface, while gentle waves lapped against his back and made his shadow sway. Water dripped off every tendril of fur, plopping into the lake below and sending small ripples radiating outward. Lazily, the bear swung his head to the side and looked toward me, a calm expression on his face. Yellowstone Lake is notoriously frigid all year, so I could only imagine the cooling relief the bear must be enjoying. The bear's head nodded from side to side as he became increasingly relaxed, as if the waves were lulling him to sleep.

After spending at least half an hour in the lake, the bear finally stood up in the water and slowly walked back to the shoreline. When he climbed onto the pebbled beach, he gave a violent shake of his fur and sent water droplets flying in all directions. Nonchalantly, he crossed the road and disappeared into the forest. I wondered if the bear had ever swum in the lake before, or if any other grizzlies regularly cooled off in its refreshingly cold waters. I do believe bears, and all wildlife, only show themselves on their own terms, making me grateful for any time I can spend observing their wild lives.

◀ A grizzly escapes the July heat with a swim in Yellowstone Lake.

I never pretend I know a bear; one can never truly know the wildness that lies beneath such rugged and pure beauty. But there are many grizzlies I photograph regularly, including one that will always remain my favorite regardless of how much time passes. She is known by several names. To the National Park Service, her official name is the Nine Mile Sow, while to others she is Snow, named for her exceptionally blond fur. I've been watching her since she was a cub, though she has become a beautiful adult bear. I almost see parts of myself in her, especially her carefree and independent spirit, though I know she is undoubtedly wild; that intense wildness constantly inspires me.

On a late summer evening I watched as she and her two cubs, her first set, slowly ascended a hillside while foraging through thick vegetation, often completely hidden from view by the lush summer growth. Near the top of the hill and just below where I sat waiting in my car was a vibrant patch of yellow wildflowers almost glowing in the evening light. I began desperately hoping Snow would walk through the flowers.

Snow was still lumbering in my direction, but far slower than I had wished, taking only a few steps at a time between long pauses to dig for roots. Her breaths were audible in the quiet air, even and rhythmic. Suddenly her head rose; she smelled the air and began walking toward me at a steady and determined pace. As the last of the evening light filtered through the surrounding pines, Snow stepped perfectly into the wildflowers and paused for a few seconds while her cubs wrestled in a nearby berry bush. She had made the image I envisioned become a reality.

Maybe part of my love for Snow comes from her ability to deliver incredible wildlife encounters, yet I will never let my love for any wild animal change the way I view them. Snow will always be unwaveringly wild regardless of what name she's known by or how much time I spend watching, and that is why I love Snow.

▶ A grizzly known as Snow amidst the summer wildflowers.

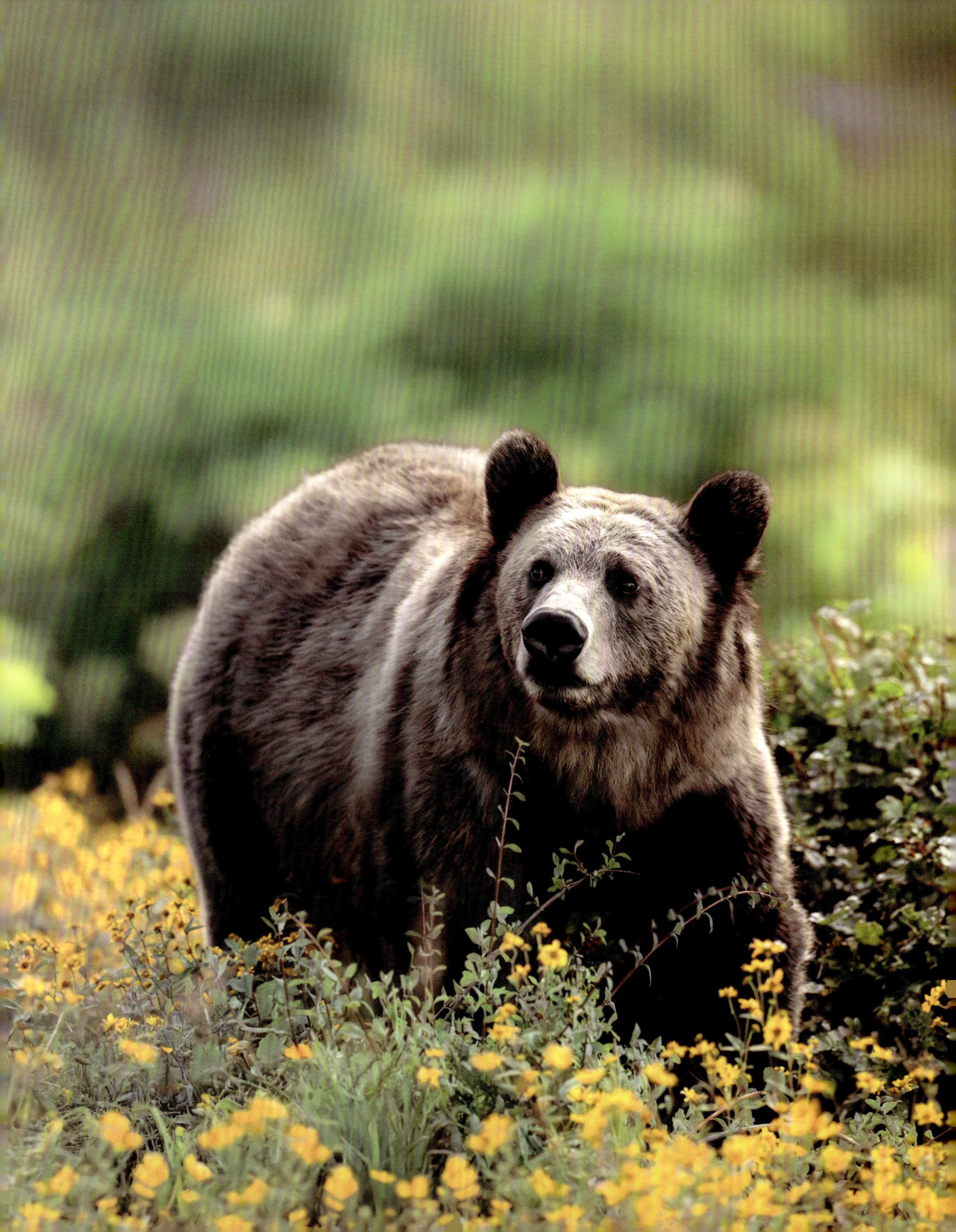

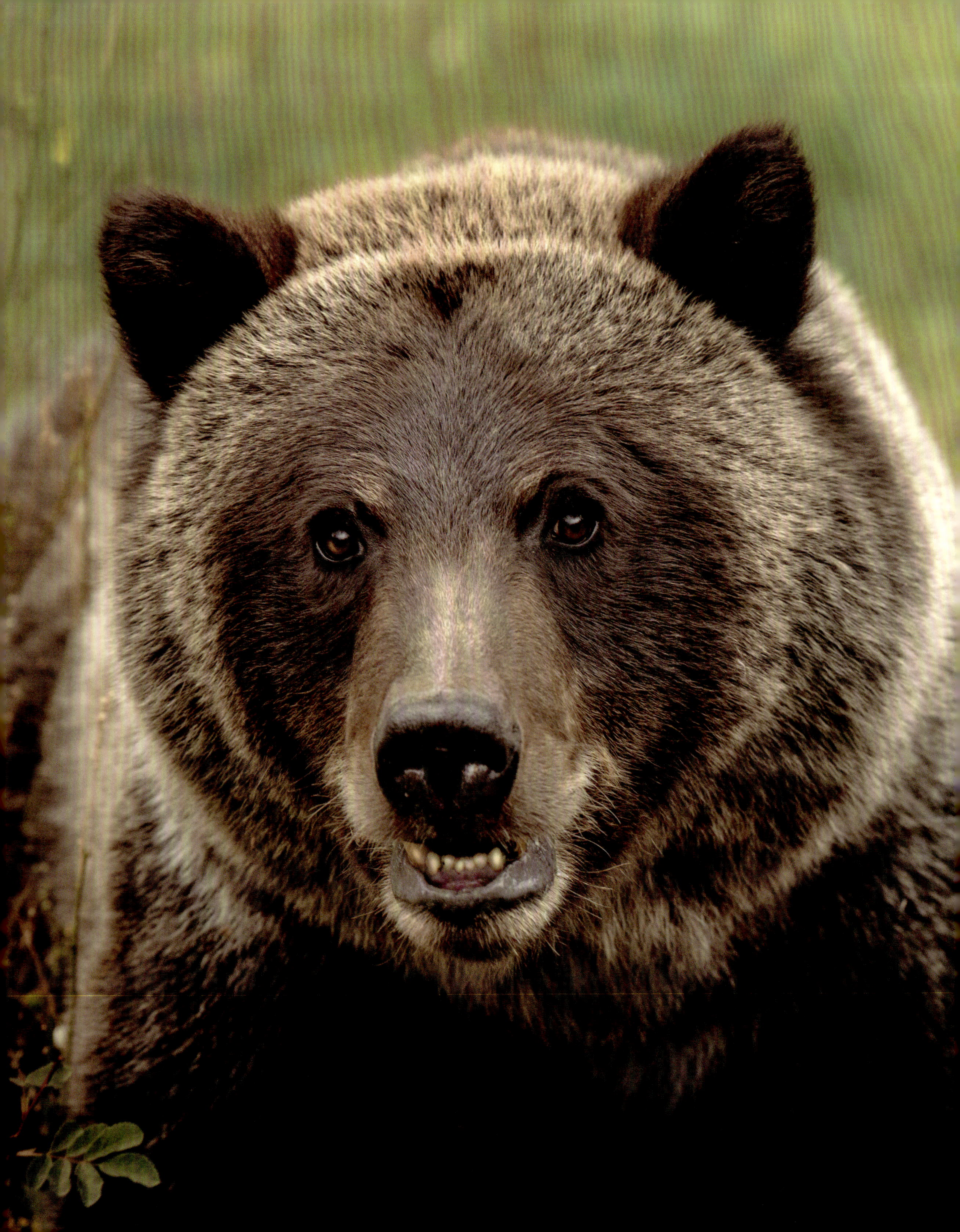

During the transition from summer to fall, bears enter hyperphagia: a state of intense eating to gain weight prior to hibernation. At the same time, berries across Yellowstone ripen, providing a sweet and vital meal to many hungry bears. As summer days begin to fade, I excitedly await berry season and the bear encounters that come with it.

Early in the morning on the first cold day of the season, I was surprised to see a grizzly almost completely hidden in thick berry bushes. It was mid-September, and I assumed berry season was over; the raspberries and huckleberries had come and gone, and even the other berries had mostly been picked over by hungry bears and birds. What remained wouldn't last under this bear's eager onslaught. The bear's white teeth were revealed with each bite, though the canine teeth weren't worn down at all. This was a young grizzly, likely experiencing its first fall alone.

Fueled by instincts and the knowledge acquired from its mother, the young bear had learned to survive and thrive in its wild world. I wondered if the bear had visited this berry patch as a cub, or if this was a new discovery found through an incredible sense of smell. Regardless, the bear feasted with an insatiable hunger. With surprisingly delicate movements, the bear used its lips and tongue to effortlessly pluck the berries from their stems and swallow the sweet morsels whole. At times, the bear all but vanished into the thick vegetation, only betraying its location via a swaying branch or rustling leaves and making photography difficult. I waited with my camera raised, sometimes only capturing the bear's round ears or grizzled fur between branches.

The bear slowly moved as it ate, eventually stopping in a thick berry bush at the base of a pine tree close to where I sat in my car. Looking directly at me, the bear opened its mouth and began plucking berries, completely unbothered by my presence. I could hear its teeth snapping while it chewed. Before long, the bear had efficiently cleared the bush of its berries and disappeared back into the thick vegetation in search of another feast.

◀ A young grizzly bear raises its head from feasting on berries in preparation for hibernation.

I never know which bear of the season is the last, the fleeting beauty of all things that end. Most grizzlies head to hibernation around the time the park roads close, so the last days of October are spent wondering if the bear I've just observed will be my last.

I spent several hours on a gloomy fall day watching a mother grizzly and her cub as they foraged for any remaining edible vegetation. The grasses were dead but a striking dull orange color in the dreary light. The wind howled sporadically through the dead and burned trees, causing an eerie creak as they swayed under its force. The grizzlies' thick blond winter coats perfectly blended into the autumn hillside. Clearly content with whatever grubs or roots they had dug up, the pair remained in the same place, rarely moving more than a few steps over the course of an hour. I waited patiently, knowing they would eventually continue down the slope. After several hours, the bears broke from their foraging routine and started to head directly toward my car.

The sow, despite her large size and typical slow gait, was determined in her path. As she approached the edge of the hill just above the road, she paused, and our eyes locked for a second. Locking eyes with a grizzly is the rarest and most pure connection to the wild; it feels as if you're looking into the eyes of Mother Nature herself. I didn't dare break eye contact. After another glance over her shoulder to locate her cub, she continued down the hill and crossed the road behind my car, heading east into the woods. The slopes of her familiar mountain were just a few miles away, her winter retreat, and I wondered if I would see her again or if she had just become my last grizzly of the year.

► With her tawny fur, a female grizzly blends into the autumn landscape.

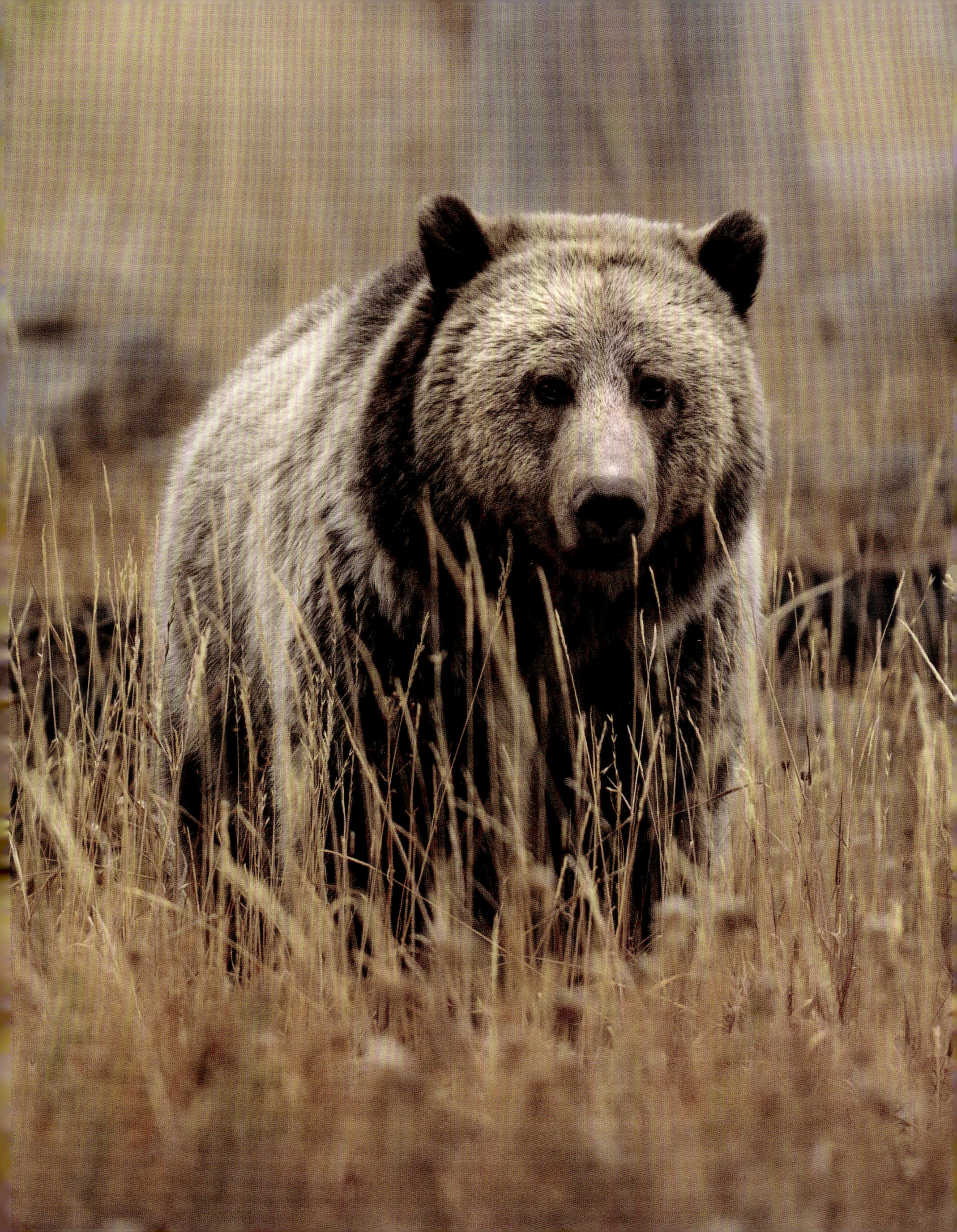

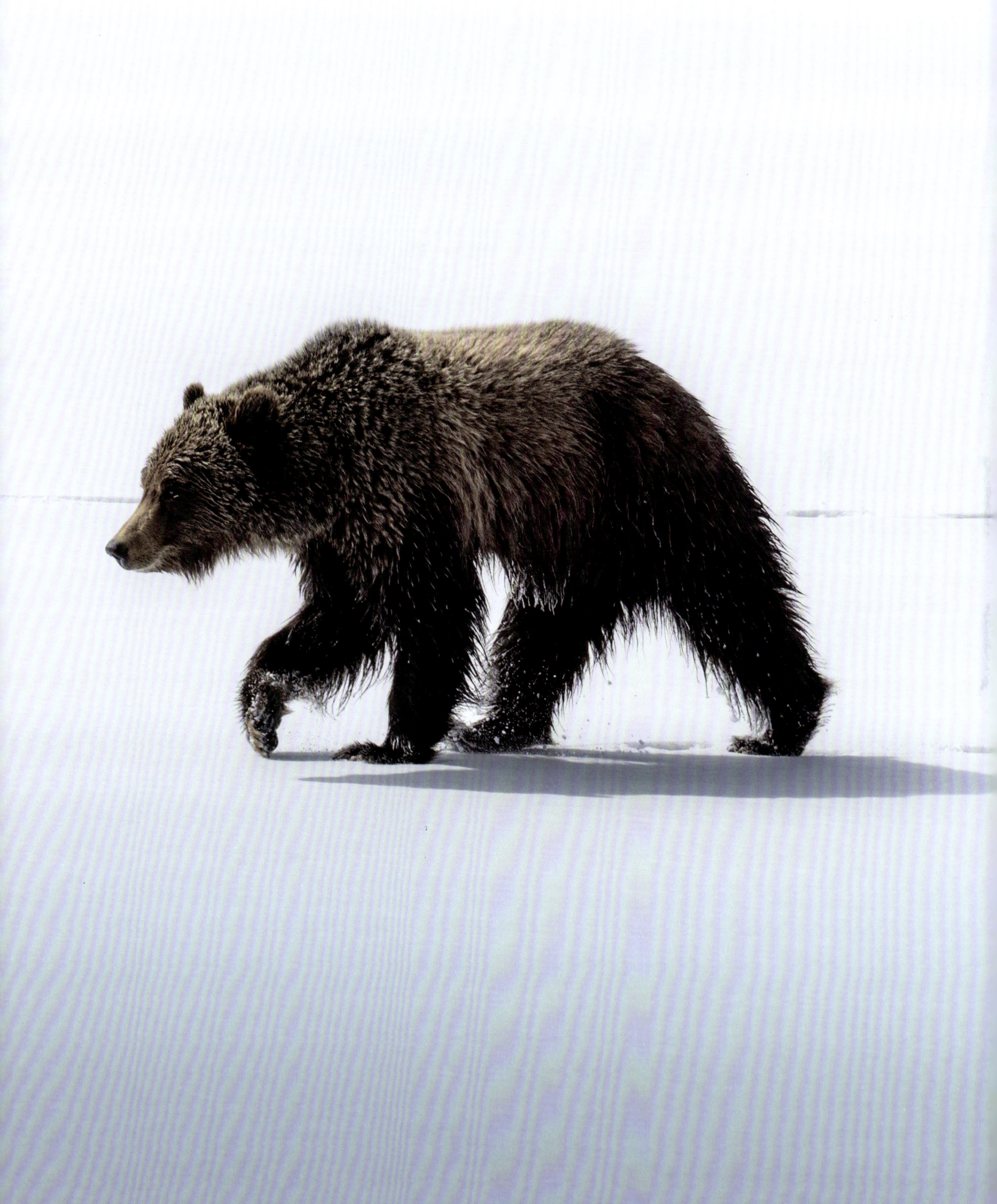

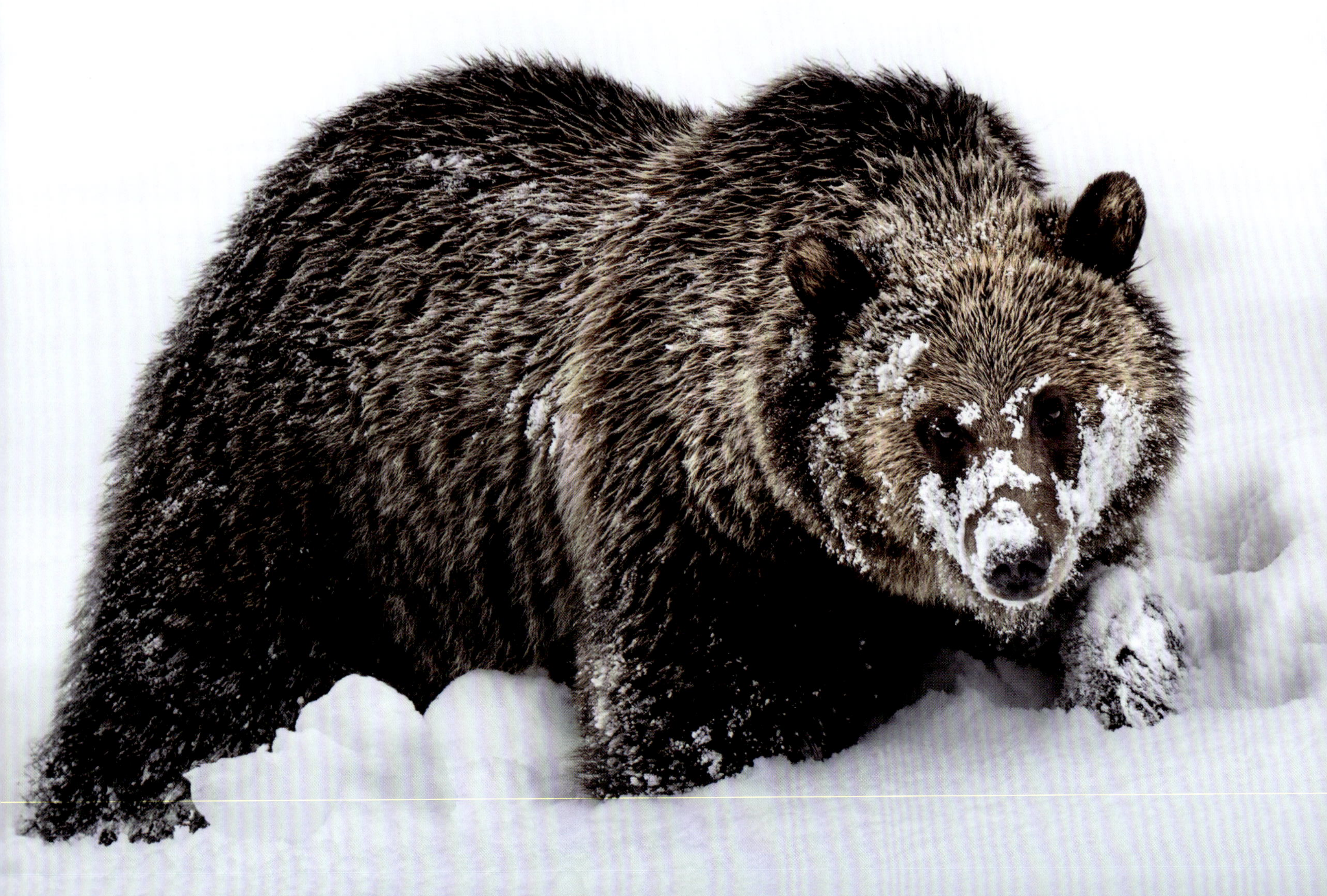

There are specific times in the spring and fall when it's possible to photograph grizzlies in snow, either at the beginning or end of their long winter hibernation. The thought of seeing bears in snow is always exciting. With a deep blanket of snow covering the mountains one late autumn afternoon and more falling straight down onto the fog-drenched hillsides, I began the search for a grizzly, venturing to an area frequented by a mother grizzly and her cub. I soon found two lines of bear tracks leading up the mountain. Disheartened and assuming they were well on the way to hibernation, I continued my search without much luck for most of the day.

But in the late evening, as the snow continued to fall, I found the mother grizzly and her then two-year-old cub walking through deep drifts and climbing over fallen timber. This struggle through the deep snow was their final hardship before the promise of peace during hibernation. I began photographing the pair, capturing the snowflakes softly collecting on their already light-colored fur and the snow that clung to their legs and paws, weighing them down with each step. The cub showed her usual goofy personality as she rolled through the belly-deep drifts, often kicking her paws and sending clumps of snow flying. To her, this journey wasn't a challenge but a game.

Eventually, the satisfied cub regained a level of composure, though the snow still covered her face. For a moment she looked right at me. Her eyes shone through the gray air, golden and fierce amber pools. I couldn't bring myself to blink. I was hypnotized by her wildness and in awe of her beauty. The second passed, and our eyes broke away. She turned and looked toward her mother, who had continued onward. Bounding energetically in her mother's line of tracks, the cub soon caught up. They disappeared into the trees, clearly headed to their den. Soon, the persistent snowfall hid even their tracks. I bid the bears goodbye, knowing I wouldn't see them again until the spring. I was now once again waiting for spring, waiting for bears.

◀ A grizzly enjoys a late autumn snowfall before beginning hibernation.
▲ *Previous*: A grizzly bear walks across the ice of Yellowstone Lake in the early spring.

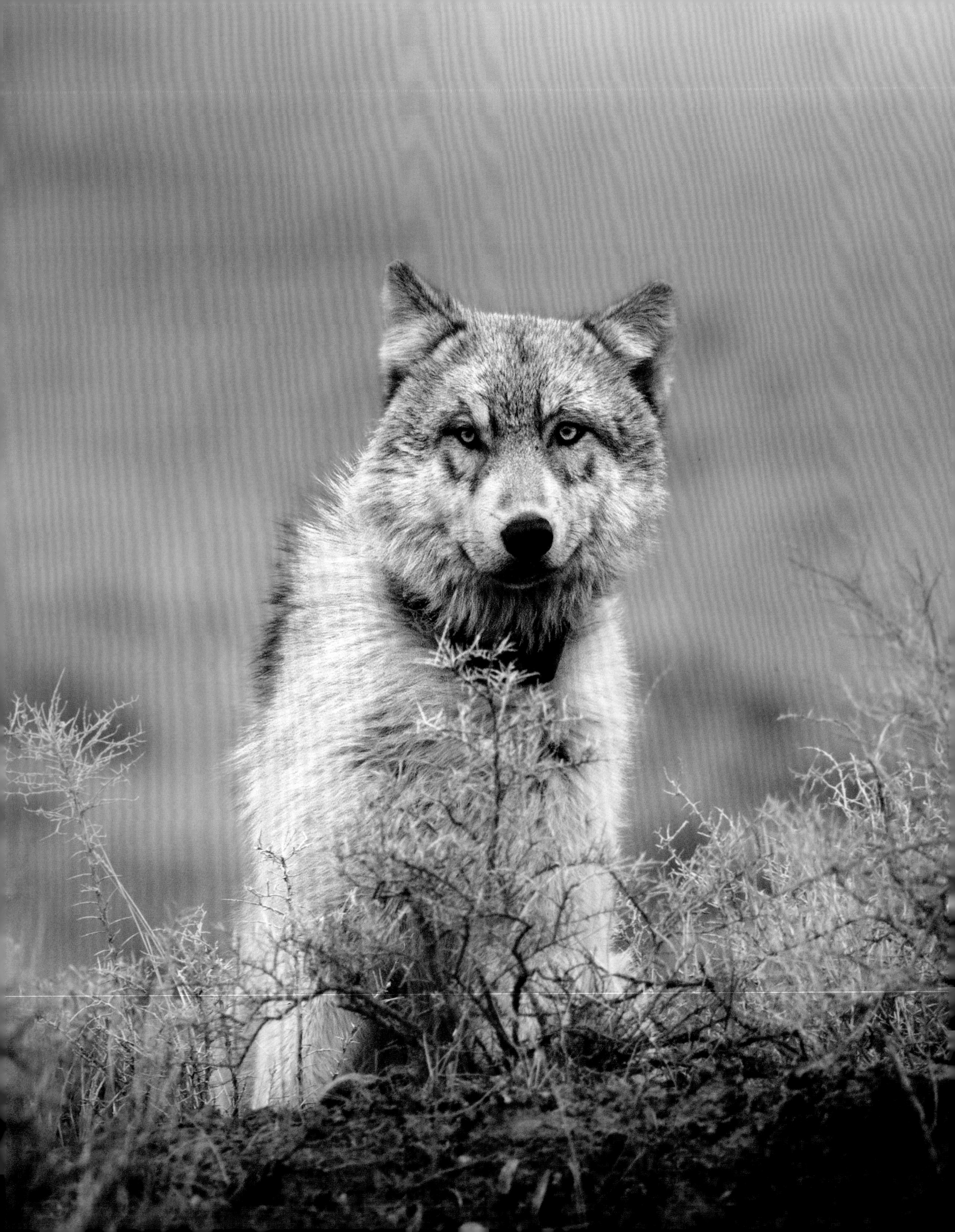

Gray Wolf

The history of wolves in Yellowstone is a fascinating one and stands as a testament to the successes of conservation, ecological understanding, and rewilding. During the late 1800s and early 1900s, wolf and other predator populations dropped as a result of westward expansion. Thousands of wolves were shot, trapped, and poisoned across the West by settlers who were fearful of the animals and wanted to protect livestock, causing the wolf population to plummet. By 1926, wolves had been completely eliminated from Yellowstone.

Without the population control wolves provided, the elk population boomed, causing overgrazing that wreaked havoc on other species. In 1995, thirty-one gray wolves were reintroduced to Yellowstone, bringing balance back to the entire ecosystem. Their impact was seen even in the flow of the rivers: Wolves dropped the elk population to a natural level, which limited overgrazing on all vegetation, thus allowing the willows to bounce back and provide vital erosion control, strengthening riverbanks. Wolves had restored Yellowstone.

Today, the wolf population within Yellowstone sits around 100 to 120 individuals, all descendants of the pioneering wolves that were first reintroduced. Some wolves have tracking collars that are used for ongoing research by park biologists. Wolves can be gray, white, or black and live in packs as large as thirty-five, though the average pack size is about eleven individuals and one breeding pair. Pups are born in the spring and remain close to the den until they become old enough to either join the pack or disperse to find a new pack. Yellowstone's wolves live roughly four to five years, though the oldest known wolf here lived to over twelve. The leading cause of death for wolves in Yellowstone is other wolves. Outside of the park and at risk from hunters, their average lifespan is only two to three years.

Wolves can be seen across Yellowstone; Lamar Valley is a world-renowned location for wolf watching. Often elusive, wolves are most likely to be seen in the early morning and late evening or heard howling from distant meadows just after nightfall.

◀ A collared gray wolf peers through the sage.

Wolves are difficult to find; I spent my first several years as a photographer in Yellowstone without capturing a single image of a wolf, though it was all I thought of. I spent many sunrises searching for them and long hours waiting at picked-over carcasses desperately hoping for even a split-second encounter with one. Finally, I gave up. I decided I would one day photograph a wolf by chance and no deliberate attempts would change that.

Not long after, I was proven right. It was late in the season, only a week before Yellowstone would close for the winter. Dark clouds hung over the mountain peaks and the wind whistled ominously through the pines. At the edge of a meadow lay a dozen wolves, members of the Wapiti Lake Pack. Their tails were curled tightly around their noses, turning each wolf into a black or white dot on the landscape. For several hours they rested with very little movement.

Abruptly, the pack awoke and stretched, shaking the sleep from their fur. As they arose, more wolves emerged from the forest. They were other pack members, and now the pack was reunited. In a frenzy of tail wags and licks the pack greeted one another, each member displaying behavior appropriate for their rank in the group. Lower-ranking wolves cowered in submission on their bellies and slowly wagged their tails. The dominant wolves stood tall with their tails held up assertively. A large black wolf was the last to appear from the forest; he was the alpha male. His dark coat faded into the shadows, but even from a distance I could see his bright silvery eyes. The rest of the pack paused to look at the alpha and await his next move. Breaking the tension of the moment, he trotted up to his pack and joined in the greeting, the occasional yip or growl audible even from across the meadow.

Soon the pack settled back down, and a few members curled up together in a close circle. Before long the entire pack had fallen back asleep, clearly at peace now that they had reunited. I reluctantly pulled myself away and left the pack, still in awe over the unique and fascinating behavior I had just witnessed. More than anything, I felt grateful to the wolves for granting me the moment I had been chasing all year. I knew I would cross paths with them again when the time was right, and not a second before.

▶ The Wapiti Lake Pack reunites on the edge of a forest.

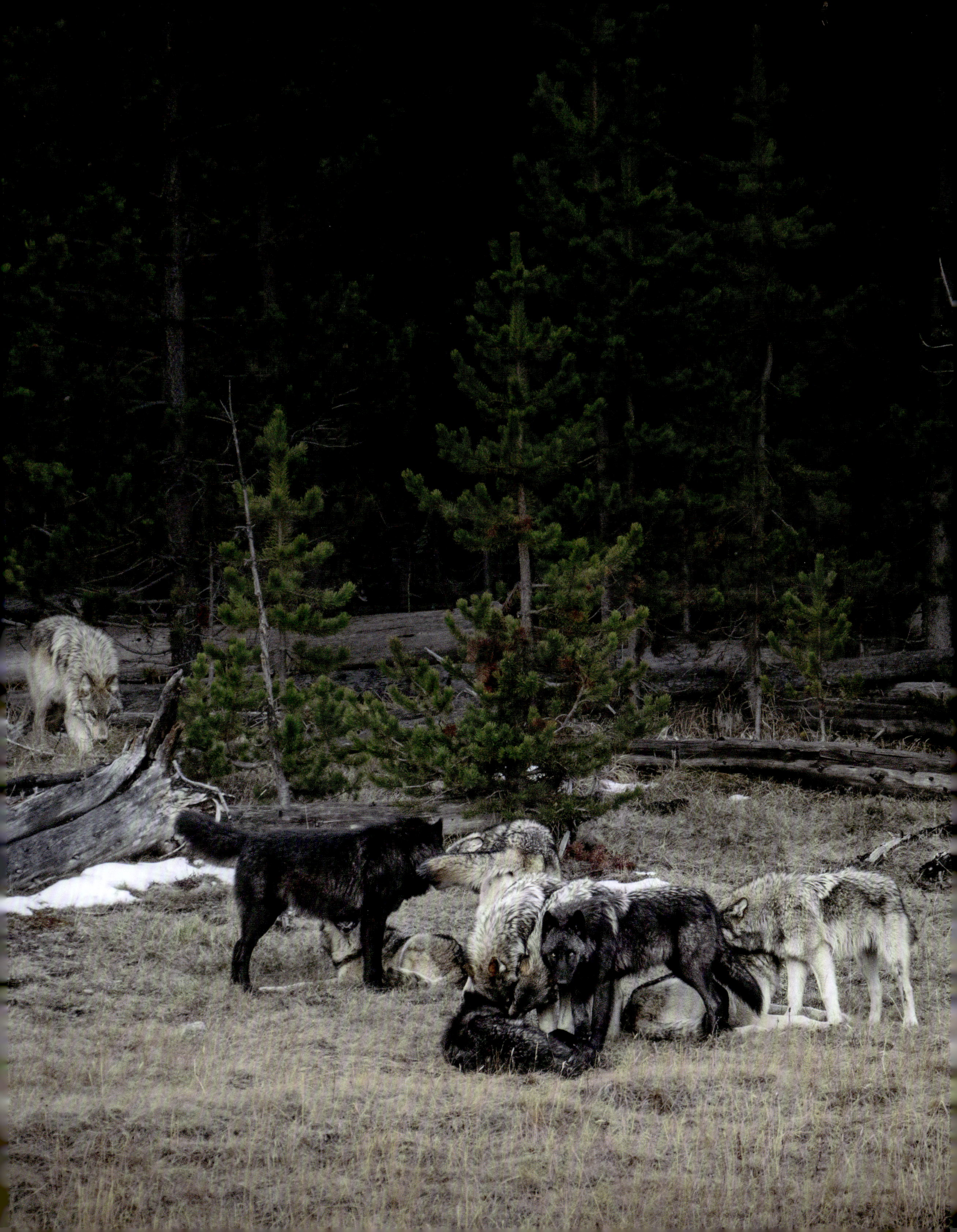

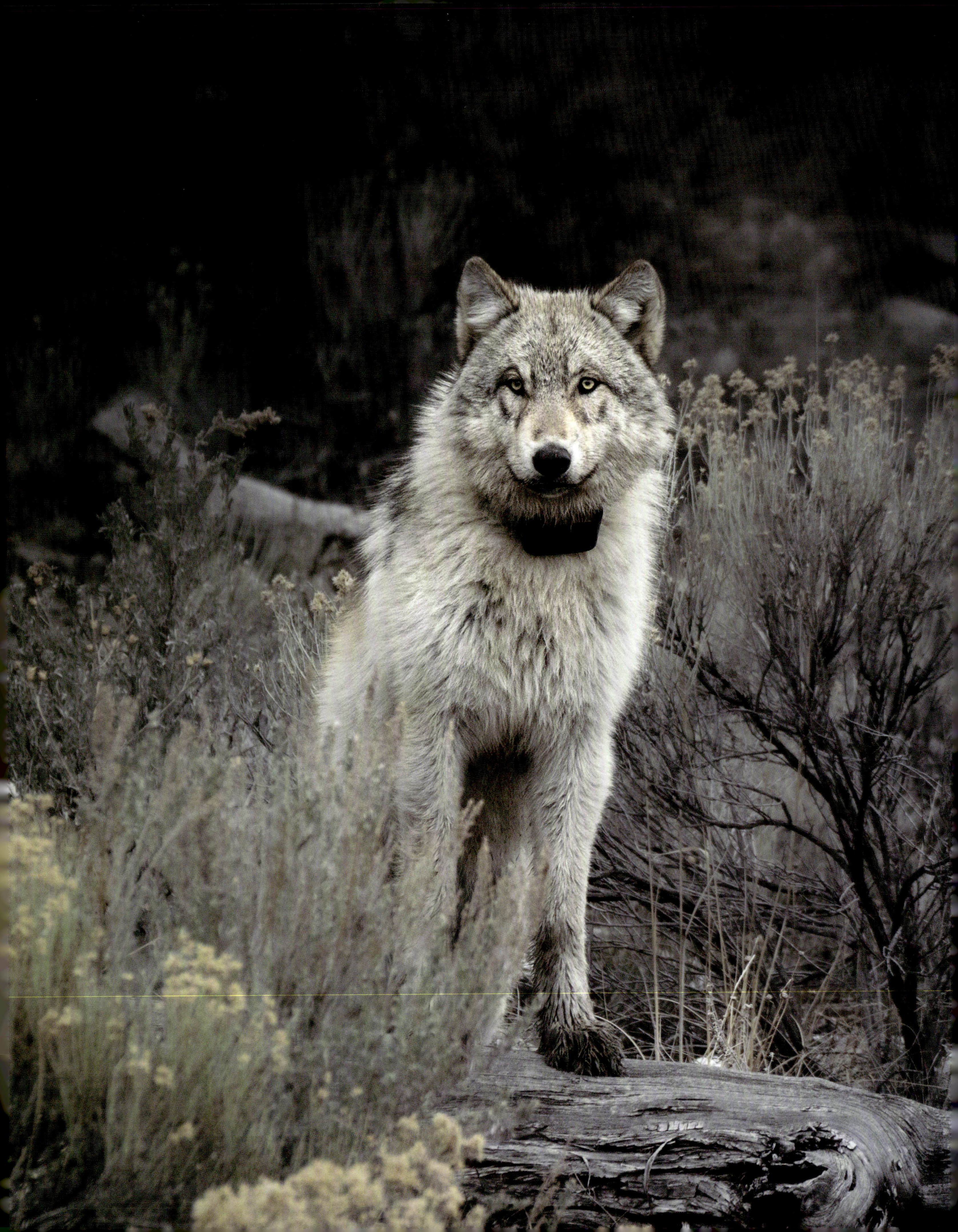

I am incredibly thankful for any time I get to spend in the presence of wolves. Photographing them is a game of chance, and I have only done so successfully a handful of times despite the hundreds of hours I spend in the field every year. Still, the best encounter I'll likely ever have with wolves occurred on my twenty-first birthday.

It was March, but the landscape remained dry with a lack of snow. The Wapiti Lake Pack had killed a deer in a small ravine a short distance from the road. At the time, the Wapiti Lake Pack numbered in the thirties, making them one of the largest in Yellowstone. Wolves came and went from the carcass. Eventually the pack retreated up the hillside for a nap, the gray wolves fading into the gray landscape, while the black wolves, curled in tight balls, resembled rocks or tree stumps.

While most of the pack rested, a young, light-gray wolf cautiously approached a nearby hillside through the shadowy sage. Watching a wolf move is incredible as every muscle works to slink across the landscape with grace and silence. Moving through the sage, the wolf stepped onto a log, revealing its mud-caked paws. Its thick fur nearly completely covered the radio tracking collar around its neck. From its place in the sage the wolf examined its surroundings with keen, observant eyes. Our eyes met.

For that split second, I could feel the powerful wildness held deep within its soulful, golden eyes and the secrets carried from generation to generation through the pack. It seemed to be searching for a small glimmer of that same wildness in me. Then, with a flip of its head, the wolf broke eye contact. The moment was one of the most powerful experiences I have ever shared with any wild animal, something that has stayed with me every day as I walk the mountains and forests that I am lucky enough to share with these untamed and beautifully ruthless creatures.

◄ A wolf from the Wapiti Lake Pack stands atop a log at the edge of some sagebrush.

Photographing a portrait image of a gray wolf had always been a dream of mine, but I never anticipated the image I captured by complete luck and happenstance. These surprise moments bring an almost addictive rush and always send a chill through my entire body; they keep me hooked on wildlife photography, always wondering what I may encounter next.

While watching the Wapiti Lake Pack later in the afternoon of my birthday, a light wolf, whom I later learned was tagged as 1330F, walked to the edge of a hill overlooking the kill her pack had made. She sat amid the silver sage for quite a while, her gray fur fading into the gray and barren landscape. Two pack members were arguing in a jumble of growls and yips over the carcass, causing her to swivel her head in investigation. I decided to capture a photo of the wolf in profile when a raven soared directly over her head. The result was an image of an incredible wild moment that represents the intricate relationship between the two species.

Equally clever, wolves and ravens have lived alongside each other for thousands of years, sharing the same mountains, forests, and rivers. Ravens, being intelligent and opportunistic, have learned to follow wolves to scavenge scraps from their successful hunts. Similarly, wolves have learned to use circling ravens to locate carcasses, like a visual dinner call in the sky. Their relationship is mutually beneficial.

The brief instant when the two species aligned in my camera was unbelievable. This image shows all the reasons why I love wolves: the wisdom in their eyes; their sleek, almost ghostlike appearance; and most importantly, their connection to everything that is truly wild.

▶ Wolf 1330F and a raven cross paths near the rest of the Wapiti Lake Pack.

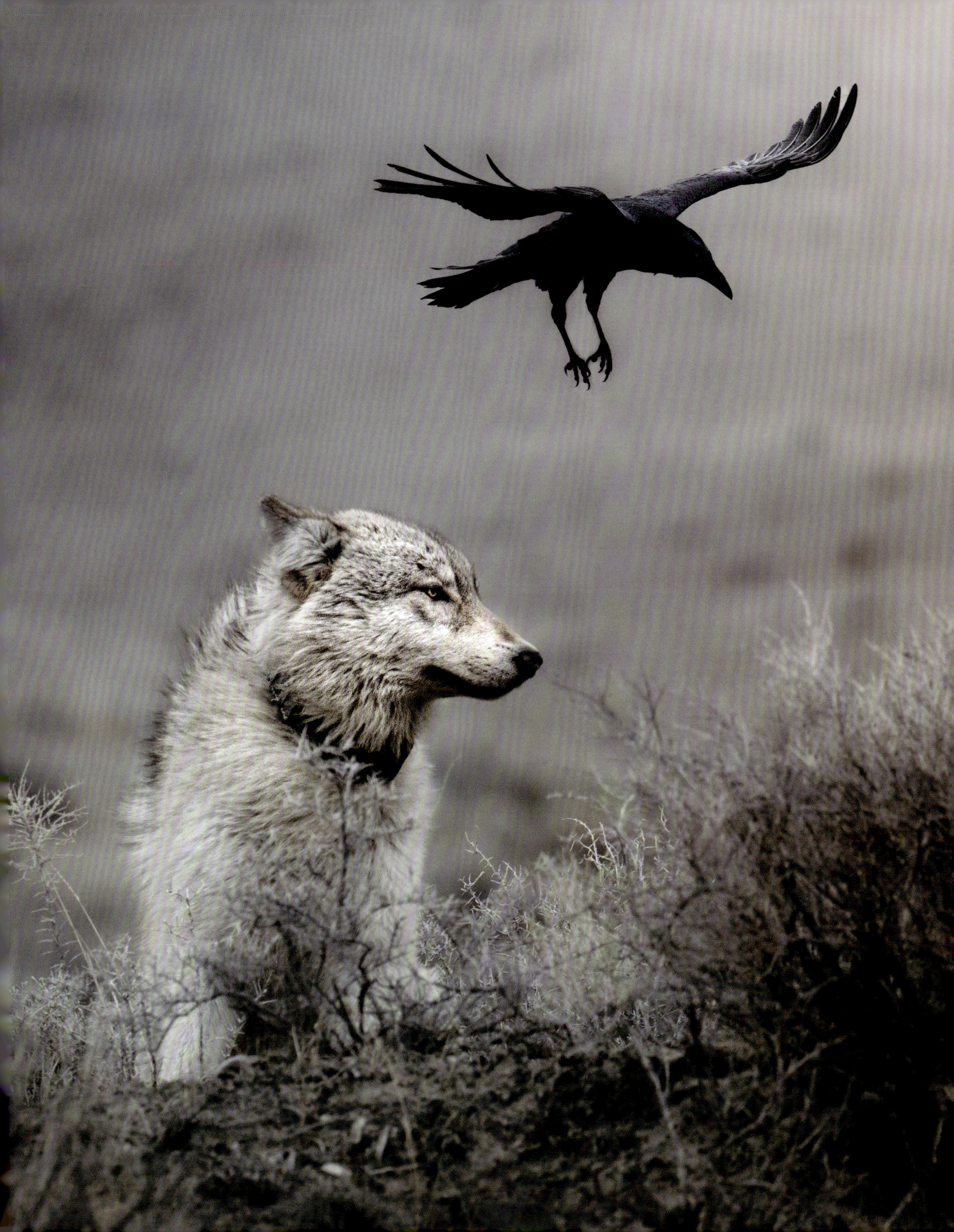

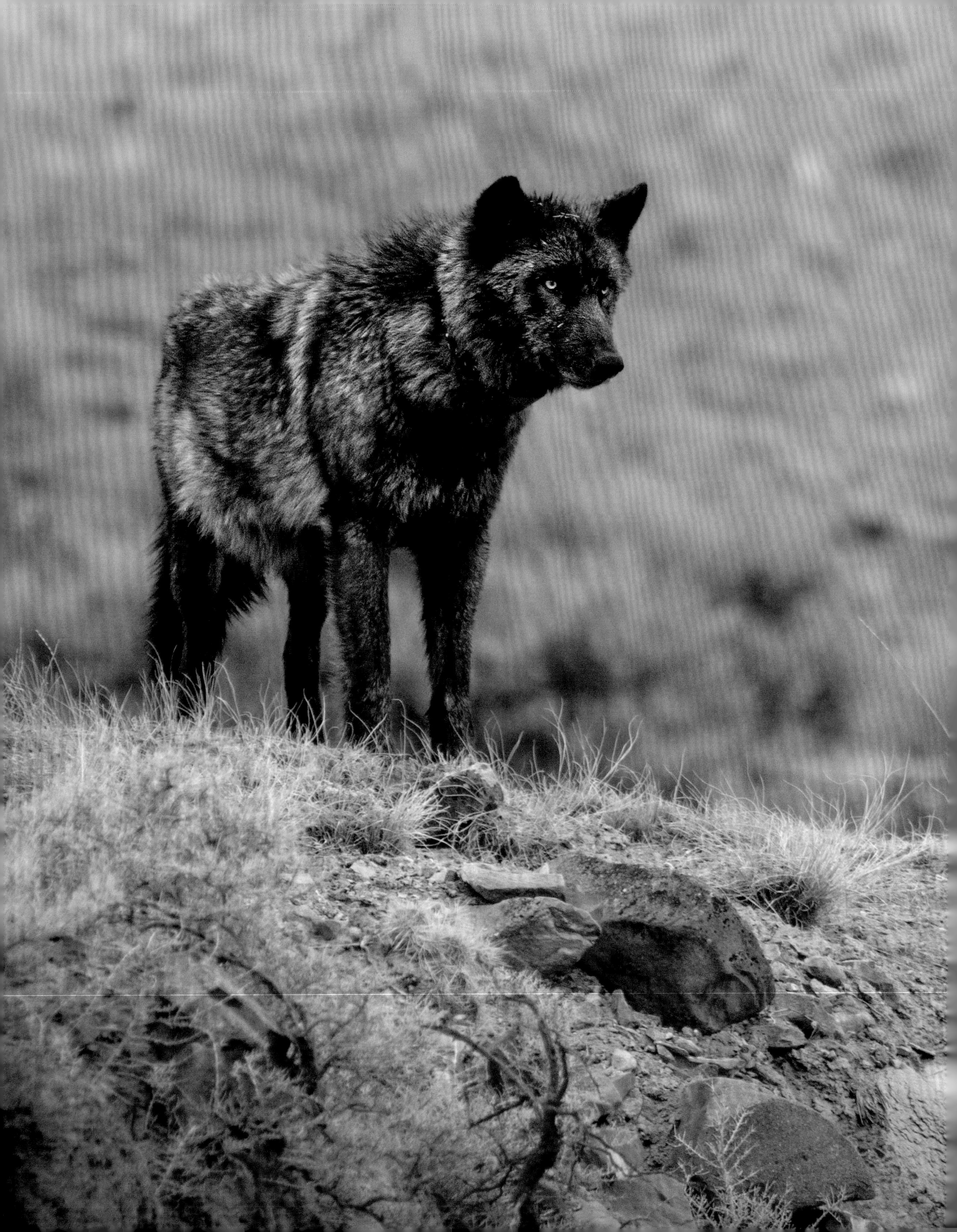

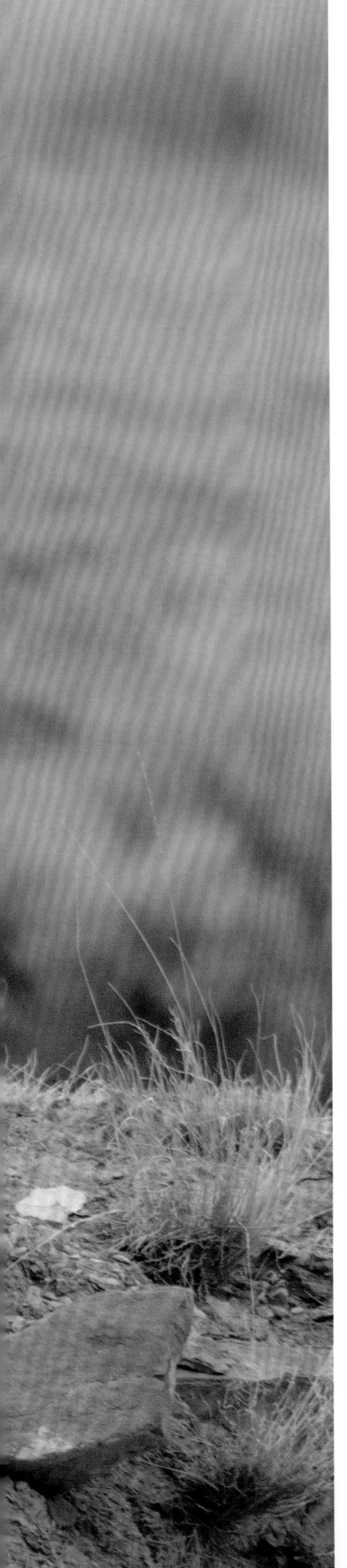

Wolves can range in color from white to black, each with their own unique coats. All wolves are undeniably gorgeous, though there is something exceptionally striking about black wolves, as their golden eyes appear more soulful against their dark coats. Sleek and sly, black wolves move like shadows across the valleys and mountain slopes. Since about half of Yellowstone's wolf population has black fur, there is no shortage of black wolves, and they are an exciting and stunning subject to photograph. Against a gray or white winter landscape, black wolves can be much easier to spot than their gray counterparts. They add contrast to the environment and even from a distance their shapes are recognizable.

During a mild winter's day, I had noticed considerable wolf activity in a river ravine where the Wapiti Lake Pack had made a kill the night before. It proved to be an eventful day as wolves came and went from the ravine, sometimes completely disappearing into the trees or over a hill. Their howls periodically rang through the cold air, echoing at first and then being answered by a chorus of howls from varying hilltops. Since they were usually too far away to photograph, I simply enjoyed hearing the pack's eerily melodious howls as every voice melded together in wild harmony. No other sound in Yellowstone compares to the howl of a wolf.

As the pack's song continued, a black wolf appeared atop a small rise overlooking the river. It stood steadfast in its tracks, looking toward a few pack members feeding on the last of the kill in the ravine below. The wolf's golden eyes were bright and intense. Through the hazy air, the wolf's fur appeared more brindle than black. Undertones of brown and gray coursed through its coat, creating lighter streaks throughout the otherwise jet-black fur. Distracted by another howl, the wolf turned, gave a brisk wag of its tail, and loped up the hillside to join its pack members in a chorus of strong and soulful howls. The wolf song continued until sunset when the pack fell silent and disappeared into the night.

◀ A black wolf watches his pack.

River Otter

River otters are one of the few semi-aquatic mammals in Yellowstone, weighing between 10 and 30 pounds (4.5 and 13.6 kg). These sleek, agile creatures have a dense, water-repellent coat that keeps their skin dry and warm despite frigid conditions. Since they spend most of their time in the water, otters have long, muscular bodies, webbed feet, and flattened tails that make them excellent swimmers. Additionally, otters can hold their breath for up to eight minutes, which allows them to travel while remaining underwater. Otters can be difficult to see because they spend so much time in the water, but they are easier to spot during the winter months when parts of rivers freeze, forcing them onto the ice. Otters can be seen in Yellowstone Lake, the Yellowstone River, and in the Lamar River, as well as various other waterways in Yellowstone.

River otters are carnivores, with a diet consisting of fish, frogs, and even waterfowl. The decline of the cutthroat trout population in Yellowstone negatively affected the river otter population, which heavily relies on cutthroat as a primary food source. However, with the ongoing recovery of cutthroat trout, otter numbers are rising in areas across the American West. Otters are most active during the early morning and late evening but can be seen at any time of day. Their slide-mark tracks can be spotted more often than otters themselves—evidence of their playful antics as they dive into and out of the water.

Otters are incredibly social animals, though it is not uncommon for them to live solitary lives until mating season in late winter, often the only time males and females come together. Females give birth to litters of one to six pups in spring, typically in a den dug into a riverbank. By summer, the young otters are skilled swimmers and begin to learn how to hunt and catch fish. Some pups may disperse while others stay with their mothers and form family groups. Threats to river otters include predators like coyotes, wolves, and bears, along with human-caused threats like entanglement in fishing lines.

► A river otter rests on the edge of a snowy bank.

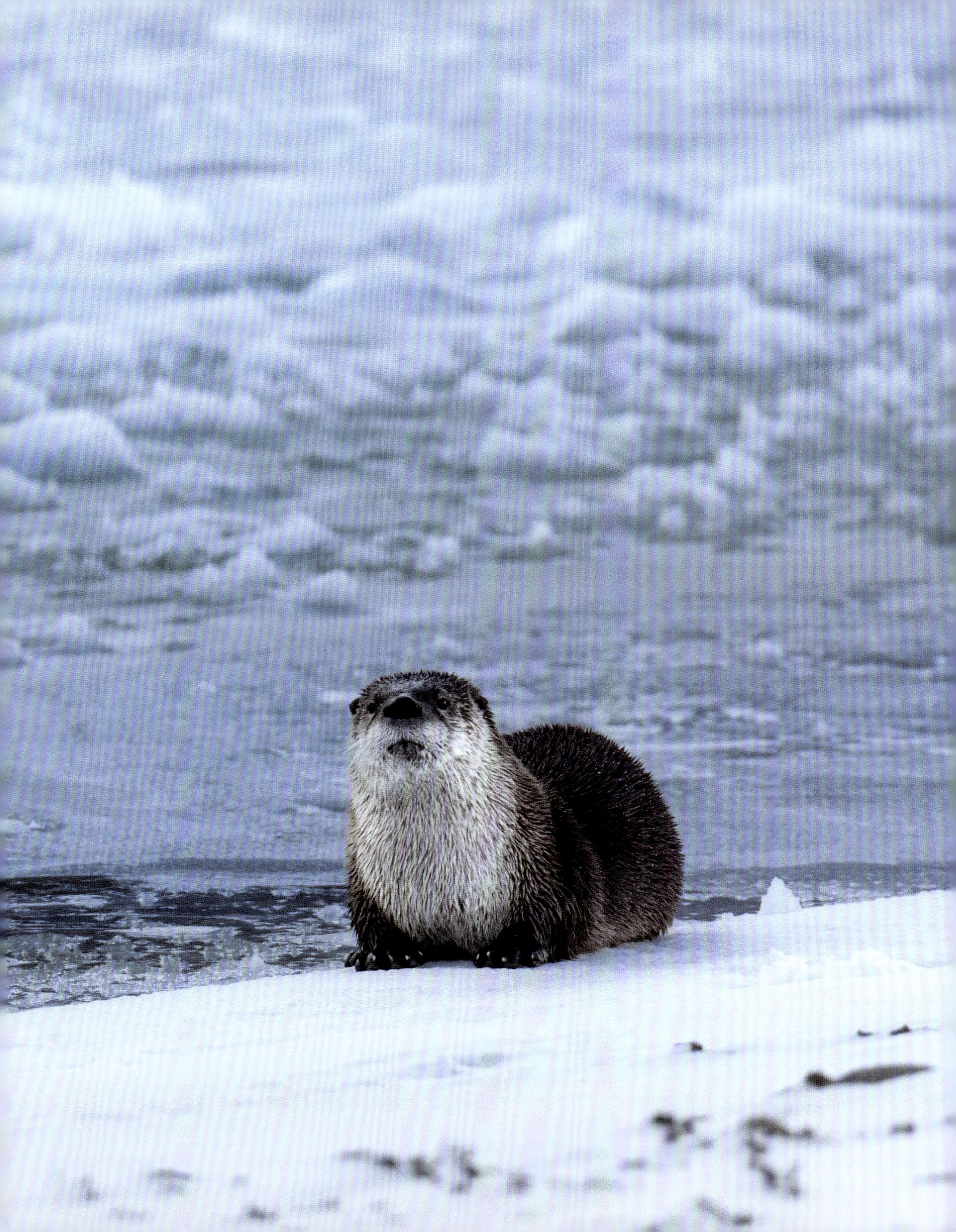

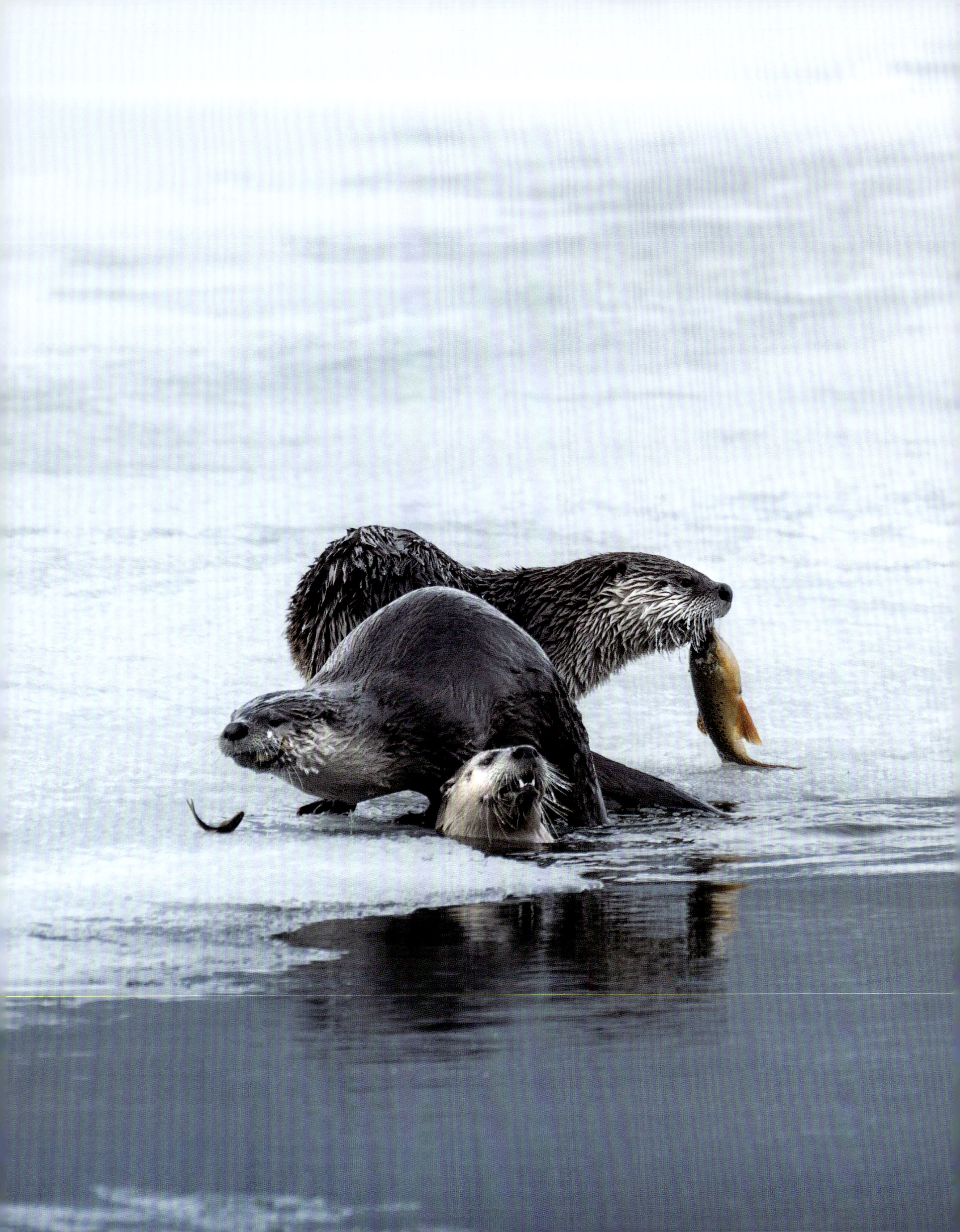

During a December trip into Yellowstone's Northern Range, I decided to search for river otters. Ice shelves and fresh snow make otters easier to spot, at least in theory, and though I didn't have high hopes, I noticed their distinctive slide tracks leading directly into the Lamar River.

Scanning the shoreline, I soon found three sleek bodies on the ice not far away: the elusive subjects I had been searching for. I slowly approached the riverbank from downstream, moving carefully while watching their body language to avoid disturbing them. After getting within photographable distance, I laid down in the snow on my stomach at the river's edge for a low-angle shot. Since their fur was dry and fluffy, I knew the otters had been on land for a while. They were completely unbothered by my presence as they played together on the opposite bank, kicking up snow in the process and releasing an occasional growl or chirp. With incredible speed, one otter leapt upwards with an arch of its back and landed atop another, causing both to roll together in a ball of fur and claws.

Then, without warning, the otters quickly and silently slid into the icy river and disappeared. But just before I was about to leave, two of the otters reappeared and climbed back onto the ice, their coats glossy from the water, while the third otter's head rose just above the surface. Each had a trout caught in its jaws. In a matter of minutes, the fish were eagerly devoured, leaving nothing but a few scales and drops of blood on the ice. I continued to watch the river otters for over an hour, amazed by their agility both on the ice and in the water. I finally had to leave the river's edge and hike back to my car to warm up, obviously not as well suited for the freezing temperatures as the river otters.

◀ Three river otters enjoy their catch on the icy banks of the Lamar River.

I never expect to see otters during the spring or summer months. With a vast network of rivers and streams and the expansive scope of Yellowstone Lake, otters have no shortage of pristine waters to disappear into. The few times I have seen otters during the summer, the encounters were always fleeting, nothing more than the end of a tail disappearing beneath the surface with a splash. When I spotted a lone otter swimming through an alpine lake, it was quite an exciting sight, especially given that he didn't immediately disappear.

It was August, the peak of fire season, and smoke hung in the air from nearby blazes. It created a unique red tint to the afternoon sunshine and left the distant mountains hazy. As I drove past one of my favorite alpine lakes, I noticed an unusual ripple on the glassy surface. I stopped my car and grabbed my binoculars. While scanning the water, I caught a quick glimpse of a flat and narrow tail before it dipped under the surface. There was no doubt; it had been a river otter.

I walked to the water's edge with my camera in hand, still looking for any movement that would indicate the otter's location. After a few minutes and no signs, I heard a soft puff of air. Swimming parallel to the shore of the lake and moving directly toward me was the otter. It dove underwater again, just to resurface and climb atop a partly submerged log near to where I knelt at the lake's edge. Beads of water rolled off its sleek fur, which glistened in the afternoon sun, and its abundant whiskers. Then, with another huff, the otter slid off the log and dove into the lake, disappearing under the water.

▶ A river otter rests on a submerged log.

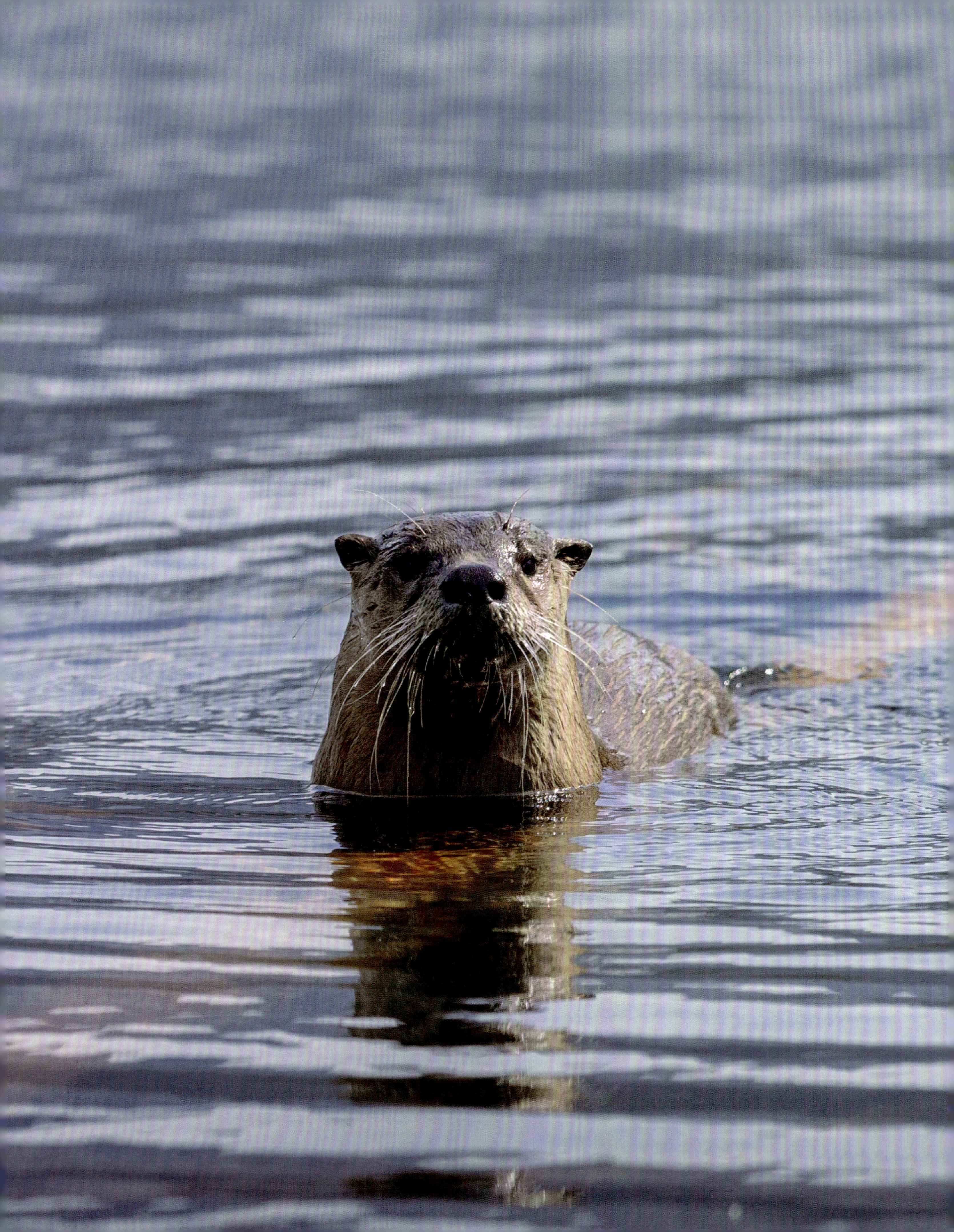

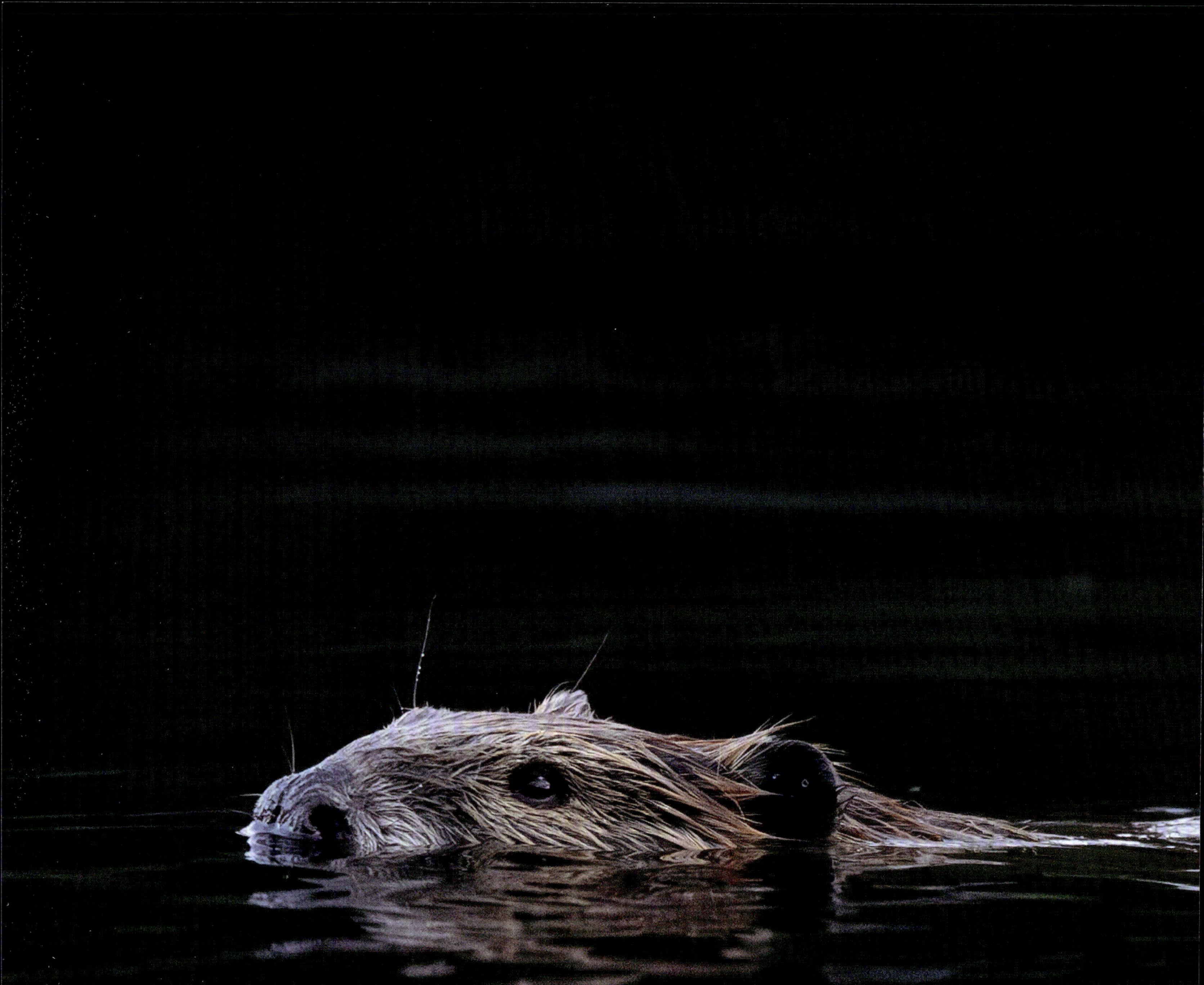

Beaver

Beavers are Yellowstone's natural builders, and their dams shape the entire ecosystem. Armed with thick and durable teeth that never stop growing, beavers can chew through trunks to fell trees, then use them to dam streams and create ponds. These ponds provide crucial habitats for many other species including trout, moose, and otters, and allow for favorable growing conditions for aspen and willows, which are favorite foods for beavers. Beavers also construct lodges as shelters but may occasionally dig dens in riverbanks instead.

Beavers live in family groups known as colonies that average about six individuals. Females give birth to litters of two to four kits in the early spring. Kits can swim within four days of birth and typically stay with their families until the age of two.

With dense, waterproof fur and webbed feet, beavers are excellently suited for life in the water; however, their fur coats were in high demand during the first half of the nineteenth century, leading to extensive trapping to supply beaver pelts for felt hats. It is estimated that today's North American beaver population is roughly 10 percent of what the population was prior to European settlement, with recent population surveys identifying over one hundred colonies within Yellowstone.

Evidence of beavers can be seen all over Yellowstone, ranging from beaver-chewed tree stumps to the aptly named Beaver Lake, where an over 600-foot-long (183 m) beaver dam has survived for more than a century; it was once believed to be the longest beaver dam in the world. Beavers themselves can be seen in a variety of wetland habitats, including near Beaver Lake, along the Lamar River, and near the East Entrance. Beavers retreat to their lodges for protection from predators including wolves, bears, coyotes, and mountain lions, and will slap their broad tails on the water's surface as a warning and alarm call when danger is nearby.

◀ A beaver glides through the water.

Beavers, although incredibly agile in the water, are rather awkward on land. With round bodies and short legs, they almost waddle while they move, and they certainly don't go anywhere in a hurry. On an overcast spring day, I spotted a beaver stroll up a muddy riverbank and disappear into the thick willows, although the thicket's swaying branches indicated the beaver's location. Assuming he would be back, I grabbed my camera and waited.

A few moments later, the beaver shuffled out of the willows with a mouthful of freshly cut branches. His thick tail left a trail in the mud as he dragged the branches to the river and slipped into it with ease. Sitting in the shallow and slow-moving water, the beaver held a branch in his nimble hands and used his large teeth to begin eating the bark to get to its nutrient-rich inner layers. Soon, all the branches had been consumed. The beaver emerged from the river and followed the same path back to the willow thicket, the water beading off his fur and wetting the bank.

Before long, the beaver waddled back, once again with a mouthful of branches. Swaying side to side while tugging the branches as if annoyed, the beaver plopped back into the water. He returned to the same spot in the river and steadily stripped the branches of their bark in the same rhythmic, monotonous way.

I watched as the beaver completed this busy cycle of branch gathering and eating several times, always in the same tedious manner. With the clouds shifting overhead, a storm clearly on the way, I decided to leave the beaver, assuming not even rain would interrupt his routine.

▶ A beaver diligently gathers a feast of willow branches.

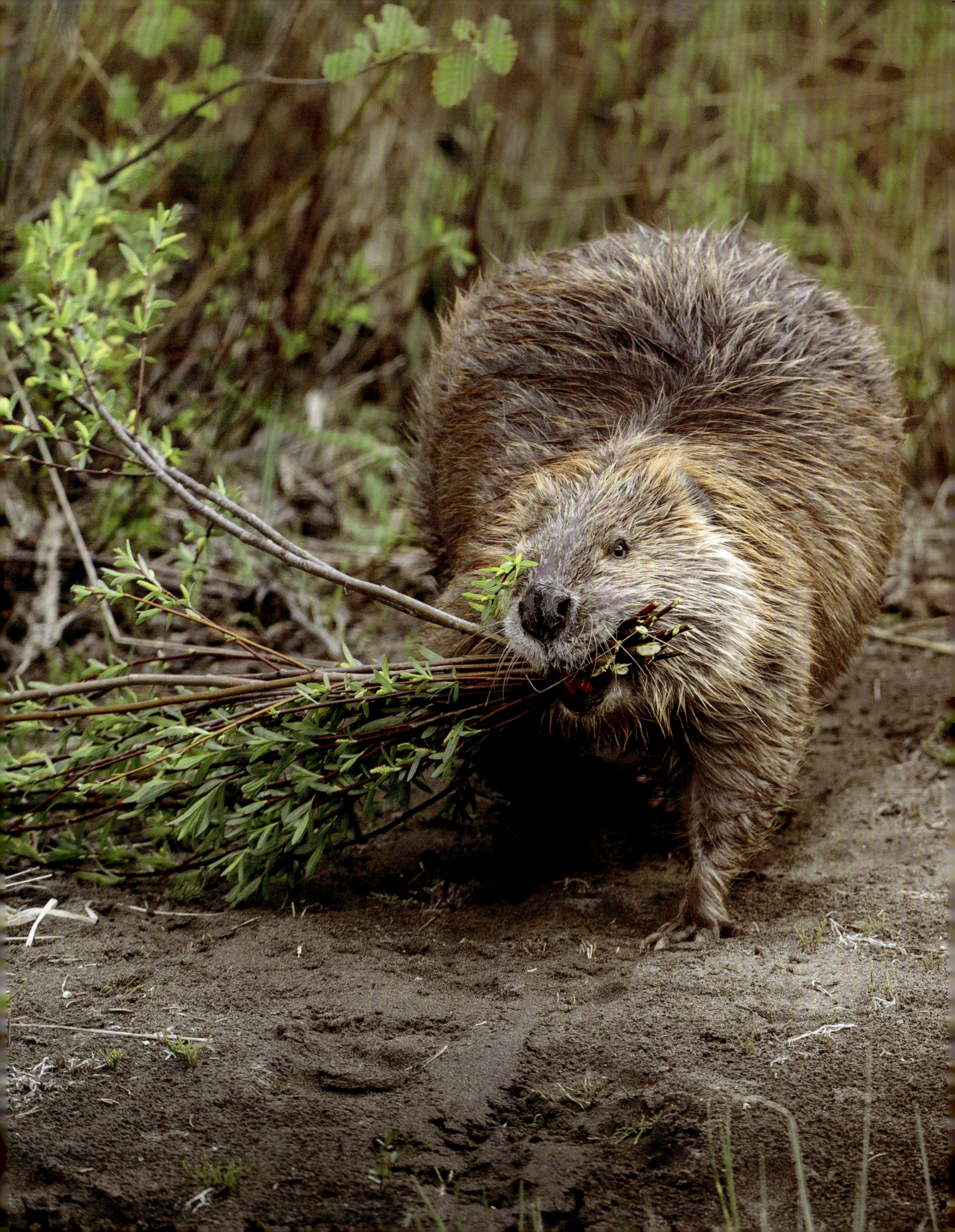

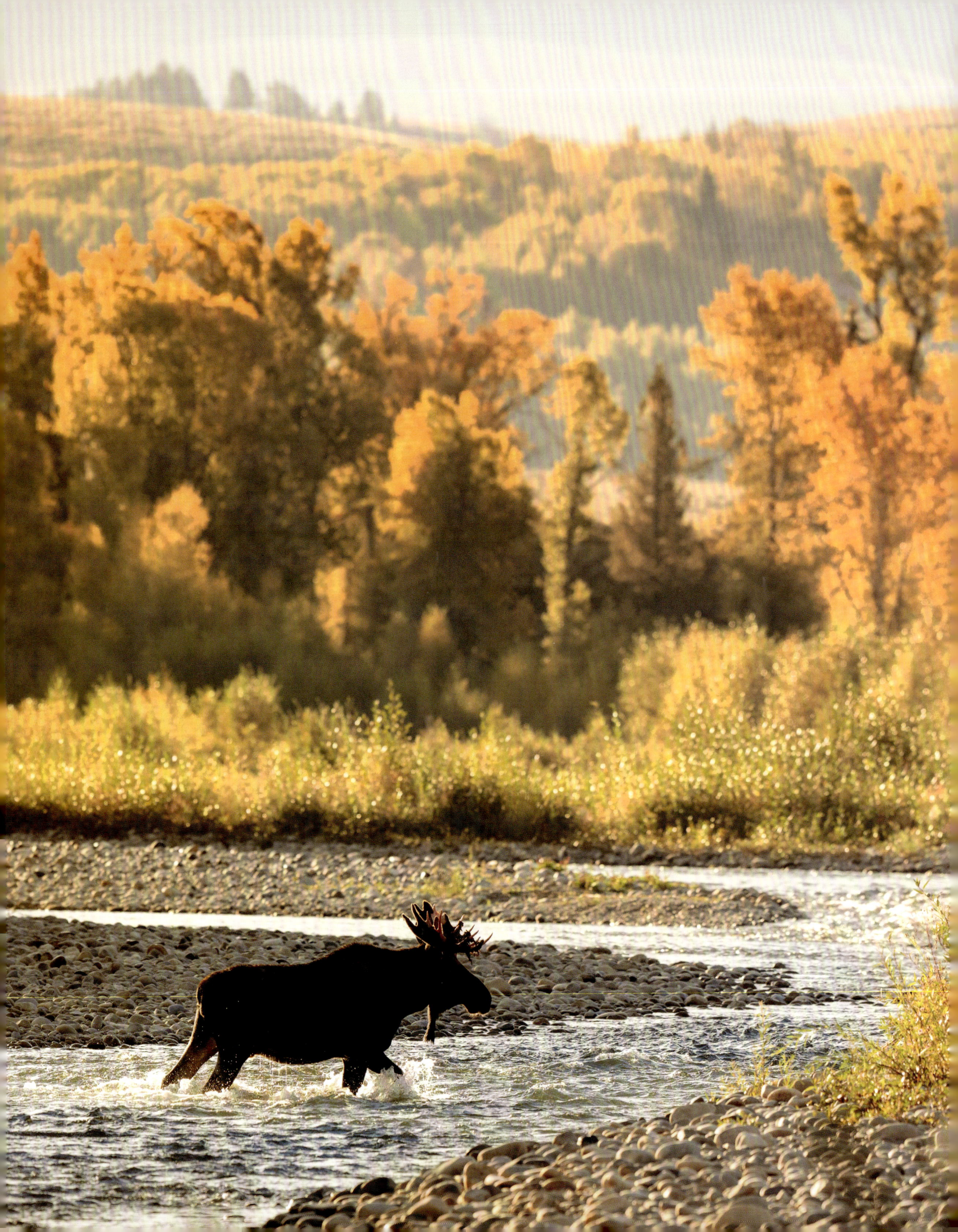

Moose

As the largest member of the deer family, moose are an impressive species. Males, called bulls, can weigh 1,000 pounds (454 kg) and stand over 6 feet (1.8 m) tall at the shoulder. Bull moose also have large, paddle-like antlers that weigh on average 40 pounds (18 kg). The antlers begin growing in the early spring and are covered with a soft tissue called velvet that carries blood to the antler, allowing it to grow. At the end of summer, moose shed the velvet and reveal the bony antler beneath. During these few days of shedding, the antlers can appear bloody as the vessels break and dry. Antlers play an important role in the fall during the rut, or mating season, when bulls fight for dominance and mating rights. The bony antlers are then shed during the winter months before starting their regrowth in the spring.

Cow (female) moose do not have antlers and are typically smaller than bulls, but they can still weigh up to 900 pounds (408 kg). Calves are born in May or June, with cows having either one or two calves at a time. Cow moose with calves can be very aggressive and protective; they have been known to successfully defend their calves from bears and wolves. Moose can live up to twenty years. Wolves and grizzlies are capable of taking on adult moose, though the risk of injury is still high, making predation attempts on moose rare.

Moose are a relatively uncommon sight in Yellowstone, but they can be glimpsed in northern parts of the park in wetland habitats and near willows, especially near the Northeast Entrance. Today, fewer than two hundred moose can be found within Yellowstone's borders, a result of population decline caused by habitat destruction, competition from other species like elk, and predators like wolves. The historic forest fires of 1988, which burned 1.4 million acres of the park, had a significant impact on the moose population and destroyed vital forests and wetland habitats. Moose are far more commonly found in the nearby Grand Teton National Park, where habitat destruction has not been such a factor.

◀ A moose crosses a river surrounded by fall colors.

During the last weeks of summer, I went for a sunrise hike in search of moose. Camera in hand, I started following the creek through marshy wetlands, the prime moose habitat. The dull colors of predawn faded to vibrant, warm sunrise hues. I took my time carefully walking over the uneven ground, puddles and thick mud sloshing underfoot with each step. Before long, my pants were nearly completely soaked from the dew-covered vegetation brushing against my legs. I made my way toward a willow thicket where I had seen moose before, but first I had to cross the small creek.

After nearly slipping on the algae-covered rocks, I made it across and stepped onto the steep bank and through the willow thicket. I remained on high alert for any movement or rustling branches; while I was hoping to find a moose, thick vegetation was the last place I wanted to accidentally surprise one. I emerged from the willows into a small meadow near the river and spotted a dark shape in the shadows. A bull moose was just rising from its resting place under a large tree.

The bull stretched rather awkwardly and lumbered toward a different clump of willows, his massive hooves thudding the ground with each step. He wasted no time stripping their branches, using his large yet dexterous lips to delicately pull the leaves from each individual twig. In the morning air, I could hear the leaves crunch as the moose feasted. The only other sounds were the soft rush of the river nearby and the pleasant morning birdsong from chickadees and robins. Amazingly efficient, the moose had soon stripped all the branches from his stand of willows. He swung his head around and briefly stared at me, ears alert, as if just noticing me for the first time. He then lumbered across the meadow and disappeared back into the shadows.

▶ A bull moose enjoys his breakfast of willows.

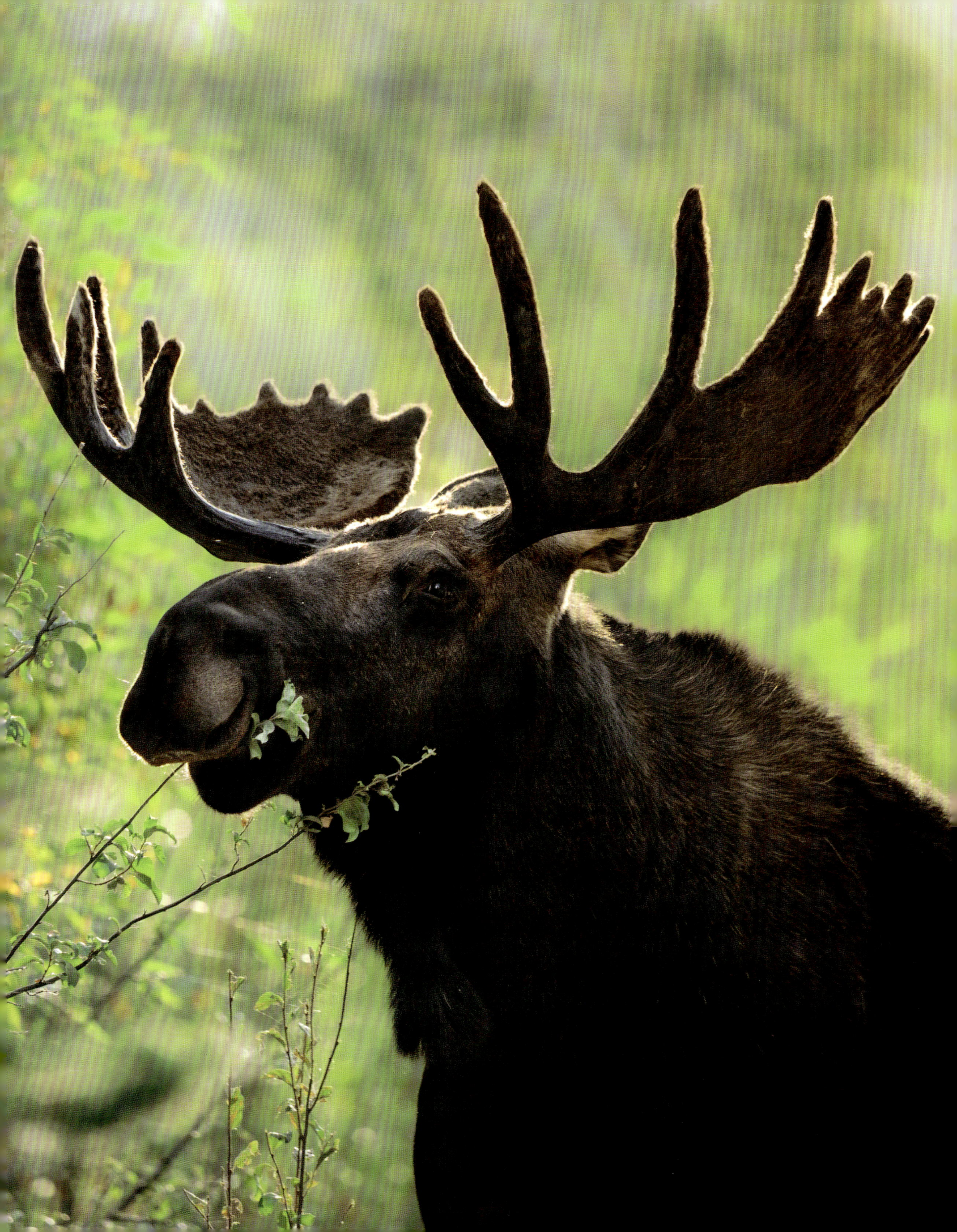

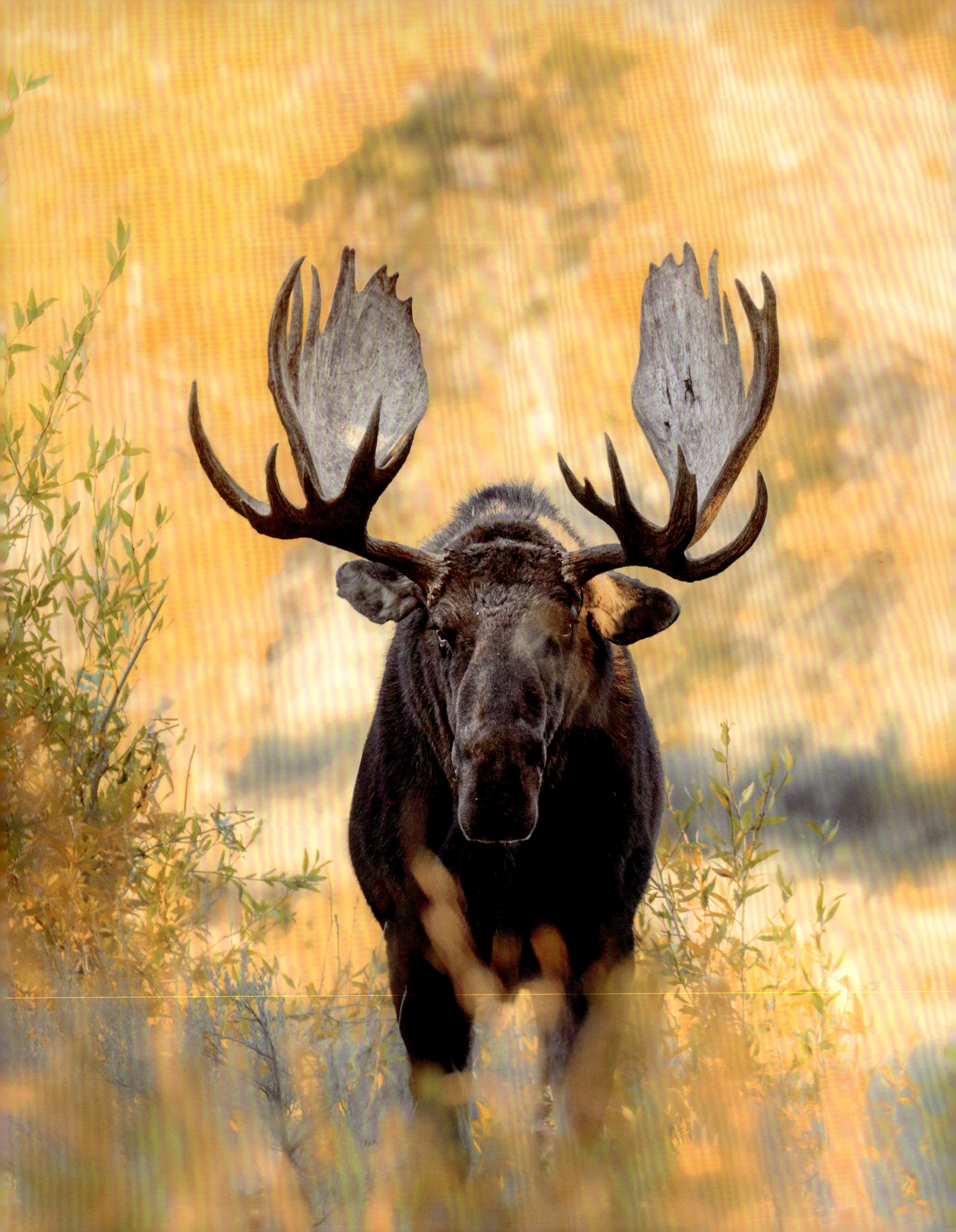

To me, moose are the ultimate sign of fall in the wild; when they return to the valleys with their velvet shed, fall can begin. On a cool early morning in September, I went looking for moose. I could tell the fall leaves were vibrant even in the twilight, and if I could find a moose, it had potential to be unforgettable.

Scanning the sage flats, I soon found a distant moose slowly moving toward the tree line. I set out with my camera. A fogbank hung low over the river, and the air was damp and filled with the sweet smell of sage. I walked quickly to get to the trees before the moose, although not fast enough. The moose had disappeared. The sun was just peeking over the horizon by the time I reached the trees, thankfully providing more light to hopefully help me find the moose again.

Eventually I heard a twig snap somewhere in front of me. I came around a corner and saw the bull moose in a small clearing. I stood in awe for a few seconds before raising my camera to capture the scene. The bull was standing tall and looking directly at me, though his body was relaxed and eyes calm. His long legs were nearly completely hidden by the bluish sage and vibrant yellow grasses. The brilliant leaves on the cottonwood trees shone in every shade of yellow and orange and surrounded him on all sides. Golden light filtered through the leaves, causing them to look even more vivid. The dappled light fell across the bull's antlers and back and gave him the same golden hue as the autumn forest. It felt as though we stood looking at each other forever, though it was likely barely a moment. He soon turned and continued walking, clearly intent on making it to the river. I watched as he disappeared, leaving me alone with the autumn colors.

◀ A bull moose surrounded by autumn foliage.

Late in autumn, I drove south into Grand Teton National Park with the hopes of photographing moose. The fall leaves had already dropped, leaving the aspens and cottonwoods barren and colorless. The Teton Range dominates the landscape and visibly loomed over the valley even in the predawn light. After a quick scan with binoculars, I located a group of several moose far away on the sagebrush flats near a creek, right where I hoped they would be.

With my camera slung over my shoulder, I excitedly began trudging through the sage toward them. The sage roots grabbed at my ankles, causing me to stumble in the dim light. My heavy breaths froze in the cold morning air. By the time I reached the moose the first rays of morning light were just touching the valley. The moose were all standing on the edge of a bank near the small creek: two small bulls, three mid-sized bulls, and one large bull with a characteristic floppy ear. I had photographed him in previous years. It was good to see him again.

As the sun rose and illuminated the Teton Range with vibrant shades of pink and purple, the largest bull made his way through the tall, golden cattails into the creek. Without much hesitation I waded into the cold water for a better angle, soaking my boots and pants. We both stood in the creek and gazed at each other. I was amazed by the scene in front of me: the bull towering in the creek, his reflection in the still water looking back up at him, the alpenglow across the Tetons. This had been a scene I had always wanted to photograph and finally everything lined up in my favor. After posing in the water for a few moments, the bull started walking toward me, splashing water with each step before climbing onto the opposite bank. He paused and glanced toward the mountains as if equally in awe of their rugged beauty, before slowly departing from the creek, leaving me there with wet boots and a dream image.

► A bull moose poses in a creek in Grand Teton National Park.

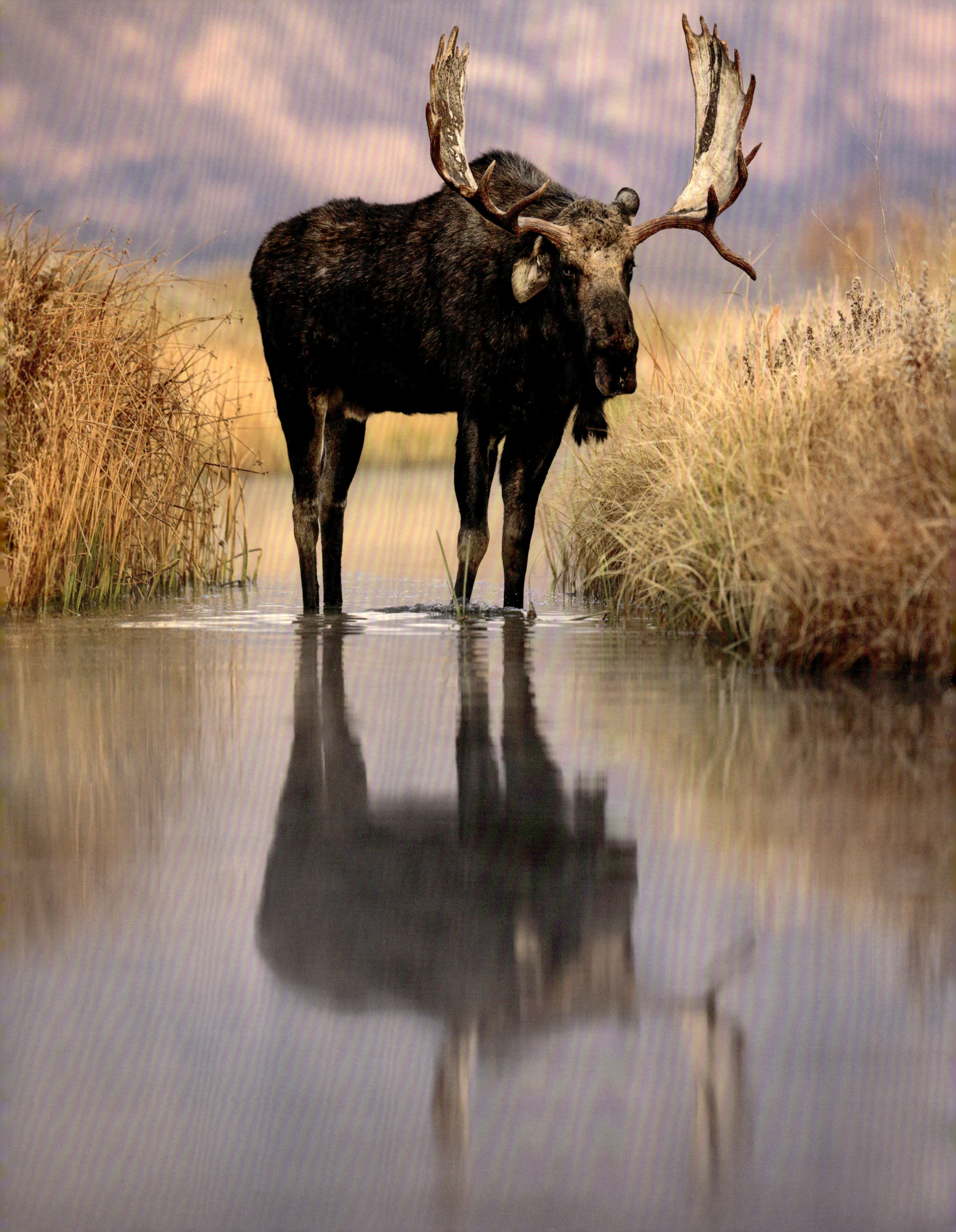

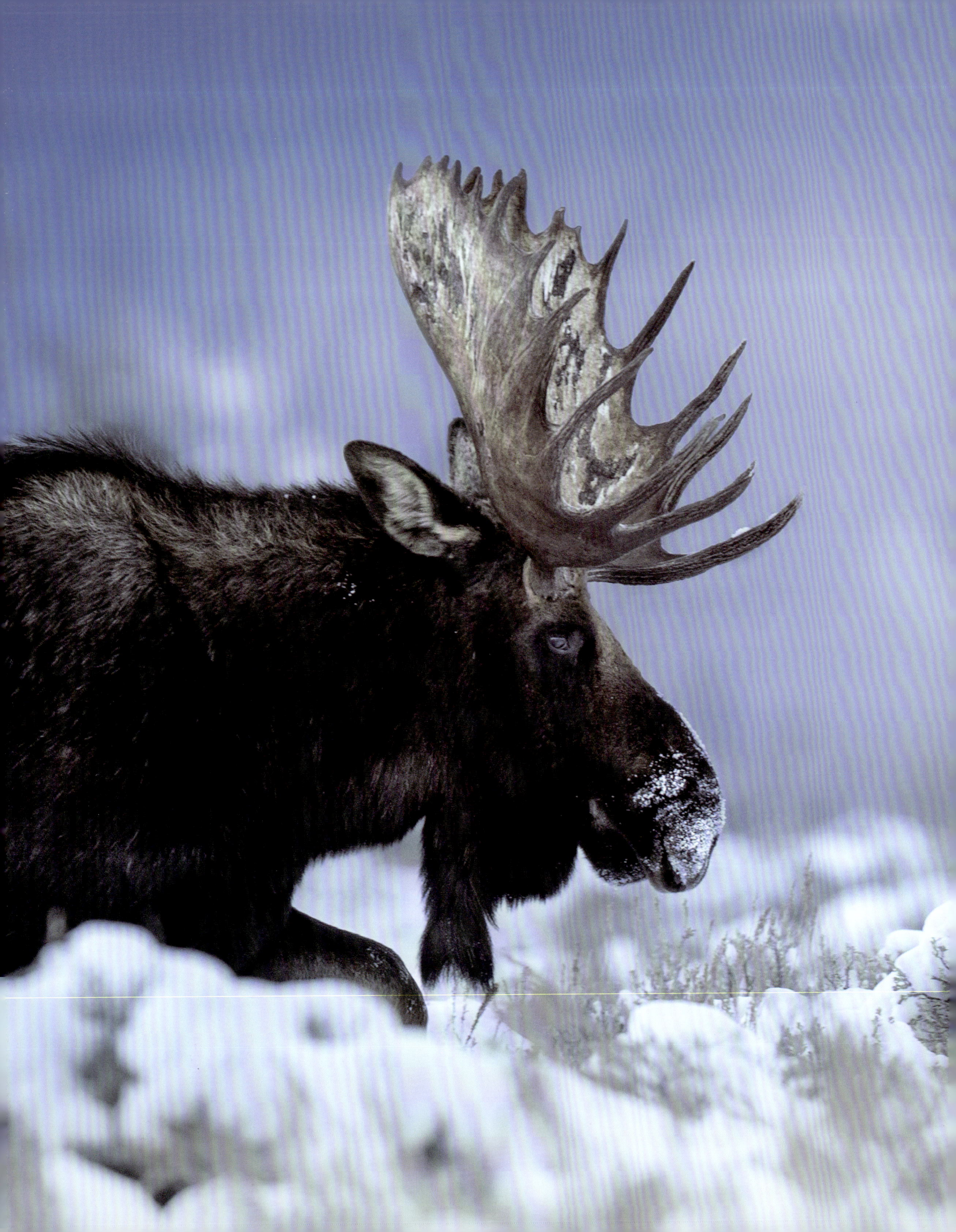

While moose are my favorite species to photograph in the fall, it is a short-lived season in Yellowstone. Winter soon creeps in and takes control of the landscape, chasing away any lingering colors and replacing them with gray and white. Winter is harsh, but wildlife still braves the weather, and so do I.

Setting out on a bleak afternoon in early November, I realized winter had returned in full force. A storm the previous day had left nearly a foot of snow across the entire valley. Only the sagebrush poked through the snowfall. Everything else was buried. The cottonwoods and aspens stood barren, their trunks strong and resilient against the frigid temperatures. Low clouds hung over the distant mountain, telling of another incoming storm. It seemed as if the valley was resting and void of life—at least until I spotted a distant bull moose, his dark coat contrasting against the white snow.

After bundling up in many warm layers, I hiked into the sage meadow toward the moose. Drifted snow crunched underfoot and made walking difficult. Soon I was breathing hard. The cold air stung my face and lungs, yet it was energizing at the same time. Once the moose was within photographable distance, I kneeled against a large sagebrush and clumsily grabbed my camera through my mittens. The bull was ignoring me, focused on browsing through the snow in search of any edible vegetation. I could hear his breaths, strong and hollow. I sat and watched the bull for a while, slowly becoming impatient and cold as sunset drew nearer. Even with my many layers, the winter air was getting to me. Just as I debated leaving empty-handed, the moose raised his snow-covered face while his large antlers gleamed impressively in the gloomy light. The moose couldn't have cared less about the snow, even though he was covered in it. I, on the other hand, was frozen and decided to return to my car, hoping the trek back would help warm me up.

◀ A bull moose forages in the snow for vegetation.

Mule Deer

Mule deer are one of the most common large mammals in Yellowstone and can be seen in open meadows, at forest edges, and along riverbanks where food is abundant; their browsing habits actually help shape the vegetation patterns of the park. They are well adapted to the park's varied terrain and can be found at elevations ranging from the plains to the higher subalpine regions. Mule deer are identifiable by their reddish-brown to gray coats, white rumps, and black-tipped tails. Their large ears, reminiscent of a mule's, give them their name.

Bucks begin to grow antlers in the early summer and use them during the rut in the fall, when bucks compete for the attention of does. These bony antlers are covered in soft velvet, which provides blood flow while they're growing. By early fall the velvet has shed, exposing the hard antler beneath, and bucks shed the antlers themselves in winter to help conserve energy. Each year as a buck matures, his antlers will grow larger than they were the year before, increasing his chances of dominance and success in the breeding season.

Fawns are born in the spring, usually one per doe, though twins aren't uncommon. Born with spots that help camouflage them from predators, fawns are completely reliant on their mothers for their first few months. In the winter, mule deer usually form into larger herds, with fawns staying with their mothers.

Mule deer serve as prey for many predators including wolves, mountain lions, and bears, and remain ready to flee at any sign of danger.

Mule deer have long migrations, with herds moving to lower elevations during the harsh winter months to find food and returning to higher grounds in the summer. Over 1,500 mule deer can be found in Yellowstone during the summer, though that drops to less than four hundred in the winter as herds search for more favorable conditions. Human-made barriers like interstates and fences cause habitat fragmentation and interfere with migration patterns, making conflicts like vehicle strikes a major threat to deer.

► A mule deer buck walks through an autumn meadow.

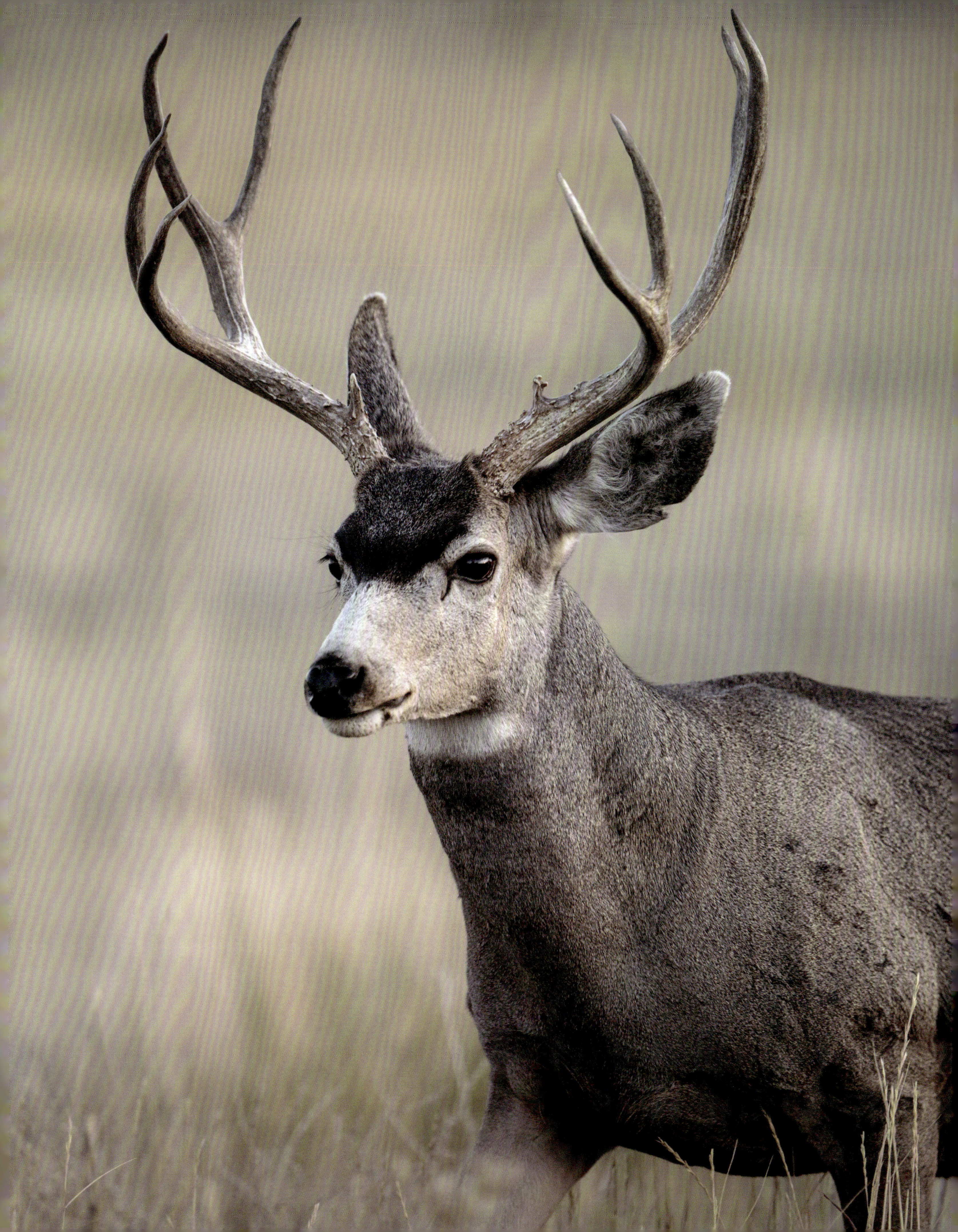

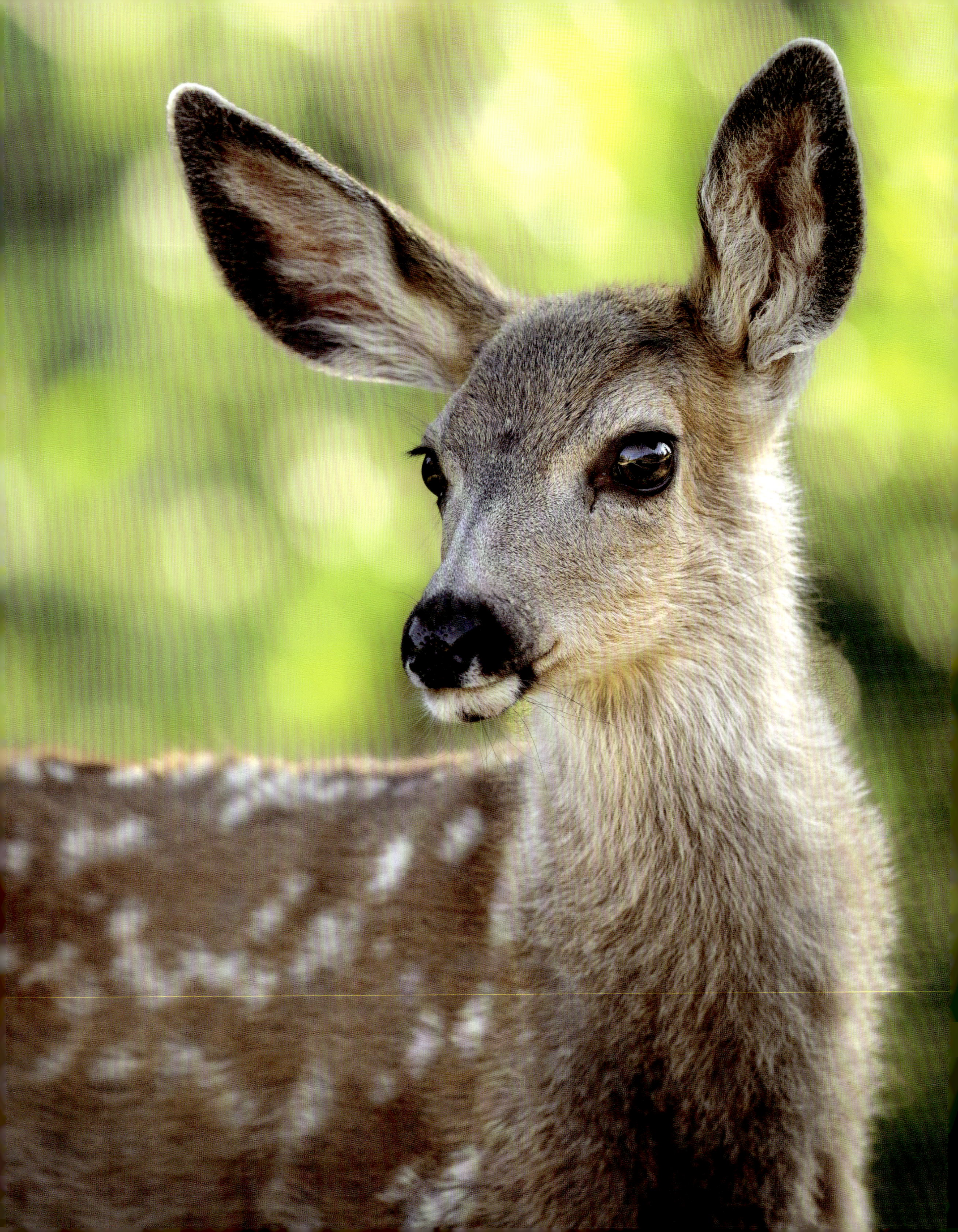

On a late summer evening while looking for grizzly bears, I came across a small group of mule deer does and fawns. Deer are a species I see every day, and I often drive past them without stopping. However, something about the fawns caught my attention. I kneeled alongside a large boulder, remaining still and cautious to avoid startling the notoriously skittish species. For a few moments the does stared at me with ears forward on high alert; they were ready to bolt if needed. Meanwhile, the fawns had completely disappeared into the tall grasses thanks to their camouflaging spots. As I sat motionless, the deer soon became comfortable with my presence and relaxed to resume grazing.

One by one, the fawns emerged from the protective cover of the forest and slowly walked through the tall grass. Each enthusiastically bounded back to their mother's sides on still-wobbly legs. I noticed one that repeatedly looked my way, clearly the most curious of the group. Gradually the fawn took a few steps closer, its mother not far behind.

The two grazed alongside each other close to where I kneeled, their large ears twitching at any minor sound. While the doe was feasting on the rich green summer grasses, the fawn soon became distracted. Any small movement or sound was worth investigating, including the soft buzz of a bee flying through a nearby flower patch. I watched in amusement as the fawn's ears swiveled independently of one another, as if each had a mind of its own. The fawn's eyes were a soft golden brown lined with thick, dark eyelashes. Every few seconds, the young deer's nostrils flared as it breathed in the fresh summer air. The evening light filtered through the surrounding aspen and birch trees, illuminating the leaves like a kaleidoscope in endless shades of green and blending with the tiny white speckles on the fawn's soft fur. Soon the dots would fade completely, but for now they remained, along with the fawn's youthful curiosity and wonder for its wild world.

◀ A curious mule deer fawn on a summer evening.

In the last few weeks before Yellowstone closes every year, I'm eager to find any animals to photograph. The fall colors will soon be completely gone and replaced with winter's grays and whites.

Although it was cold, I drove with the windows rolled down. The brisk October morning air helped wake me up, and it carried a scent of sweet pine and musty leaves. It was the smell of fall in Yellowstone.

Just as the sun rose above the horizon, I spotted a mule deer buck on a sloping hillside. The first rays of sunlight illuminated the entire hillside in a soft, warm glow that turned the fall colors even more vibrant. The buck was peacefully grazing through golden grass and looked at me momentarily before returning to his morning feast. Nearby was a brilliant red and orange bush, its leaves popping in the morning light. Taking a few steps up the side of the steep hill, I positioned myself at the ideal angle to capture an image of the buck against the red colors; he just needed to walk a few steps in the right direction.

Ignoring my presence, the buck continued grazing and rarely raised his head, though his ears were constantly twitching as they surveilled for danger. He took a step or two every few minutes, slowly moving closer to the red bush. The morning sun warmed my back while I patiently waited for him to provide the image I had envisioned. Finally, he strolled past the red bush. The sun reflected off his shiny antlers and gave them an even whiter and sharper appearance, contrasting with the shaded hillside in the background. Equally illuminated, the buck's eyes were as bright as the brilliant red and orange leaves on the bush at his feet. It was the perfect last display of fall foliage. Soon winter would return, but for now color still dominated the mountainsides.

▶ A mule deer buck grazes across a hillside covered with fall foliage.

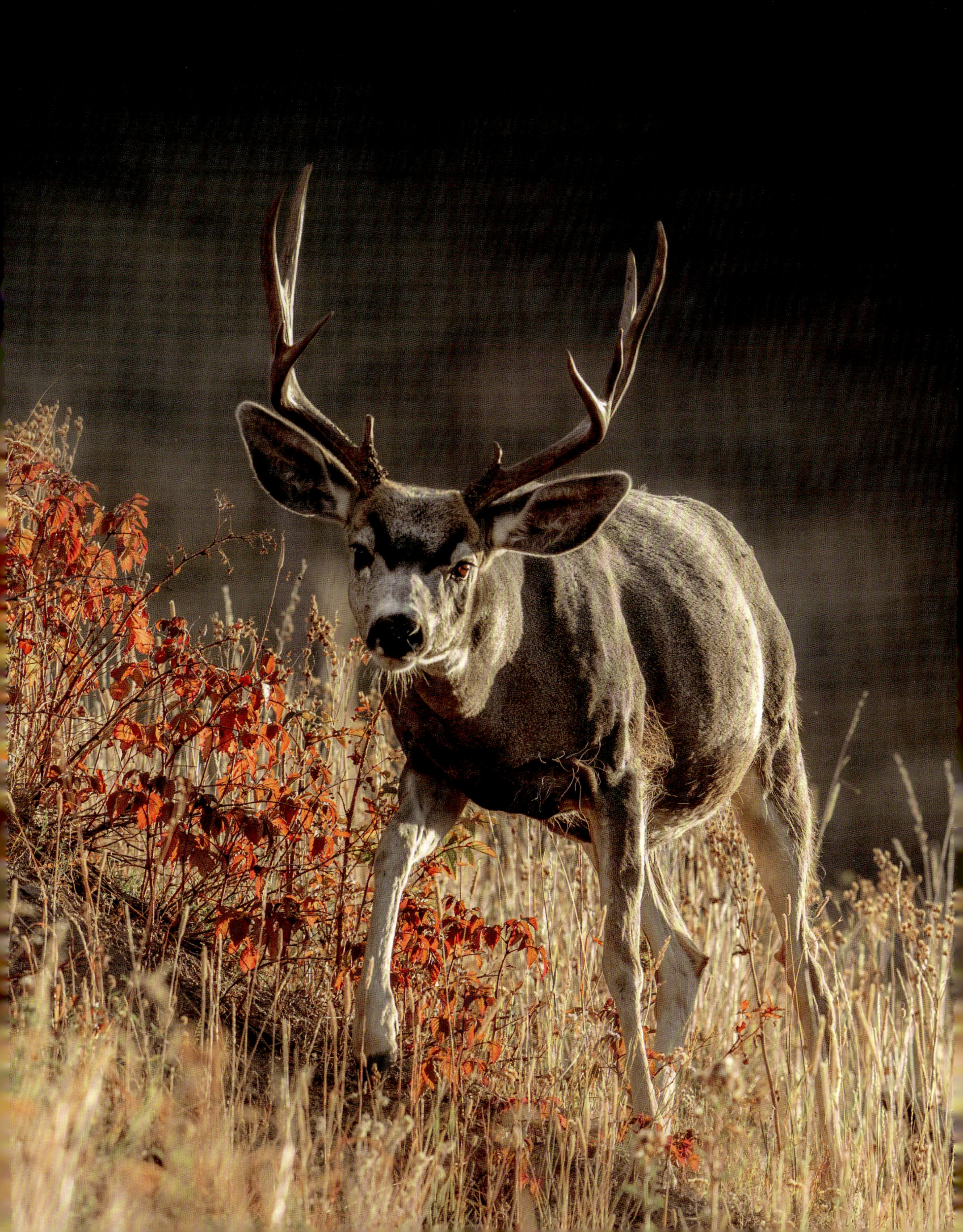

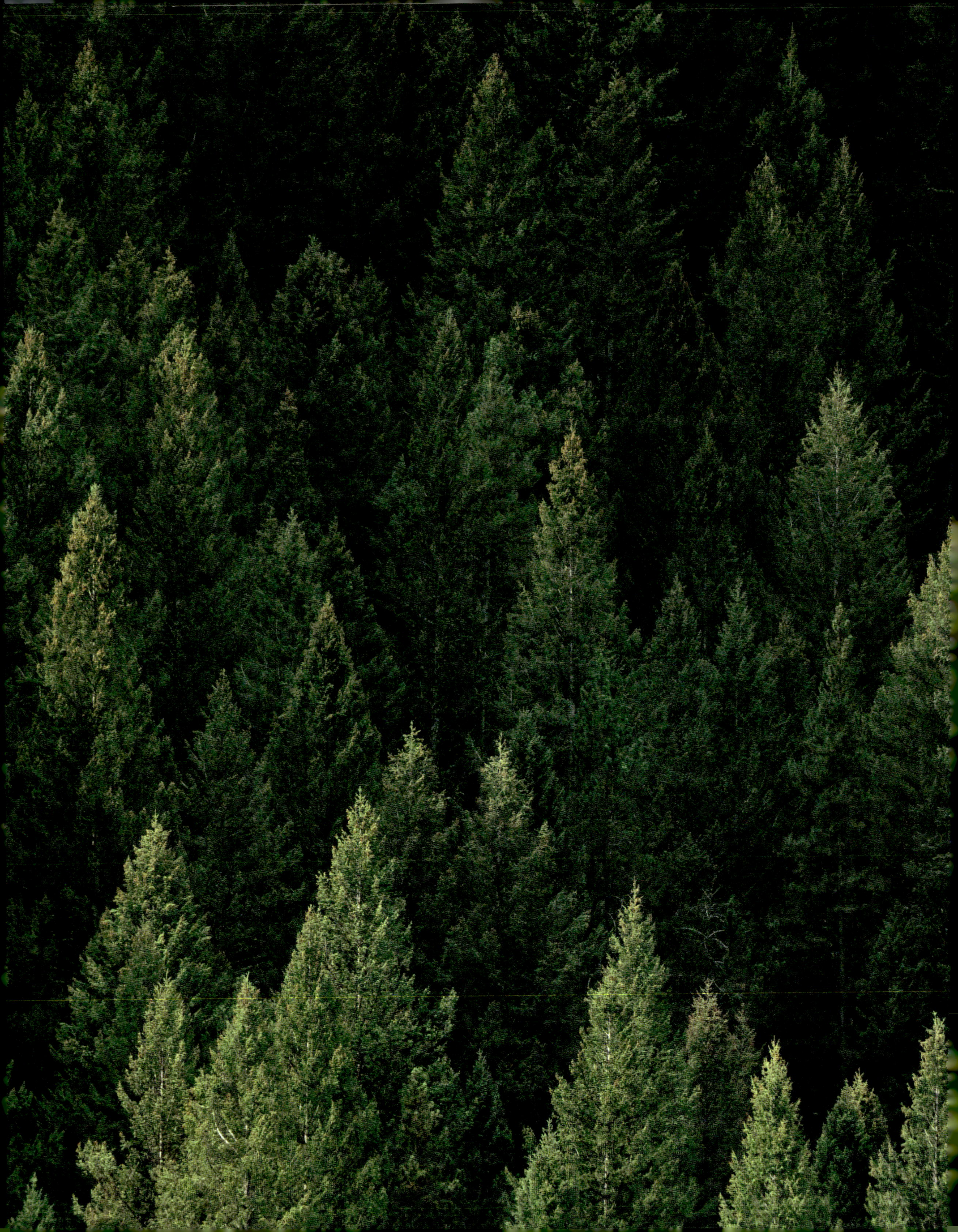

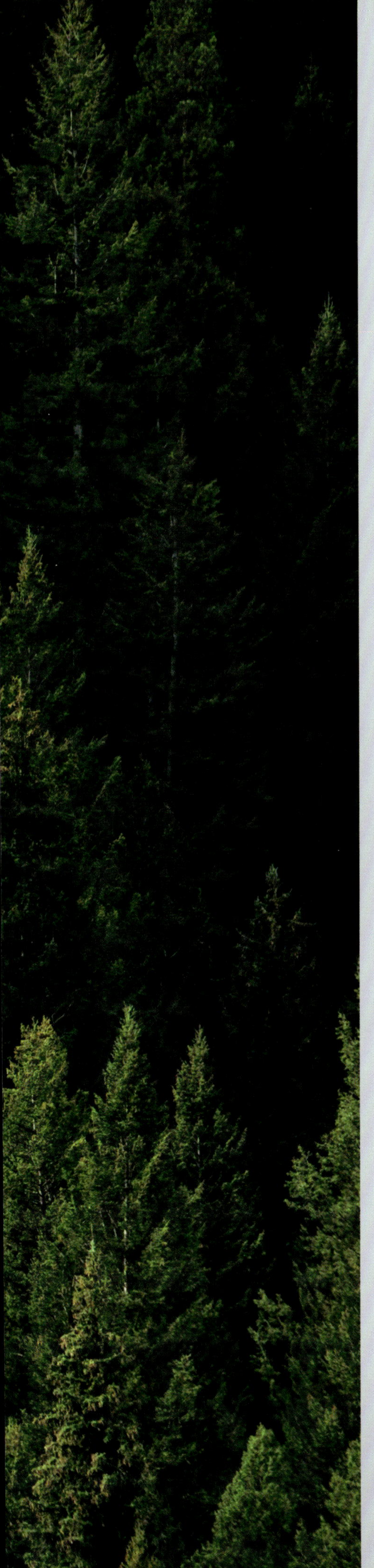

FORESTS

Forests cover much of Yellowstone, largely dominated by towering lodgepole pines. Some trees have stood for hundreds of years, bearing scars from past fires. Other trees are mere saplings, just beginning their long growth to maturity. Forests here are diverse, with both deciduous trees and conifers, though evergreens are the most abundant. The evergreen trees of Yellowstone include the lodgepole pine, Engelmann spruce, subalpine fir, limber pine, whitebark pine, Douglas fir, and Rocky Mountain juniper. Aspens and cottonwoods grow in some areas of the park, along with willows and other smaller shrubs. Forests provide a rich and diverse habitat for many species.

Much of Yellowstone burned to the ground in the devastating wildfires of 1988, which left the landscape charred and blackened. However, forests are resilient, and new seeds germinate in the aftermath of fires, allowing for regrowth. Today, areas around Old Faithful, Norris, and Madison are covered with dense pines, the regrowth that began after the fires of '88. While fire is destructive, forests need fires to rid the forest floor of debris, remove dead trees, and even to open their seed cones. Lodgepole pine seeds are covered in a thick wax that only opens under intense heat; the trees themselves need fire to thrive.

While they can appear dense and uninviting, Yellowstone's forests are home to numerous species of wildlife, many of whom can often be seen along the forest edge or relaxing under the cool cover of trees. Black bears roam between the thick trees, occasionally even climbing into the branches for protection. Squirrels and chipmunks dart from branch to branch busily looking for food, while elk take shelter between trunks. Welcome to the forests of Yellowstone.

◀ One of the many pine-covered slopes of Yellowstone.

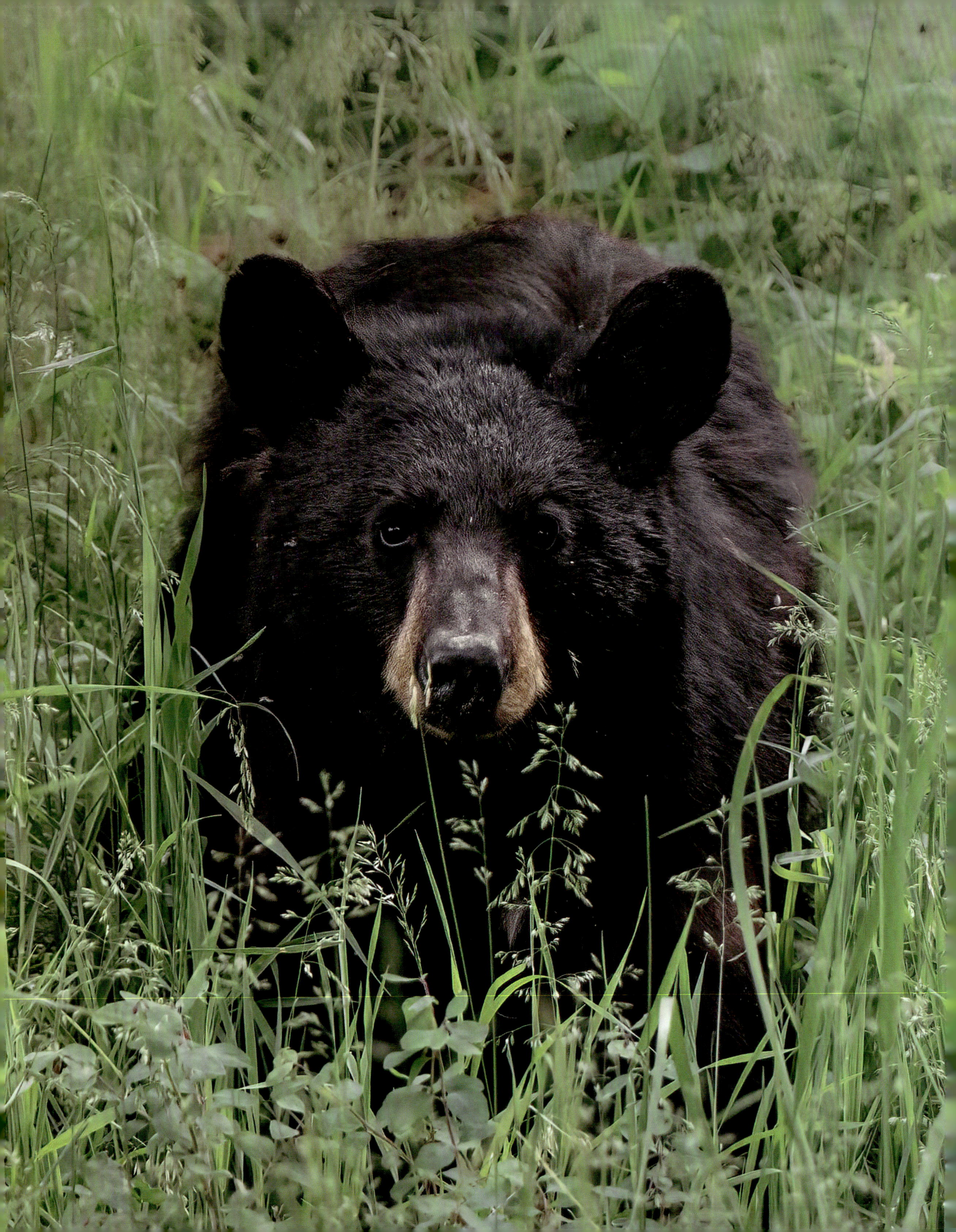

Black Bear

Black bears are often mistaken for their larger cousin, the grizzly, especially in Yellowstone where the two species coexist. Although they are called black bears, they are not always black. Coat variations include brown—known as cinnamon—or even blond, though roughly half of black bears in Yellowstone are indeed black. A few key features can be used to differentiate black bears from grizzly bears, including their large, disk-shaped ears and lack of a prominent shoulder hump. With sharp, curved claws, black bears are skilled climbers and will climb trees to escape threats such as wolves and grizzly bears. Black bears can often be seen in forested areas or in small clearings near tree cover, including on Dunraven Pass and near Tower Fall.

Black bears are typically smaller than grizzlies, weighing between 135 and 300 pounds (61 and 136 kg). Incredibly opportunistic feeders, black bears will eat almost anything, including small mammals, insects, pine nuts, grasses, berries, and other vegetation, as well as occasionally scavenging carcasses. Their summer and fall months are spent eating as much as possible in preparation for hibernation, with most black bears heading to den in November; males will emerge starting in April, while females with cubs will remain in the den until May or early June. Females give birth to cubs during hibernation, usually in litters of two or three. They are born in late January and early February and spend the first few months of life nursing and rapidly growing. After emerging from hibernation the following spring, yearling cubs are sent to live as independent bears. Black bears can live for fifteen to thirty years, with natural causes and old age being their most common cause of mortality in Yellowstone.

We don't know exactly how many black bears live within Yellowstone; while grizzlies have been extensively studied in the last fifty years, few studies have focused on the black bear population or how the growing grizzly population has potentially affected them. Black bears are more skittish and wary of people than grizzlies, making conflicts rare.

◀ A black bear walks through tall summer grasses in Yellowstone.

While I enjoy photographing any baby animal, black bear cubs are the young subjects I have the most fun watching. Helplessly tiny when they first emerge in the spring, black bear cubs are heavily reliant on their mother's protection, but that doesn't stop them from occasionally causing mischief.

Bear cubs abound in the early spring and are usually front of mind after a long and bear-less winter. While looking for black bears along a forested slope on a warm spring day, I found a beautiful sow calmly lying in the shade below a tree. My eye caught movement in the branches above; two tiny cubs were perched on a limb. From their lookout, the cubs watched curiously as their mother began to graze and soon disappeared into the thick bushes not far away. Mothers often send their cubs into trees for safety, giving themselves a much-needed break. I remained in my car a safe distance away, eagerly photographing the cubs.

The cubs, clearly not in the mood for a nap, soon began scampering up and down the trunk and balancing precariously on the swaying, moss-covered branches. For such young bears, they had already mastered the art of climbing. Without hesitation, one cub leapt upward, and the pair chased each other onto the farthest end of a limb, which began to bend under their weight. I had a moment of panic when one cub slipped and fell, but thankfully, the agile little cub caught himself on a branch below with his tiny hooked claws. Once he regained his footing, he darted back up the tree to rejoin his twin. The two paused for a moment and glanced in my direction, perfectly posed side by side on their jungle-gym tree. Before long, they were back to playing just as wildly as before, as if nothing had happened.

► Two black bear cubs play together high in a pine tree.

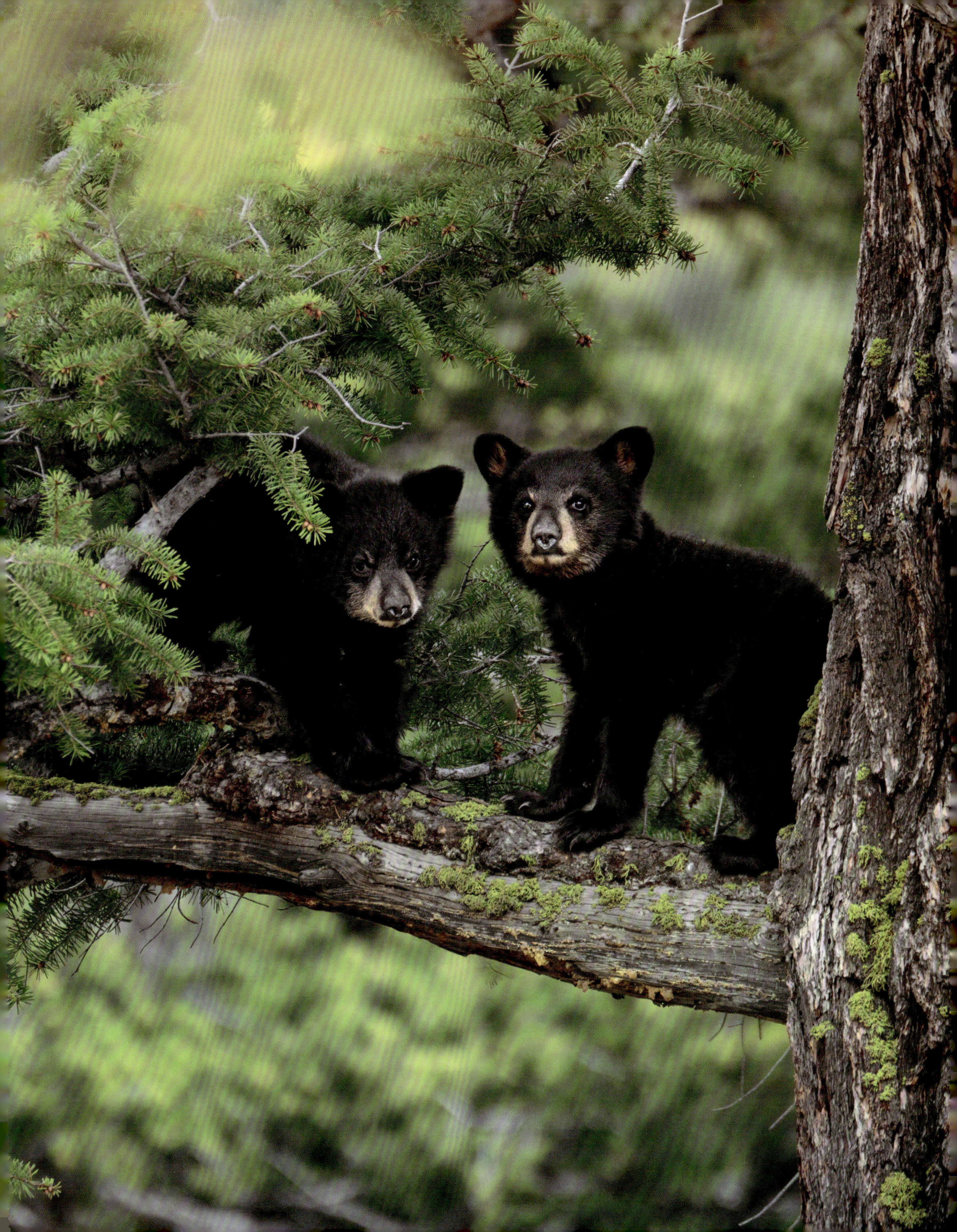

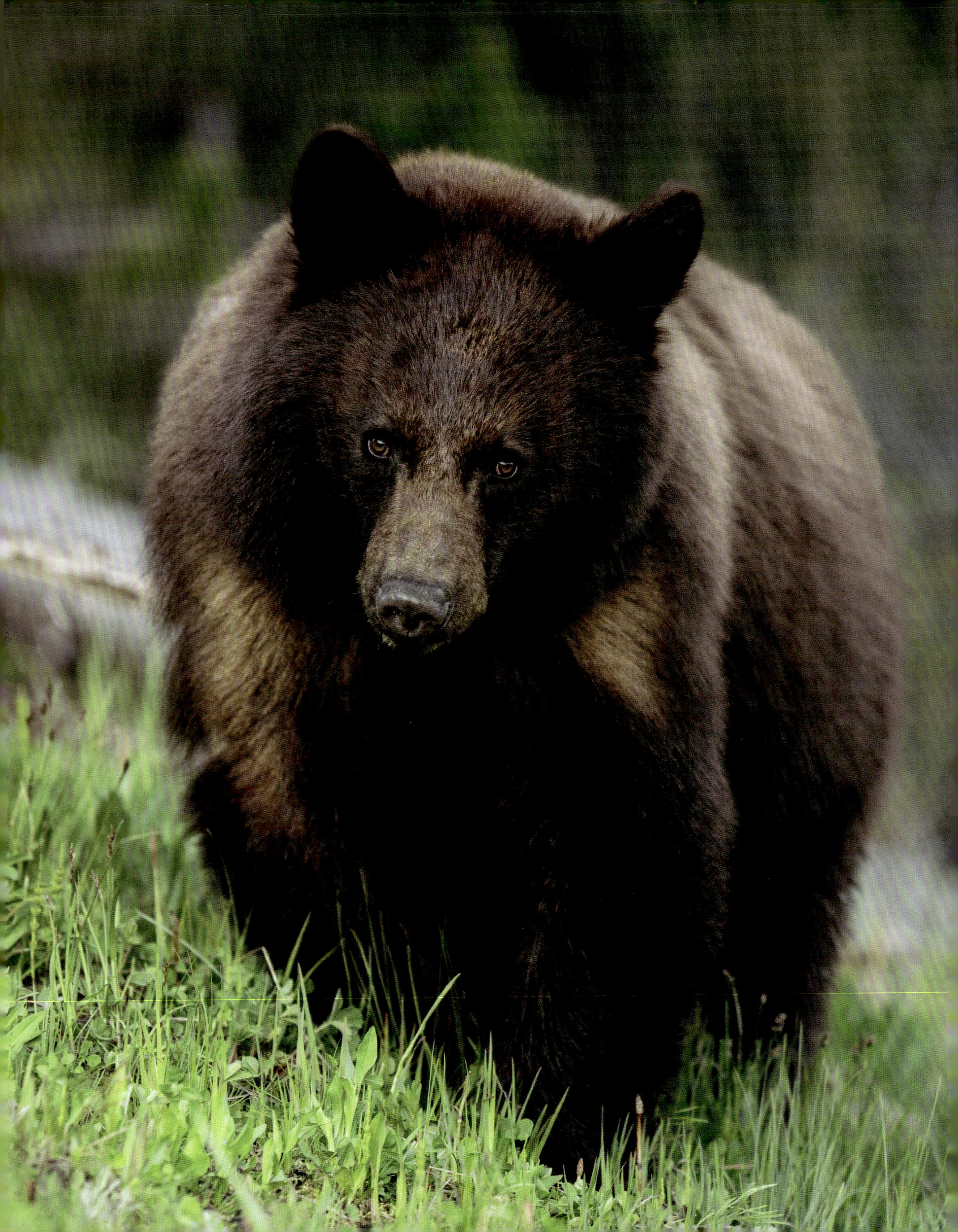

Late in the evening while slowly driving home, I spotted a black bear—likely a female based on size—grazing in some dense trees at the edge of a grassy slope. With the last bit of sunlight shining between the thick cloud layer, I decided to wait and try to capture some images of the bear. At first, only a few patches of fur were visible through the branches of several pine trees, until finally, the bear emerged into the open.

I was immediately in awe of her beauty. Instead of the usual jet-black or ginger-cinnamon coat, this bear was a very dark reddish color, except for blond patches along her shoulders and back. I had never seen a black bear with such interesting coloration before, so I excitedly began photographing her. Calmly and slowly, she grazed in a zigzag pattern up and down the hillside, her head almost always down. From where I sat in my car, I could hear her teeth delicately snipping blades of grass and the twigs that occasionally snapped under her paws. The only other sound was the annoying buzz of mosquitos.

After traversing nearly the entire small hillside, the bear raised her head and stared directly at me, as if she was noticing me for the first time. Her brown eyes looked beautiful in the last golden rays of the setting sun. With her ears pinned forward in an alert position, she was assessing if I was a threat. Then, she raised her nose, taking in several audible breaths of air and undoubtedly learning more about me from my scent. I was obviously determined to not be a threat; she walked right past my car on her way to the next green slope. Deciding I had captured enough images of the beautiful bear, I left her in peace in the dwindling light.

◀ A striking female black bear grazes on a hillside.

Adult bears are usually solitary, except in the spring when mating season begins. Males will roam large spans of territory in search of females to mate and continue their lineage with. Well into the late evening of a long day in June, I came upon two black bears in a small meadow alongside a swift-moving creek. It became obvious the two were a courting pair, brought together by the wild instincts of the season.

The female was slender and beautiful, her shiny black fur almost looking blue in the evening twilight. She clearly was not interested in the male, a large and burly cinnamon black bear who could have very easily been mistaken for a grizzly. A few scars crisscrossed his nose, evidence of past battles. He steadily pursued her; she steadily moved away. Over the gentle rush of the creek, I could hear the male's demanding gruffs as he became increasingly agitated by the female's lack of interest. His eyes never wavered from his target. She never even looked his way. Clearly wanting to cross the road, the male repeatedly circled the female, insistently trying to push her in that direction. With defiance, the female consistently sidestepped him, focused on eating flowers and avoiding his persistent pursuit.

Twice the male crossed the road alone, standing on the opposite side just long enough to give a few grunts before circling back to the female. Finally, with an air of annoyance, the female caved and moved toward the road, while the male watched her intently in the background. The couple disappeared into the thick forest on the other side of the pavement. The male's gruffs finally ceased as he got his way.

▶ A male and female black bear during mating season.

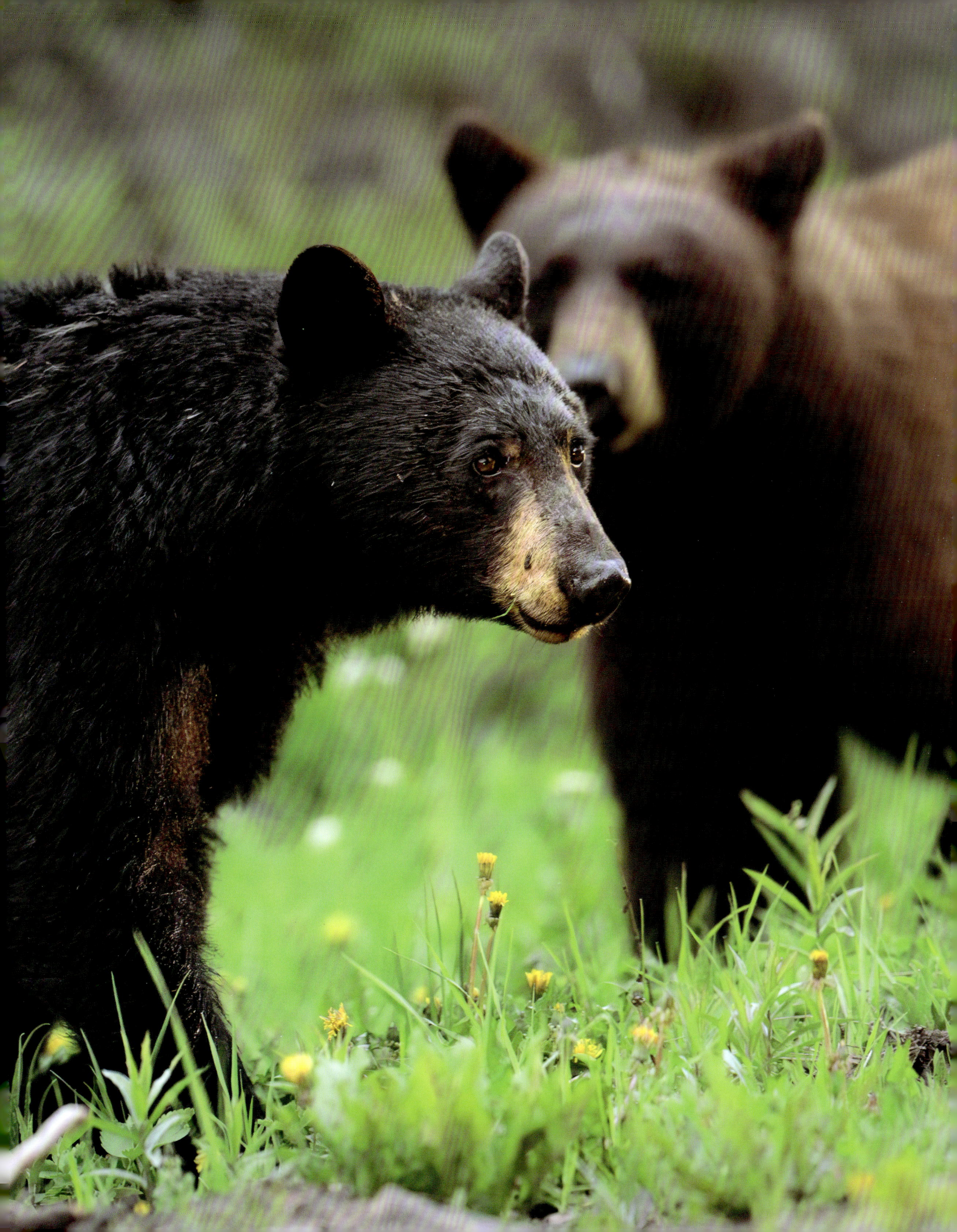

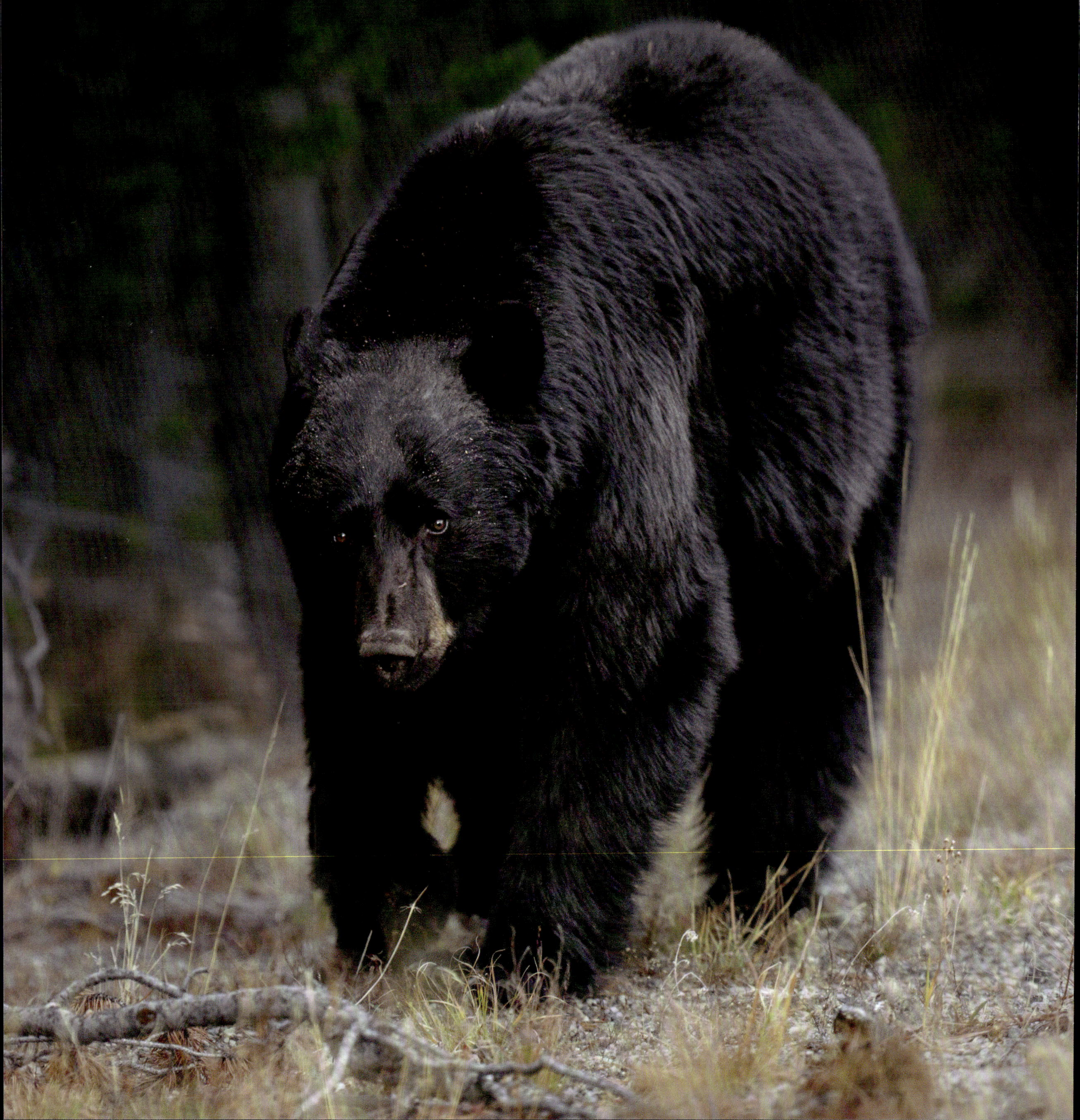

As autumn days pass and winter looms, black bears begin to seek a den for hibernation. By mid-October some black bears have already retreated to the warmth and comfort of a den, where they will pass the long and frigid winters of Yellowstone. Still, some of the larger male black bears remain, roaming the forests for any last bites of food.

On a late fall evening, just a few days before the first snowstorm of the season, I came across one such bear as he walked along the forest's edge. With a summer of eating behind him, the bear had put on a considerable amount of weight, evidenced by his round shape and sagging belly. As he lumbered along the tree line, twigs cracked under-paw and his plump belly swayed. He moved slowly but with intent, always keeping his head down. The bear's black coat nearly faded into the shadows, especially in the muted twilight. Had he been standing still, he easily could have been mistaken for just another dark patch in the forest.

The only color on the bear was his tan snout and dark-brown eyes, which seemed dull and fatigued. I wondered how old the bear was and whether he always looked this way prior to hibernation. Even the way he moved seemed drowsy, as if raising each paw was a huge undertaking. I didn't watch the bear for long. He soon turned and strode into the thick pine forest, where he disappeared surprisingly quickly. Perhaps he was on his way to hibernation and keenly focused on returning to a familiar den. I hoped that was the case and that he would soon be greeted by a sweet, and well-deserved, slumber after a long and busy summer.

◀ A bulky male black bear lingers in the forest.

Deep amid heavy fall foliage in late autumn, I found a mother black bear and her two cubs hungrily devouring a feast of late-season berries. I was surprised to encounter a sow with cubs so late in the season, though the weather had been warm with a lack of snowfall.

Through the thick cover of vegetation, the bears were rarely visible except for a few seconds when one would raise its head over the bushes; rustling leaves and snapping branches otherwise indicated their location in the thicket. As I hoped for a better photographic opportunity, one of the cubs reached its head above the dense mess of grass and shrubs. In a haphazard way, the cub continued to pluck berries from their stems with ravenous delight despite the presence of many sharp thorns. The cub had striking dark cinnamon fur that complemented the red and orange foliage surrounding him. The shadowy pines in the background only made the fall colors appear brighter.

With baffling efficiency, the cub cleared the bush of every berry but a scant few on one high branch. Looking longingly toward the last of the berries, the cub placed one paw around the branch, grasped it in a tight grip with his hooked claws, and pulled it closer. Only a few berries and vivid orange leaves clung to the branch, but the cub was not going to pass up those sweet morsels. After precisely plucking the berries with dexterous lips, the cub released the branch, causing it to snap back to its natural position. A couple of leaves fell off in the process and drifted to the forest floor.

Its hunger satisfied for now, the cub bounded energetically to its mother, who was digging behind a rotting log nearby. The other cub soon joined them and the twins started wrestling, occasionally giving voice to defensive growls. When the mother had finished digging, she led them deeper into the thicket and they all three disappeared into the colors of fall. Only three days later they were huddled in a den for the winter (still visible from the road through a protective hole in the sunny, sloping hillside), where they would remain until spring.

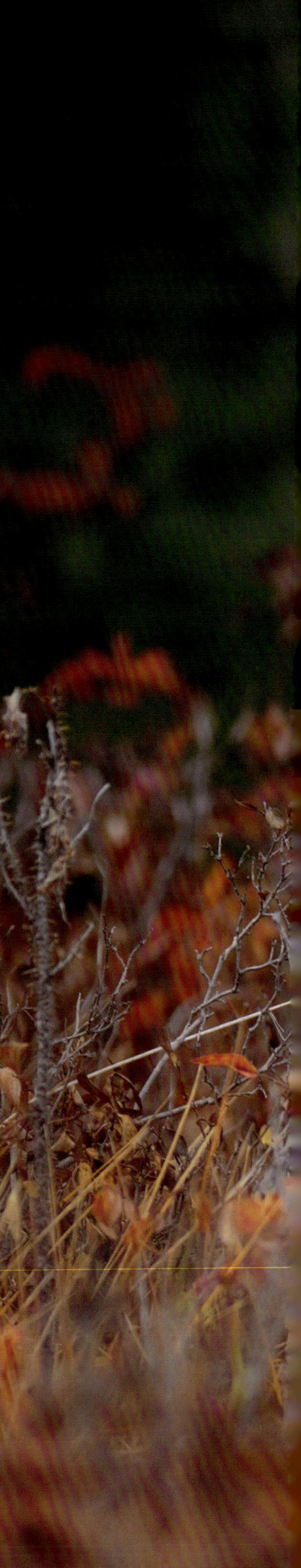

▶ A determined black bear cub forages some of the last berries of the season.

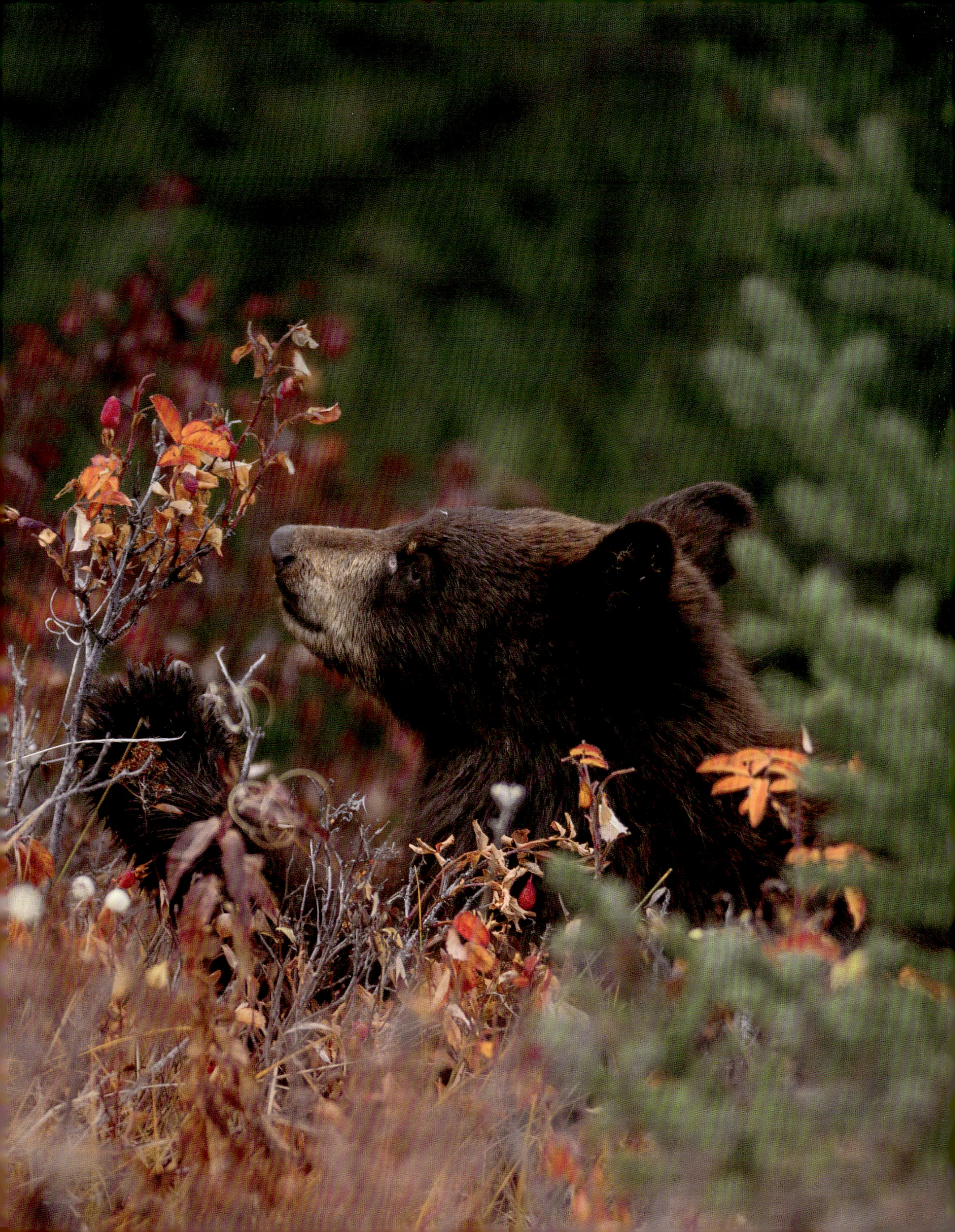

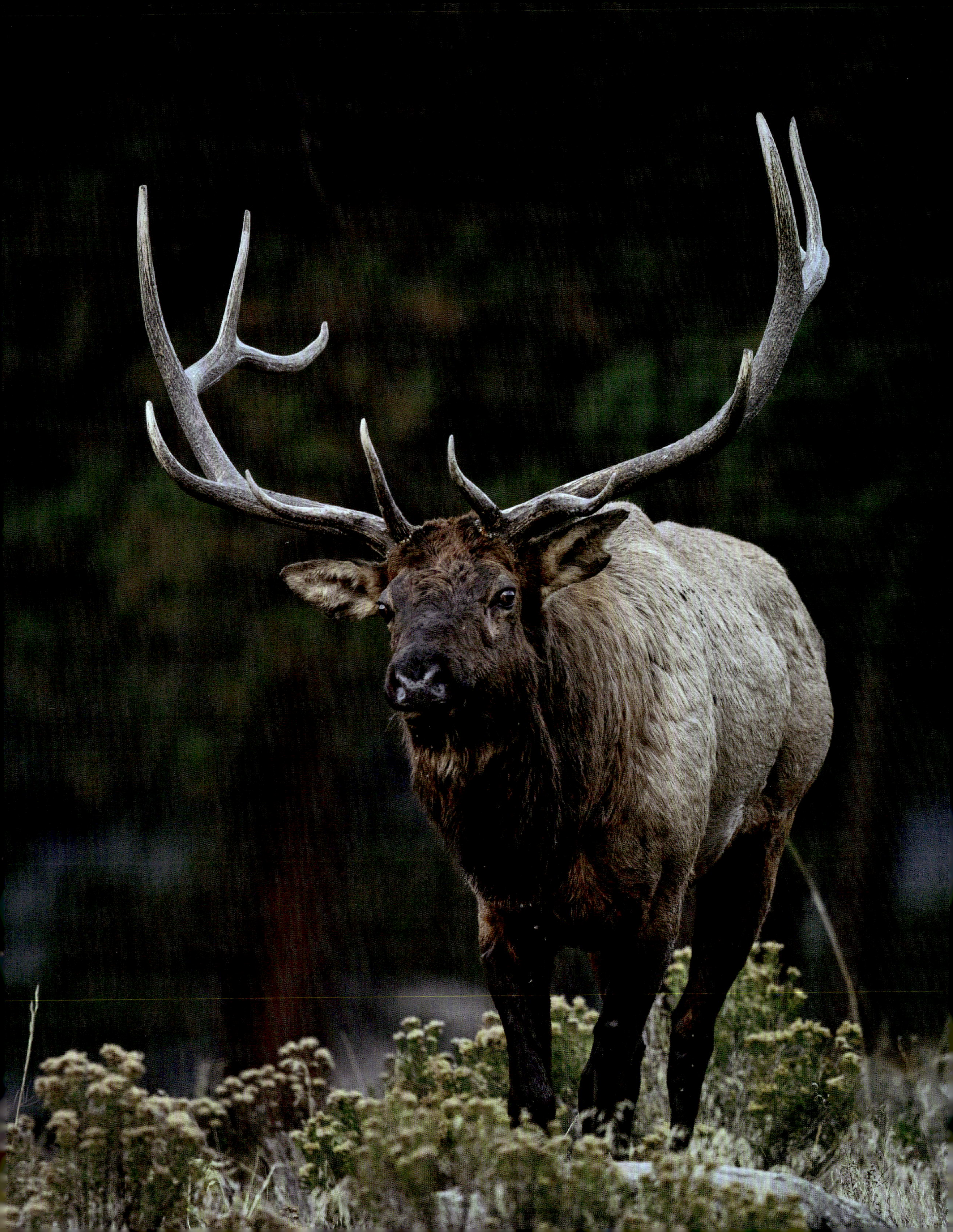

Elk

Elk are the most abundant large animal in Yellowstone, with well over ten thousand spending the summers within the park. They can be seen grazing in herds in Lamar Valley, Hayden Valley, near Mammoth, along the Madison River, and in various green meadows across the park. During the winter many will migrate along ancient migration paths to lower elevation wintering grounds where food is more plentiful, though many others can still be seen near the North Entrance and Mammoth. Bulls stand about 5 feet (1.5 m) at the shoulder and can weigh 700 pounds (317.5 kg), with cows being slightly smaller. They have a light-brown coat with large ears and a white rump.

Bulls are identifiable by their antlers, which develop through the summer and are covered in velvety tissue that allows for bone growth. During the peak period of antler growth, a bull's antlers can grow nearly 1 inch (2.5 cm) a day. In the fall, the velvet is shed and the white, pointed antlers—which can weigh more than 30 pounds (13.6 kg)—are revealed. Antlers are used in the fall during the rut, or mating season, to compete for dominance between bulls. Bulls also bugle to assert dominance, with distinct, deep, resonant calls that end in a higher-pitched squeal ringing out across the landscape.

Calves are born from early May to late June. They are born scentless and able to stand within an hour of birth, protecting them from predators like grizzly bears and wolves. Cows will fiercely defend their calves, using their front hooves to attack and ward off predators. Elk are an important food source for many animals in Yellowstone, including grizzlies, wolves, mountain lions, and scavengers like coyotes, foxes, ravens, and eagles.

◀ A dominant bull elk, complete with an impressive set of antlers.

Though elk are the most photogenic in the fall with their full-grown, white, bony antlers, bulls are interesting to watch and photograph throughout the spring and summer as their antlers grow at remarkable rates.

In early June, I stumbled upon a bull whose antlers were already impressively large given the time of year, suggesting he would become a very large and imposing creature by the fall. The lower half of his antlers had already taken form in a typical shape, with their first few tines completely finished growing. The upper half of his antlers, on the other hand, was still developing. At the top of one tine, I could barely see the divot where the branch would soon split into two. Velvet covered the entire set of antlers, which would stay until late August. The softness of the velvet mirrored the softness of the summer landscape, everything showing signs of regrowth in the new season.

Surrounded by vibrant summer greens, the bull calmly grazed across a small hillside clearing, working his way in my direction. Yellow wildflowers—the first blooms of the season—dominated the hill. They added a welcome pop of color to the landscape, which only a few weeks before had lain under a blanket of snow. I sat down in the soft grasses, the afternoon sun warming my back. With the clearing empty except for the elk and I, the air was quiet, only the occasional buzzing bee or rustle of branches breaking the silence. The elk only raised his head when stepping to a new grazing spot, just long enough to snap a few photos each time. His ears occasionally swiveled from side to side, listening to the sounds of the forest. A raven cawed somewhere in the distance. Without warning, the elk folded his legs and laid down in a patch of wildflowers. Feeling sleepy myself, I stood up to hike back to my car to take an afternoon nap, leaving the bull to do the same.

▶ A bull elk in the summer with a still-growing set of antlers.

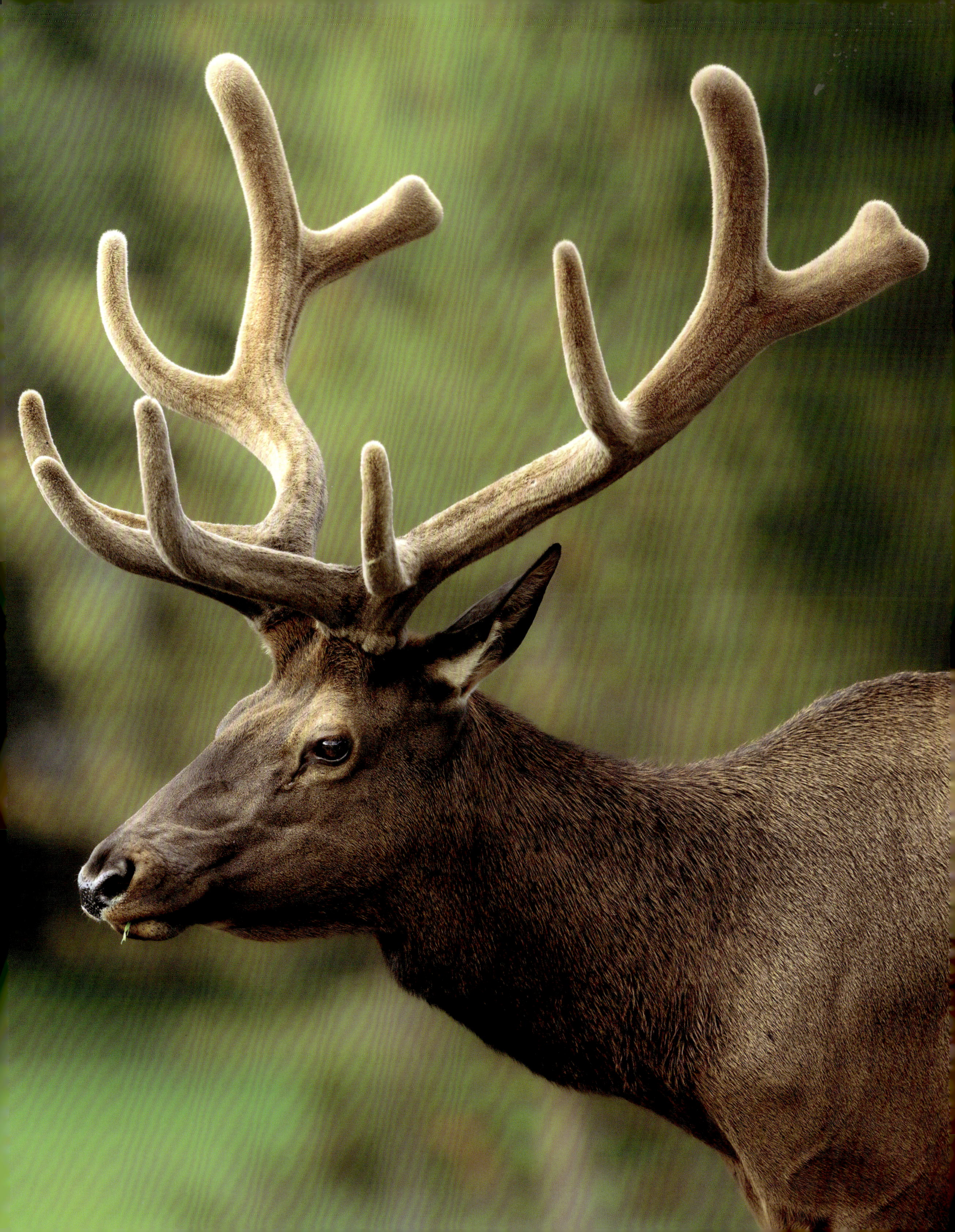

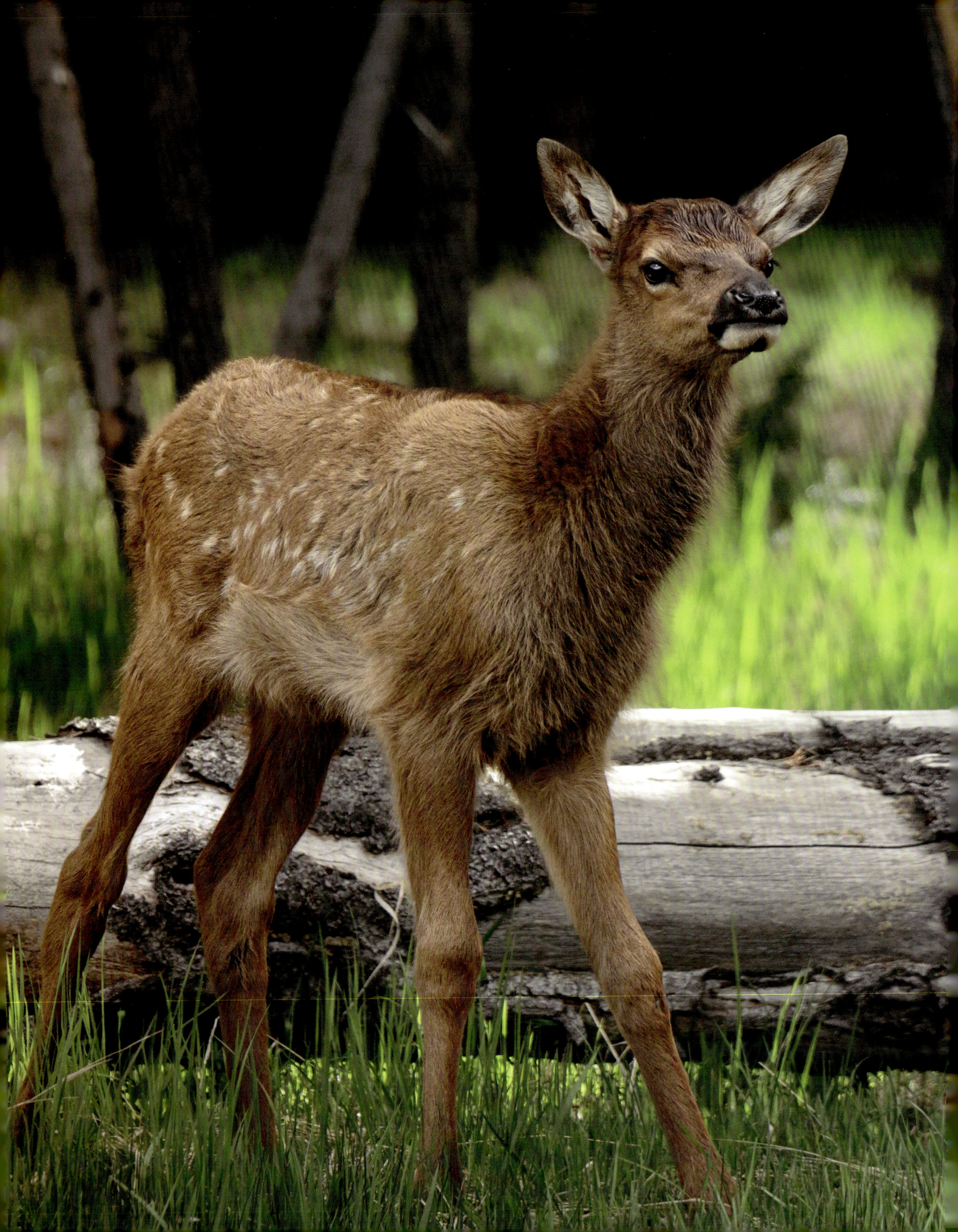

Elk calves are born incredibly vulnerable to predators like wolves and grizzly bears, and, as a result, mothers tend to keep the calves hidden for their first couple weeks of life. But as the summer progresses and calves grow stronger, they can be seen playfully bounding through meadows or calmly grazing with their herds.

On an unusually hot summer evening in Yellowstone, I decided to search for wildlife under the shady protection of the lodgepole pine forest. Before long I came across a herd of roughly a dozen cow elk, most of whom had calves. The mothers grazed through the vibrant green grasses growing along the edge of the forest, completely ignoring the antics of their offspring.

Meanwhile, on awkward and lanky legs, the calves bounced around the open forest with the wild energy of youth. Occasionally a calf would toss its head back, causing another to kick its hind legs in excitement. The group of calves raced around the meadow playing together like a group of schoolkids at recess; while to the calves the chase was simply fun, it was also strengthening their legs and teaching them the agile steps necessary to escape predators in the future. For now, though, the calves remained blissfully unaware of the brutality and harshness of their wild world.

One by one the calves returned to their mother's sides exhausted, except for one who remained apart, clearly not yet tired. With frizzy fur that stuck out in all directions and a calf's characteristic white-spotted sides, he glanced around with a perplexed expression as if confused why his friends had stopped playing. After a few moments of longing for more fun, he too laid down in the cool, tall grass for a much-needed evening nap.

◀ An elk calf takes a break from playing in the forest.

Bull elk convey a certain regality when they walk, their heads usually held high despite the weight of their antlers. Larger, and therefore more dominant, bulls are especially prideful in their movements, sauntering around the forest's edge with grace and determination. When summer fades to fall, their impressive shows of strength reach another level.

While hiking through small clearings surrounded by pines, I was met by a group of several cow elk and their now weaned calves. It was early September, and during the fall months cow elk are usually watched over by bulls. I glanced around the clearing, but there was no bull in sight. Assuming it must still be too early for the elk rut, I decided to photograph the group and kneeled in the tall grasses to begin shooting.

After spending some time with the herd, I stood up to continue my search for other wildlife when I noticed an unusually white branch in the shadows of the forest. Then it moved. It was the tine of a bull elk who had been resting in the shade, but he was now standing tall at the edge of the small clearing. He looked first toward his herd of cows and then directly at me. His ears were up and alert. Shooting from behind a young pine, I was able to capture a photo of him framed between two branches. The late afternoon sunlight reflected off his antlers, the tips of each tine whitened from rubbing them on tree trunks. The sunlight also caught the edge of dark, thick, spiky fur along his neck. Even when simply standing his muscles were visible along his shoulders and legs, while a few faint scars showed his experience battling with other bulls. Every detail of the bull added to his majestic appearance. Finally, he looked away from me and glanced back at his herd of cows. Without warning, he bugled—just one clear, crisp call. It was the first I had heard since last fall. The rut had begun.

► A majestic bull elk stands tall, ready for mating season.

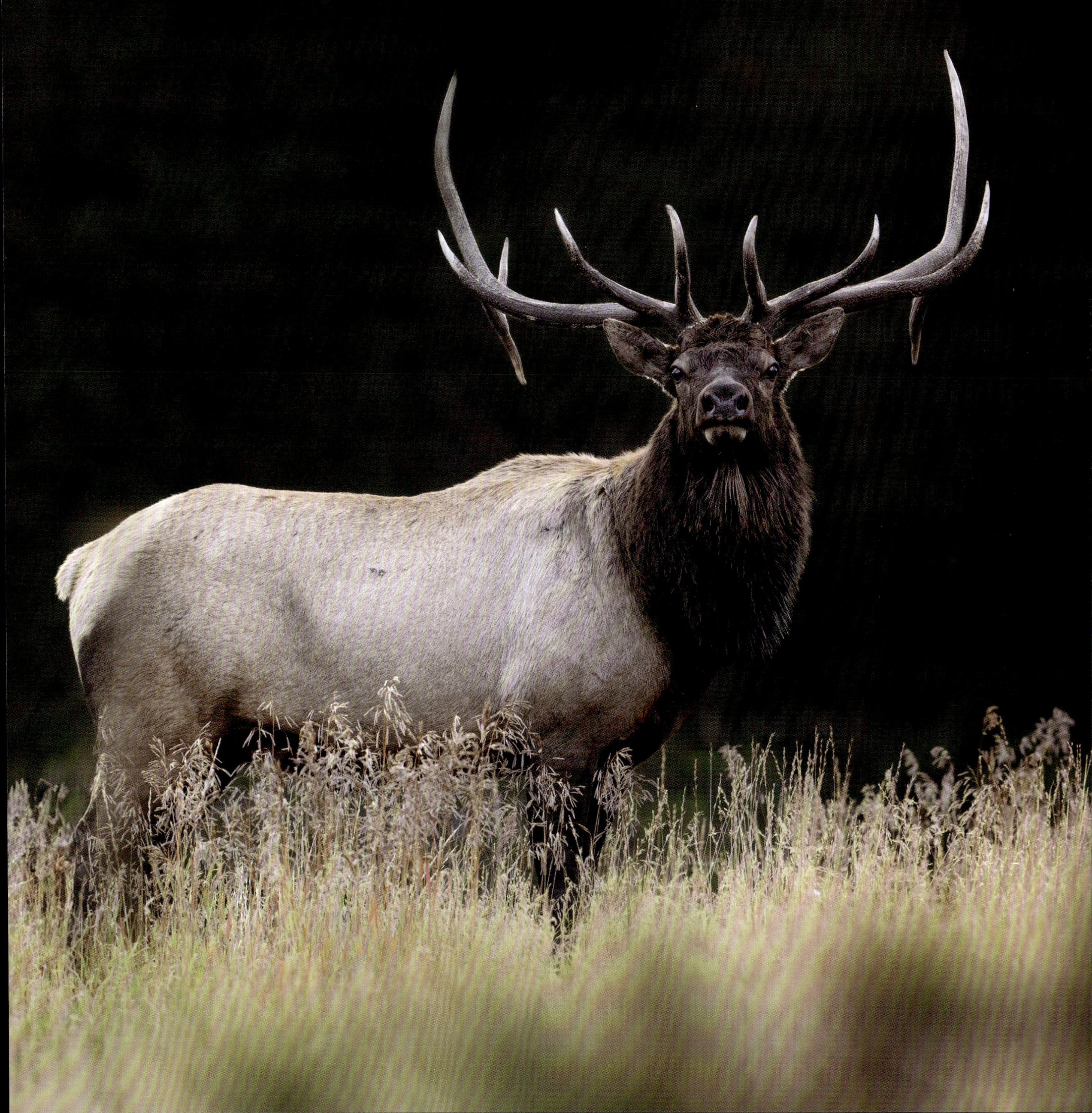

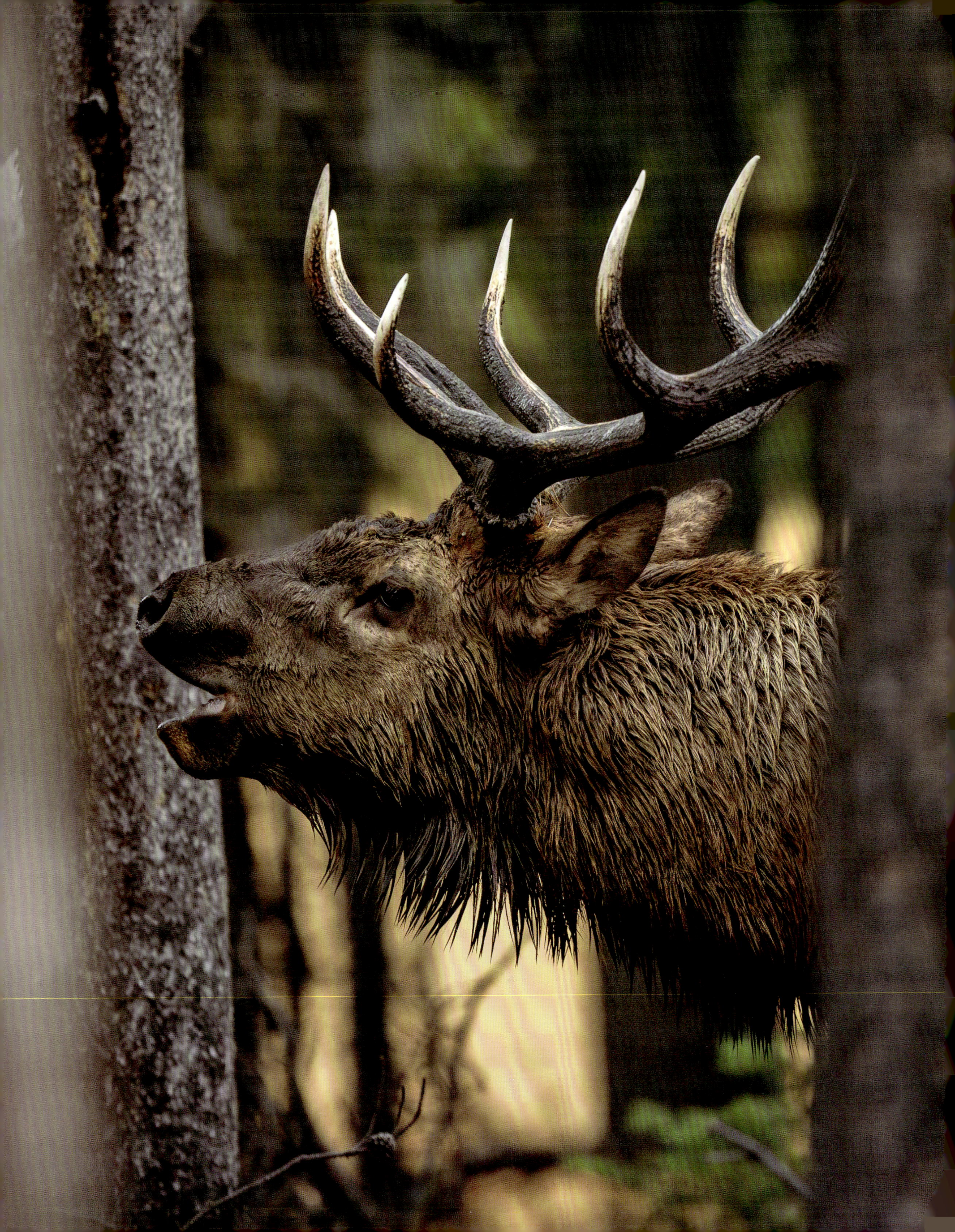

To me, elk bugles are synonymous with fall in the same way as golden leaves on aspens. Nothing compares to the hauntingly powerful yet somewhat squeaky sound of an elk bugle. It is Yellowstone's most unique sound; an exciting signal that fall has officially arrived.

I don't often see elk bugle. Instead, I will hear the call echoing through the forest or down a hillside from a bull hidden in the protection of the thick trees. While a bugle is meant to announce his presence to cows and challenge the dominance of any nearby rival bulls, it also reveals his location to any wolves who may be listening. The same way a wolf pack may follow a bugle, on a rainy autumn day I, too, wandered through the forests, guided only by the raspy call. When I first heard his bugle, it was almost inaudible over the soft but persistent breeze. I trudged through the damp forest aimlessly before I heard the bull again, and this time we were much closer. I spun in a circle, scanning for any movement between the trees. He had to be nearby.

My ears caught another sound: not a bugle, but the soft thud of hooves on the forest floor. Whipping around to my right I saw him, a large, rain-soaked bull who was carefully navigating around the thick tree trunks, disappearing then reappearing between them. Raindrops dripped from his antler's tines and his nostrils flared with each breath. I watched as his rhythmic strides carried him through the pine forest. Suddenly he stopped, tilted his head backward, and bugled, his head framed by two pines. The sound shook the forest, sent a chill down my spine, and resonated out through the rainy autumn air. He listened for a reply for a few seconds then continued into the forest, eventually fading into the shadows.

◀ A bull elk bugles in the forest.

Like all mothers, cow elk are incredibly protective of their young. They will fiercely defend their calves from any perceived threat, including wolves and grizzlies, and these powerful maternal instincts make cow elk dangerous subjects, especially in the spring. I often avoid hiking in dense elk habitats during the spring and summer months for that very reason.

Come fall, the calves have matured, and elk have usually formed into larger herds as the bulls fight for mating rights and dominance. It is an exciting time to photograph elk. The bulls' large antlers and charismatic demeanor are impressive, and I admit I am often guilty of overlooking the cows.

While watching a herd of elk move through the forest, I scanned for the dominant bull. His raspy bugles rang out through the quiet evening air, but the thick trees hid him from view. Slightly frustrated by the lack of photographic opportunities with the bull, I decided to instead shift my focus to the cow elk who happened to be in clear view.

She was slowly walking along the edge of the forest in a small meadow while the light softly filtered through the trees' remaining golden leaves. Most of the leaves had already fallen and were now covering the forest floor. They crunched softly as her hooves landed. An elk calf, its white spots faded with age, followed at a distance. It was likely hers from the spring who had been weaned but nonetheless stayed nearby. Suddenly the bull ran out of the trees with his head tilted to the side. He was trying to herd her back into the trees with the rest of the group; she completely ignored him. Instead, she walked proudly with her head held high, her ears pinned confidently to the sides. She seemed unimpressed and frankly a bit irritated by the testosterone-fueled antics of the bull, who soon took the message and returned to his other cows, leaving the independent cow alone along the tree line with her grown calf.

► An independent cow elk walks along the edge of the forest.

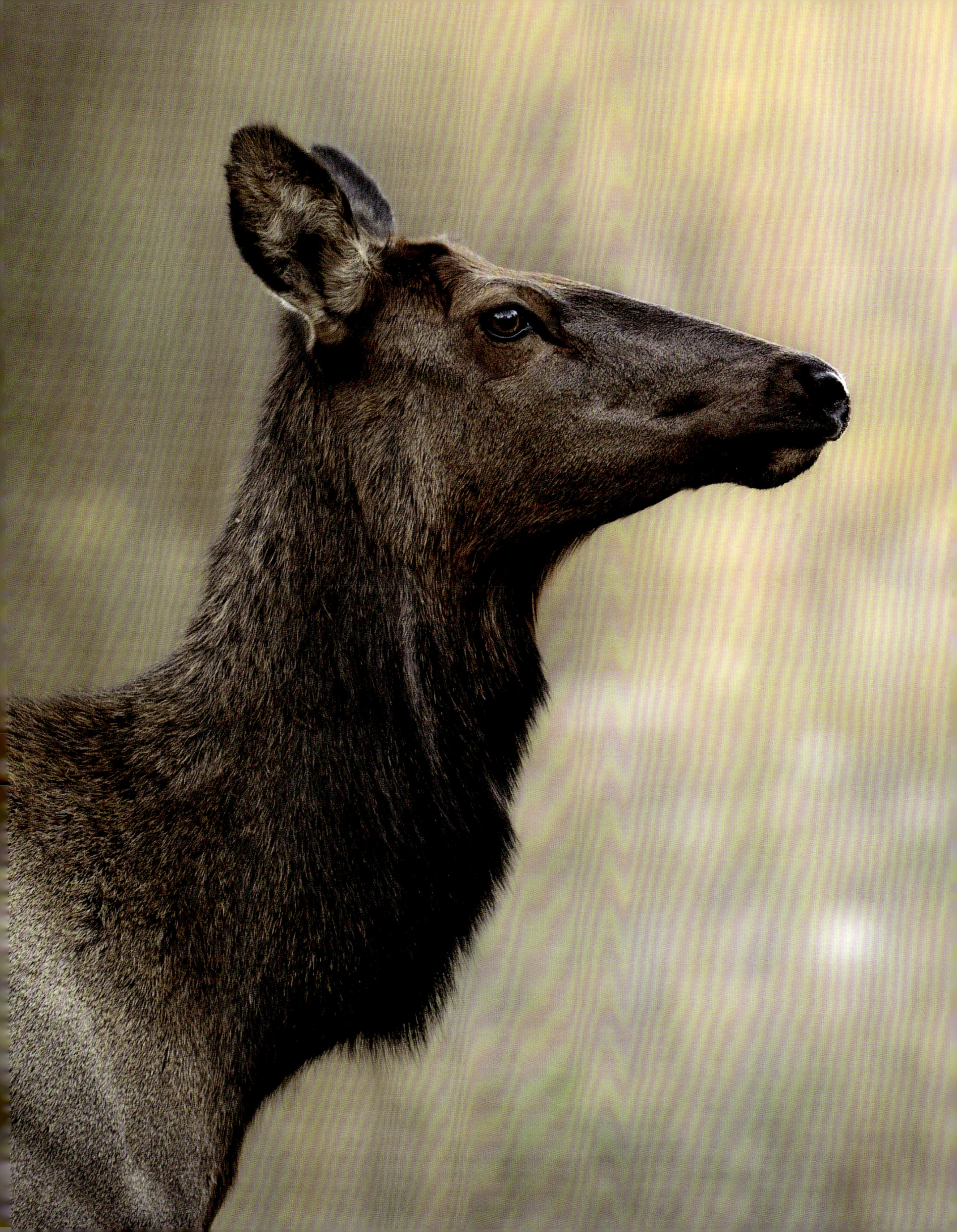

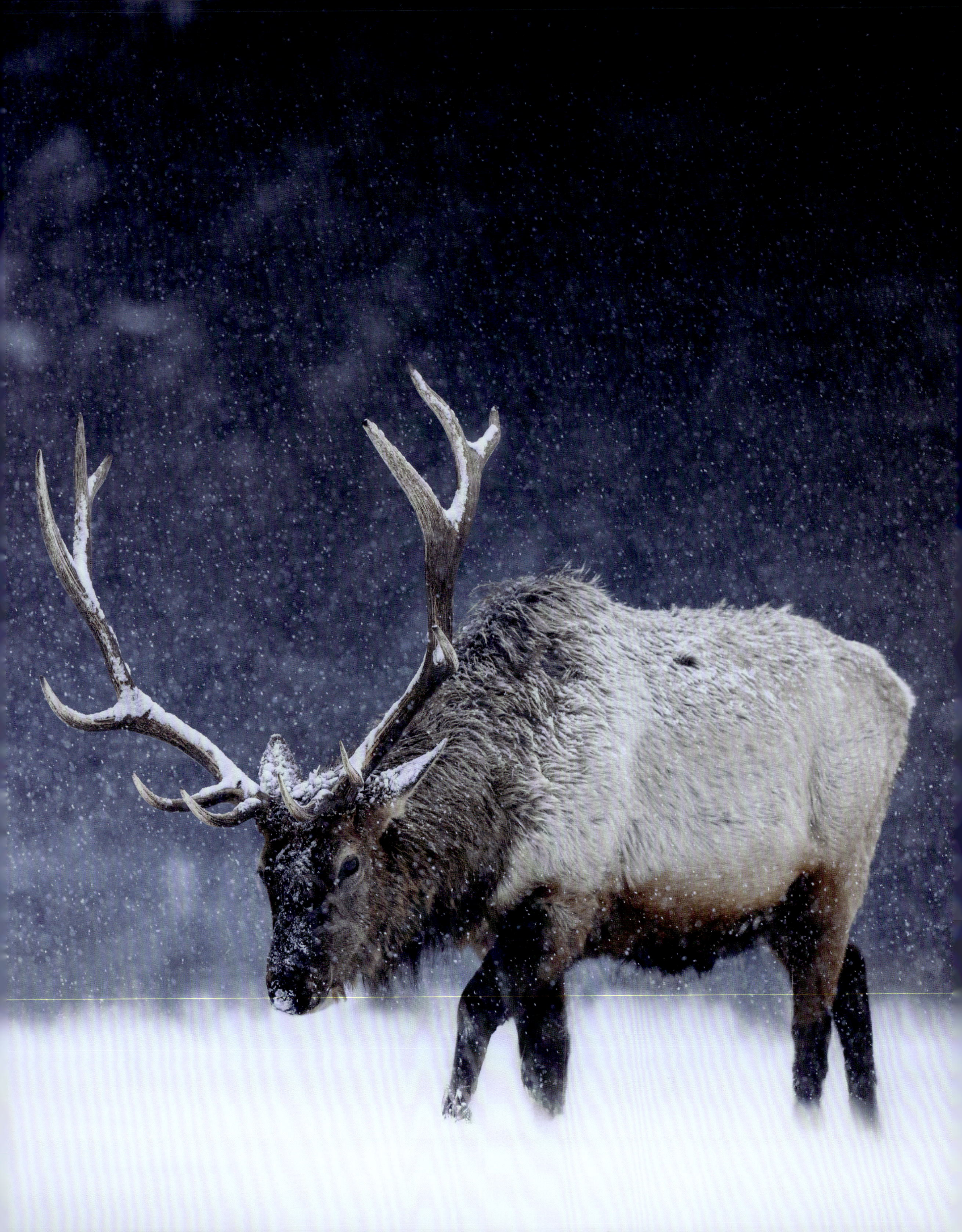

Winter snowstorms in Yellowstone can occur at any time and without warning. Storms roll into Yellowstone with intense power and turn the landscape into a chaos of windblown flakes and drifts. The animals have no choice but to endure or die.

In typical Yellowstone fashion, the weather on a cold winter's day changed with remarkable speed. Shortly after sunrise I drove into the park in hopes of photographing wolves. Thin white clouds hid any patches of blue sky, but the morning was calm without a breath of wind. Before long, the white clouds turned ominous and gray as snow started to fall. I drove deeper into Yellowstone, and as I went, the storm intensified. Large flakes were coming down at a steep angle, tossed by the now whistling wind. Visibility was dwindling.

Deciding I should stop driving, I pulled off the road and immediately noticed a lone bull elk; I couldn't help but photograph him despite the storm. Bracing against the cold, I stepped out of my warm car and into the furious gale. Snow had already accumulated on the bull's antler tines and fur. With visible effort he trudged onward, his head down as if bracing against the wind which tugged at his shaggy winter fur. He certainly was more insulated against the weather than I was in my coat. The drifted snow reached above his knees, and he left a line of deep tracks behind him that the snow quickly filled in, as if he had never even been there. In the gloomy light the nearby pine trees looked dark and cool, except for the piles of snow that clung to their boughs. Against this murky background the snowflakes were even more noticeable flying through the air, some colliding with the bull and covering his face and back. He seemed unbothered by the snow and wind. To him the storm was a normal part of life and something that he would simply do his best to ignore until fair weather returned.

◀ A bull elk braces against a sudden winter snowstorm.

Red Fox

Red foxes are the smallest canine species in Yellowstone, weighing about 10 to 12 pounds (4.5 to 5.5 kg). Despite their name, red foxes can be a variety of colors including dark gray or black (but red is the most common). Red foxes usually have a white chest, black legs, and pointed black ears, as well as a characteristic fluffy, white-tipped tail.

Red foxes feed on a diverse range of foods such as small mammals, birds, insects, and even occasionally vegetation like berries. They can be seen in a variety of places throughout Yellowstone, including throughout forests of the northeast corner, the outskirts of open plains like Hayden Valley, and any other small meadows across the park.

They are solitary creatures, except during the breeding season in January or February. In the early spring, females give birth to a litter of usually four to six kits. The kits are born blind and rely entirely on their mother for nourishment and protection during the first few weeks of life. As they grow, both parents take part in raising the young, teaching them essential survival skills. By the late summer, the kits are ready to disperse and establish their own territories. The average lifespan of a red fox ranges from three to seven years, but with protection against trapping in Yellowstone, red foxes here can live up to eleven.

Foxes have a keen sense of smell and hearing which allows them to locate prey even under deep snow and makes them highly effective hunters. Foxes can often be seen hunting, or "mousing" in tall grasses or snowdrifts, using a technique where they pinpoint the exact location of hidden prey before leaping into the air and crashing on top of it. Considered predominantly nocturnal, foxes are mostly seen in the early morning and late evening, often carrying small prey such as rodents back to their den. Though foxes are themselves predators, larger animals like wolves and coyotes can be threats.

▶ A red fox prances through a small clearing.

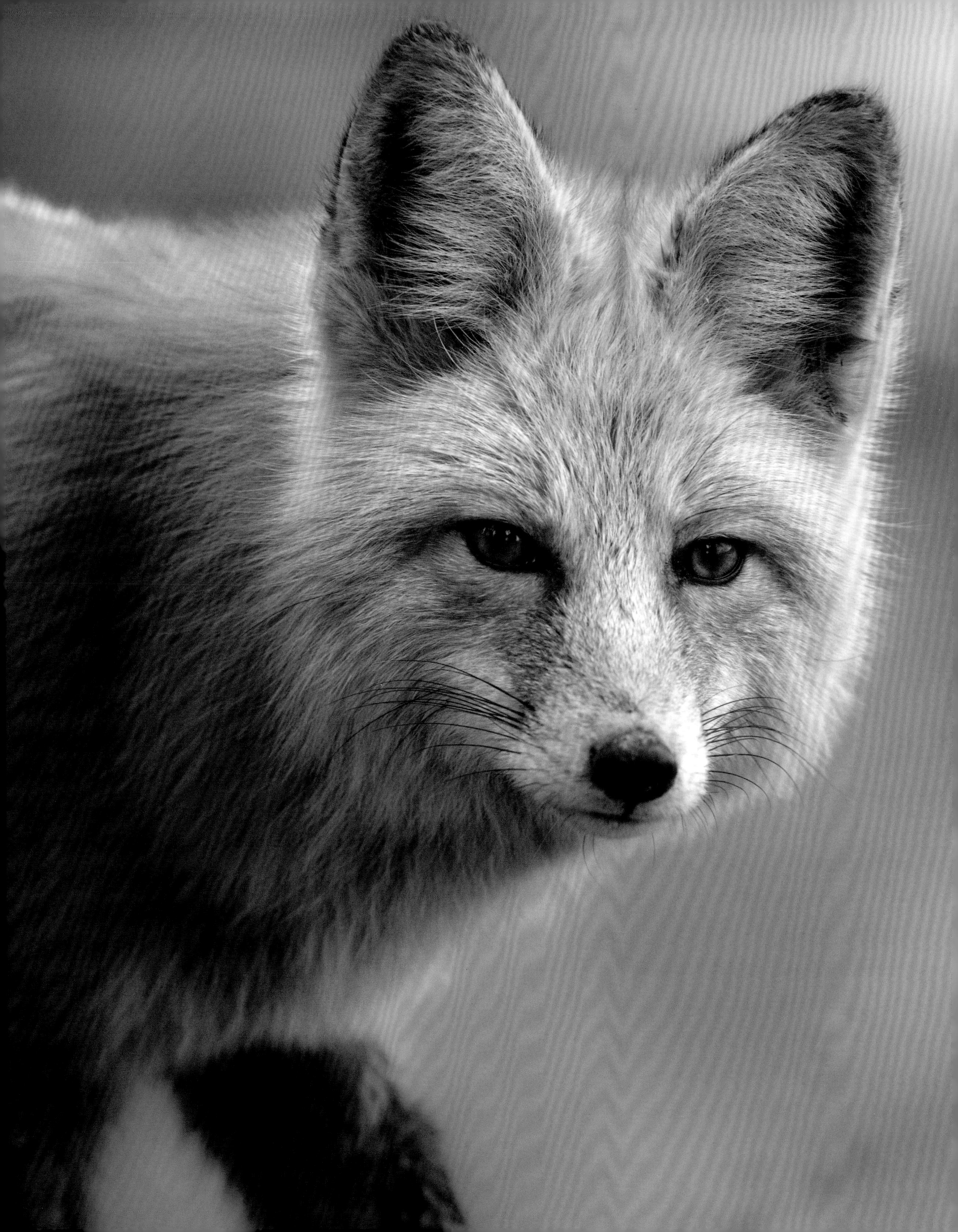

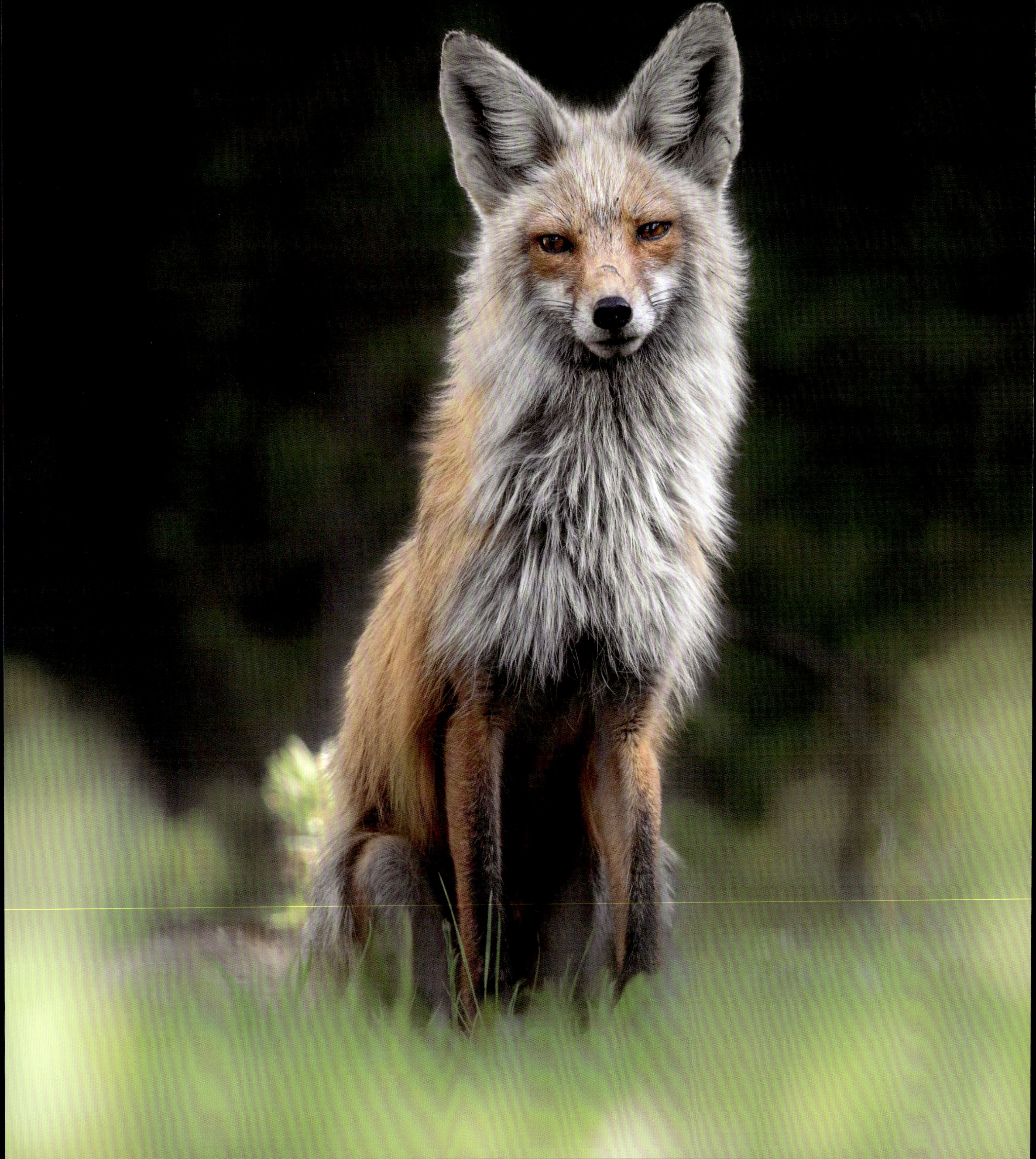

Foxes can be elusive animals, often nothing more than a flash of red fur through the trees. Exceedingly cunning and clever, they can slink silently along the forest edge, only showing themselves on their terms; however, on the occasions when foxes have revealed themselves, it has always been a memorable experience.

On a hot summer day in July, I had retreated into the woods in search of wildlife, assuming all other animals had done the same to seek refuge from the midday sun. Walking along a trail I knew well, I noticed some deer tracks in the hardened mud. Behind me, a squirrel chirped its loud and frankly annoying alarm call, likely just alerting about my presence. Signs of wildlife were everywhere, yet not of anything I had a desire to photograph. Emerging into a large open meadow, I swung my camera off my shoulder and leaned against a pine tree for a break.

Nearly dozing off in the shade, I heard a twig snap off to my left. Instinctively I whipped around, bear spray in hand, before immediately relaxing at the sight of a red fox. After trotting a few more steps into the meadow, the fox soon sat down amid the tall grasses, its eyes softly gazing toward me and a slight tilt to its head. It posed perfectly, as if begging to be photographed. I raised my camera and began capturing photos of the fox, amazed at the animal's calm.

The sunlight shone brightly off the fox's vibrant red fur in contrast with the surrounding summer greens. We sat together in the meadow for what felt like hours. Eventually the fox rose, looked around, and trotted back into the forest, but not without one more quick glance over its shoulder in my direction. I remained, reflecting over the intimate encounter I had just experienced. I've photographed the same fox several times since, identifiable by the scar across its nose, and every time I am left feeling grateful that such a beautiful creature decided to cross my path.

◀ A red fox poses in a forest meadow.

While adult red foxes are cunning, fox kits are nothing but pure curiosity. In the early spring I was lucky enough to find a fox den that I visited often that season. While their parents were away hunting, the five kits were left to entertain themselves in the small meadow surrounding the den, which they did with ease. Trying to photograph the kits was a challenge. They never sat still for longer than a few seconds, forcing me to constantly move my camera.

On a late spring evening, I watched the kits' antics as they dove into the den and came bouncing out the other side in an excited commotion. With wild energy the kits bounded through the tall grass, occasionally leaping into the air and darting back the other way in a playful frenzy. At times only the tufts of their ears were visible as they crouched down, ready to pounce on a sibling. Suddenly, and all at once, the kits crashed; after over an hour of playing, they were finally exhausted. Two kits laid together on the small mound of dirt near the den's entrance while the others retreated underground. I decided to wait in hopes of seeing the mom or dad return with a meal and watched patiently as the kits slept, their feet occasionally twitching, evidently playing even in their dreams.

After no more than fifteen minutes of rest, the two kits outside the den sat up, awoken by a meadowlark singing nearby. I raised my camera to photograph them in a rare moment of stillness. Staring curiously at the bird, both kits twitched the end of their tails as if itching to pounce, a spark of mischief in their eyes. They watched the bird flit away across the vibrant green grasses and disappear. Amazed they didn't chase after it, I continued photographing the siblings as they sat peacefully together atop their den and once again drifted back to sleep.

Over the course of several weeks, I returned to the den often and watched the kits grow up before my eyes. By the middle of summer, the den was empty, the kits having aged into beautiful young foxes and left to live their lives as independent young adults. I'll always feel grateful for watching such an intimate part of their lives.

▶ A pair of fox kits watch a songbird near their den.

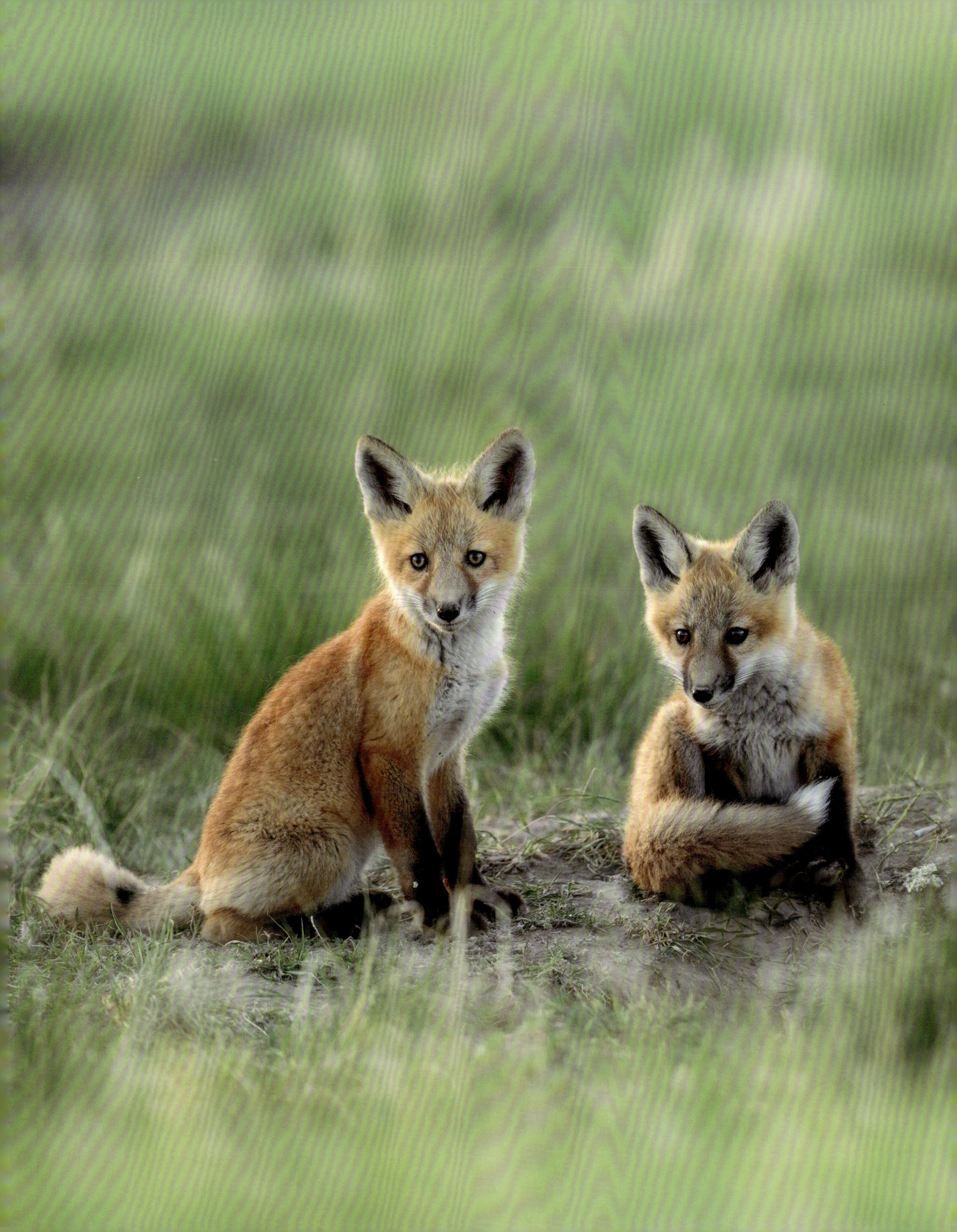

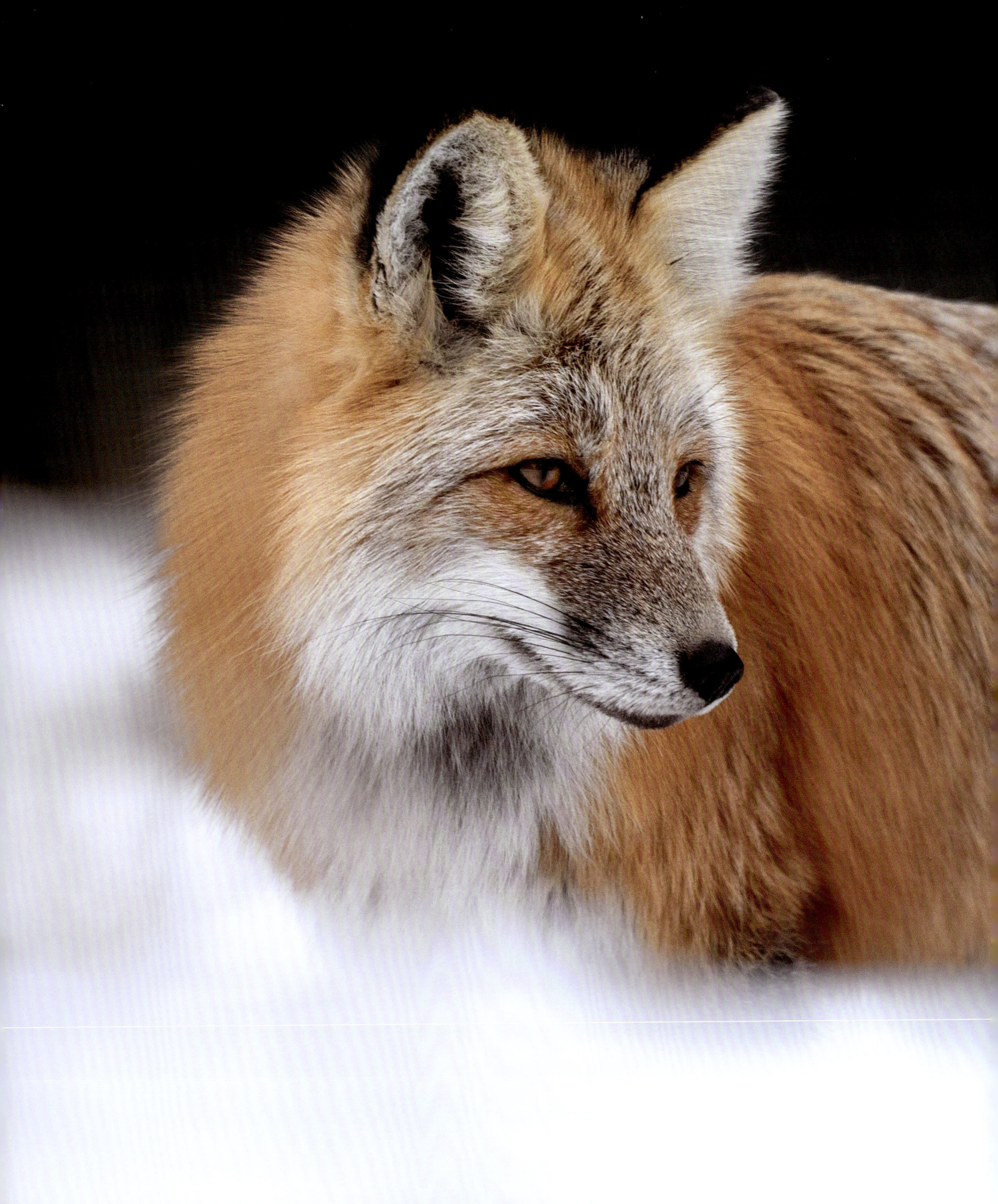

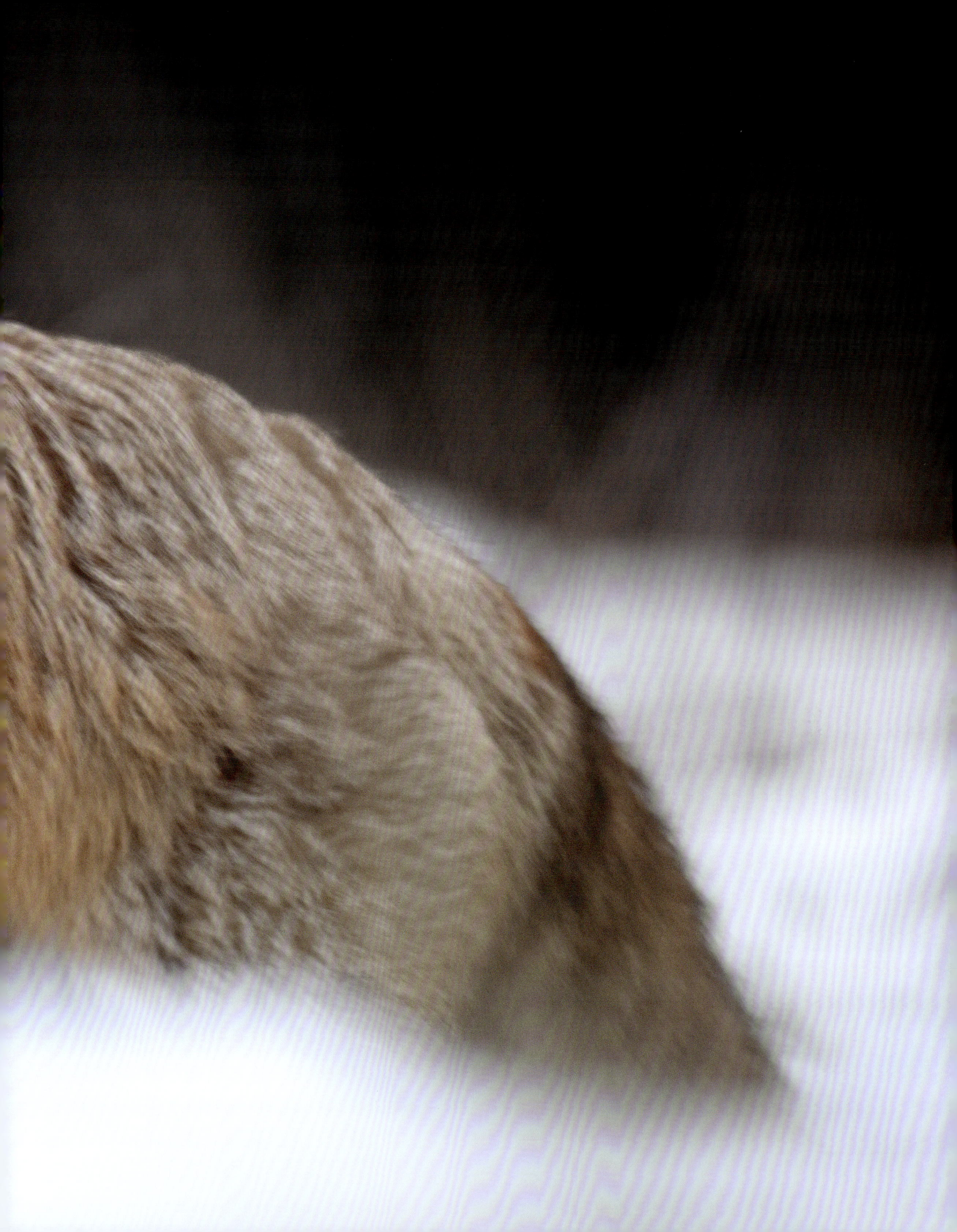

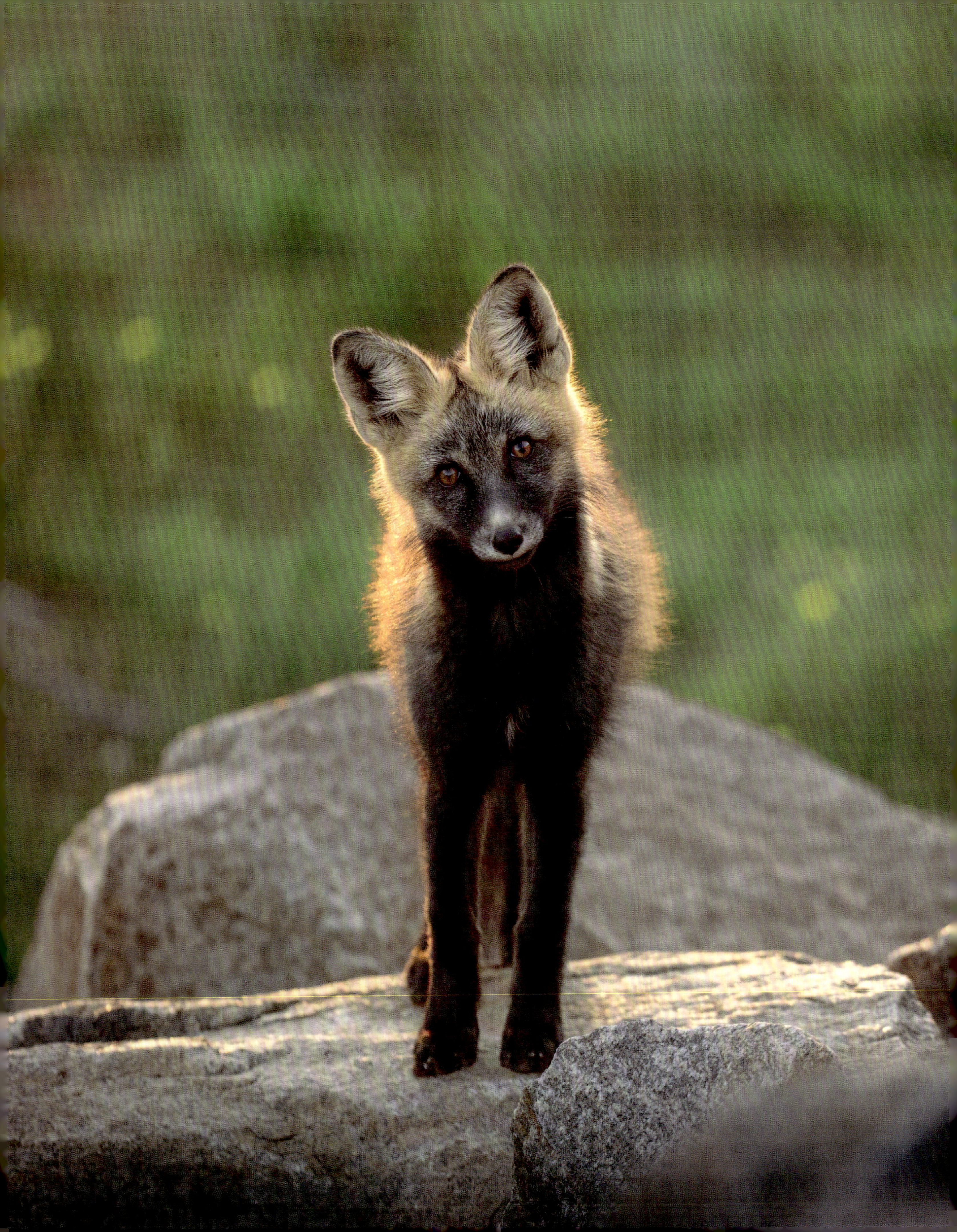

Though the name would suggest otherwise, not all red foxes are red. Some genetic mutations within certain populations can produce black and silver coat variations, or sometimes even a mixture of red and black, known as a cross fox. I had never photographed or even seen a cross fox until late one summer day when a young fox suddenly appeared in the golden light of sunset.

After a perfect day spent in the mountains, I was on my way back to my campsite when the fox trotted through a small meadow off the side of the road. Thrilled at the opportunity to photograph such a unique individual, I quietly knelt and began photographing. The fox walked a few steps in my direction before pausing atop a boulder. Ears pricked and eyes wide open, the fox gave a few inquisitive tilts of its head while studying me. A paw briefly raised in a curious motion before the fox leapt to another boulder. The fox's tail twitched with each movement I made, the white tip in deep contrast with the rest of its dark, fluffy fur. The green meadow served as a beautiful background for the fox, with the last of the summer wildflowers blooming in the distance.

With smoke hanging in the air from various forest fires, the sunset's rays were a vibrant golden red that gave everything a warm tint and illuminated the fox's frizzy fur. I was amazed how dark the fox was, its legs and spine completely black with a softer gray face, though its sides still had patches of the typical red fur which were made brighter by the smoky sun. I had never seen a more beautiful fox, or one so willing to pose for the camera. Suddenly the young fox leapt energetically off the boulder and pounced through the small meadow as if attempting to hunt, but not yet completely sure how. Before long, the sun and its vibrant light disappeared behind the mountain. Satisfied with my images I decided to leave the fox, whose gray fur now vanished seamlessly into the twilight.

◀ A distinctive cross fox poses on a boulder.
▲ *Previous*: A fox pauses in the deep snow while hunting.

I've always thought foxes are at their most beautiful in winter when snow blankets the land and their winter coats are dense and full. In the days following our first major snowstorm on the cusp of fall and winter, I was lucky enough to photograph a fox for quite a while, further cementing my opinion of winter foxes.

While looking for wildlife, I noticed a flash of red across the white landscape. A red fox was prancing across the clearing, its paws falling silently atop the drifts instead of sinking into the deep snow below. Any remaining vegetation had been buried under the fresh snowfall, except the evergreens. The small meadow seemed dull, but the fox brought a fierce color back to the landscape. Intensely alert to its surroundings, the fox glanced my way briefly before returning to the hunt.

Without a breath of wind, the air was hauntingly silent. The fox listened intently for any small sound that would indicate prey under the snow, undoubtedly aware of the intricate world of rodents' tunnels and frozen grasses that remained hidden to me. Ignoring my presence, the fox stalked toward me before pausing. I too remained still, not wanting to ruin the hunt. Our breaths sent freezing clouds into the air. While it waited and listened, a pensive expression on its face, I captured a few images of the fox. Its vibrant red fur contrasted with the dark-green background of pines.

Suddenly the fox sprang upward, kicking up snow. Arching its back, the fox dove headfirst into the snow while its tail wildly swung from side to side for balance. With a few twists and turns, the fox retreated from the snowbank and recomposed itself, shaking the snow from its fur. A vole hung delicately between its jaws; the hunt had been a success.

► A red fox waits patiently for prey during a winter hunt.

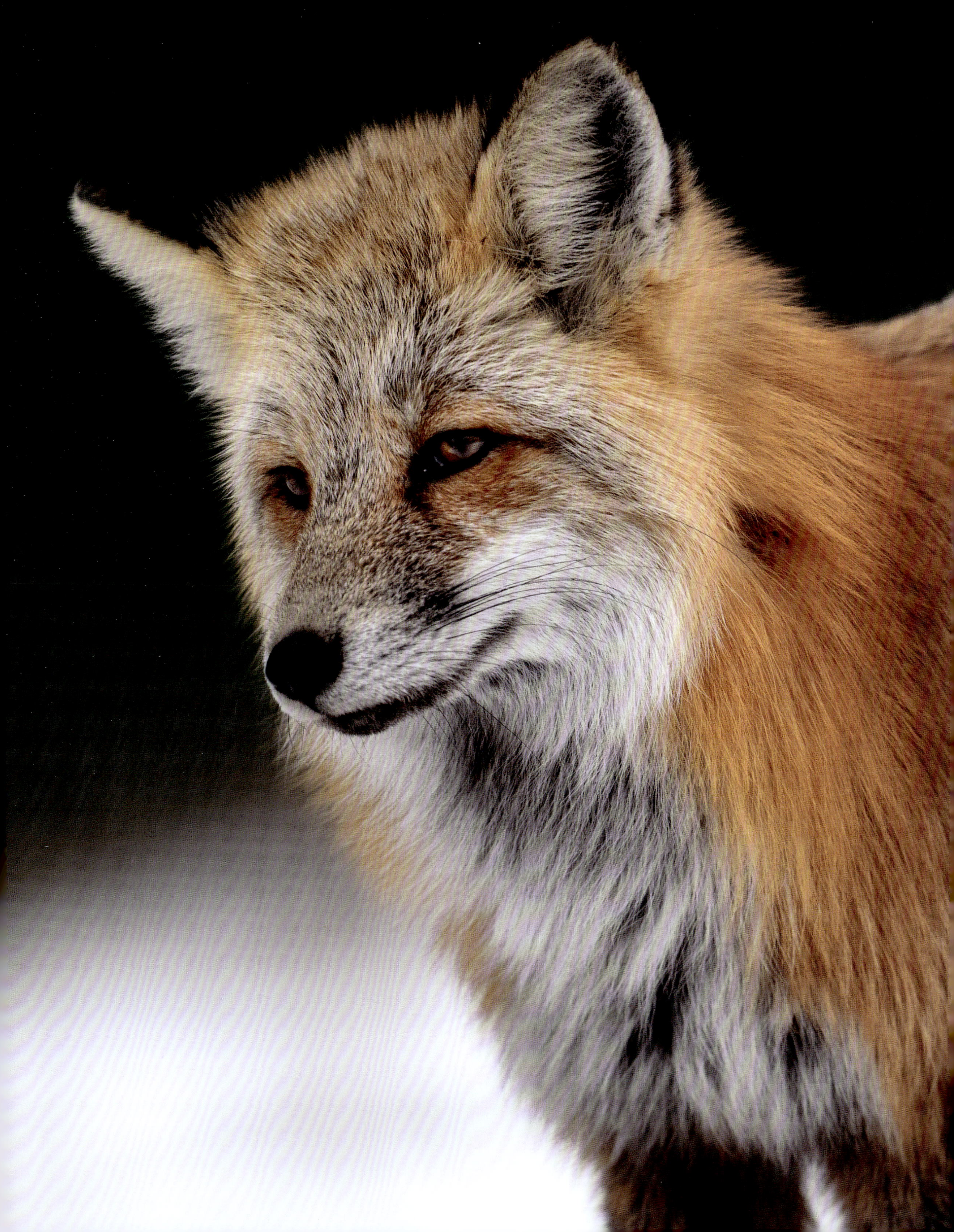

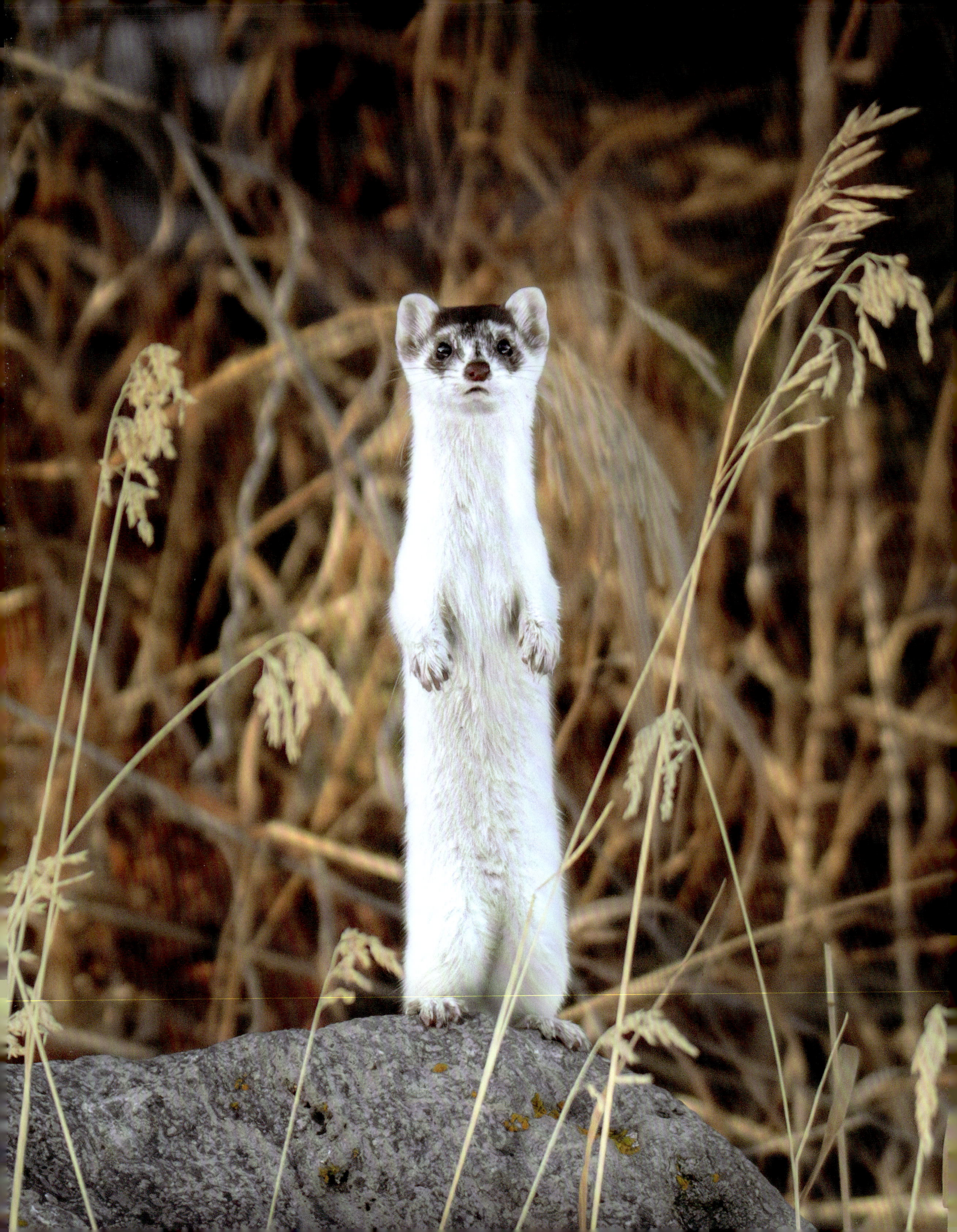

Long-tailed Weasel

Yellowstone is home to eight species within the weasel family, and among the smallest is the long-tailed weasel. Identifiable by their long, narrow bodies with short legs and pointed faces, long-tailed weasels are commonly confused for their cousin the short-tailed weasel. As the name implies, the most notable difference is length of their tail and body size, with long-tailed weasels having tails roughly half as long as their body. They are also more common within Yellowstone compared to short-tailed weasels.

Both long- and short-tailed weasels have a unique adaptation that allows them to stay hidden in any season: their fur changes color. During the summer months, weasels are brown with a yellow-to-white underbelly and a black-tipped tail. Come winter, the weasels retain their black-tipped tails but otherwise become solid white. The color change is triggered by a physical reaction to changes in the amount of daylight, which alters the production of natural pigmentation in their fur. When transitioning from their summer to winter coat, their fur can be sprinkled with lingering patches of color across the face or back before they become completely white.

Though small, weasels are ferocious and skilled hunters preying on voles, pocket gophers, mice, squirrels, rabbits, and even insects and frogs. With incredibly high metabolisms, weasels need to eat about 40 percent of their body weight every day. They are solitary animals except during the breeding season in mid-summer and while raising young. Litters consist of an average of five to seven young that are raised through the summer before dispersing during the fall. Many young weasels won't make it through their first year, but after reaching adulthood weasels can live for five to six years. Threats to weasels include predators like coyotes, badgers, foxes, hawks, and eagles, as well as habitat loss from climate change. As weather patterns shift and the average date of the first snowfall shifts later in the fall, weasels can become especially vulnerable to predators since their white coats stand out against a snowless landscape.

◀ A long-tailed weasel in the middle of its color change before winter.

Weasels are a species that I never intentionally try to photograph. Instead, I leave encounters up to chance. I rarely see the incredibly elusive, fast, and well-camouflaged mammals, and when I do, I often do not even have time to raise my camera before they completely disappear. Occasionally a weasel will prove more curious and remain visible for a few seconds before dashing away. A few seconds is all it takes to capture a handful of photos.

In early winter, following a fresh snowfall, I was in Yellowstone looking for wildlife to photograph in the snow. After an unsuccessful morning, my hopes had started to dwindle—until I saw a white flash across the road. A weasel had just crossed in front of me, clearly visible against the dark asphalt. Immediately jumping out of the car, camera in hand, I scanned the snowy hillside for any signs of it. Movement caught my eye. The weasel had poked its head out of a small hole in the snow. Had it not moved, I would never have found it. The only color against the hill was the weasel's two black eyes and tiny, brown, furiously twitching nose. Its white fur completely concealed it within the winter landscape.

The weasel remained at the edge of its snowy hole for longer than I anticipated, giving me just enough time to photograph it. With evident inquisitiveness, the weasel tilted its head and shook its long, black whiskers in sharp and fidgety movements. It briefly recoiled, its narrow body retreating into the safety of its hole before it gained the nerve to venture into the open once again. Standing amid the snow drifts, the weasel raised its paw. Snow clung between its delicate and nimble toes. An instant later the weasel flipped around, darted up the small hillside, and disappeared into the white of winter. The entire encounter lasted no longer than two minutes—unsurprising for a restless and energetic weasel.

▶ A long-tailed weasel blends in perfectly with the white snow.

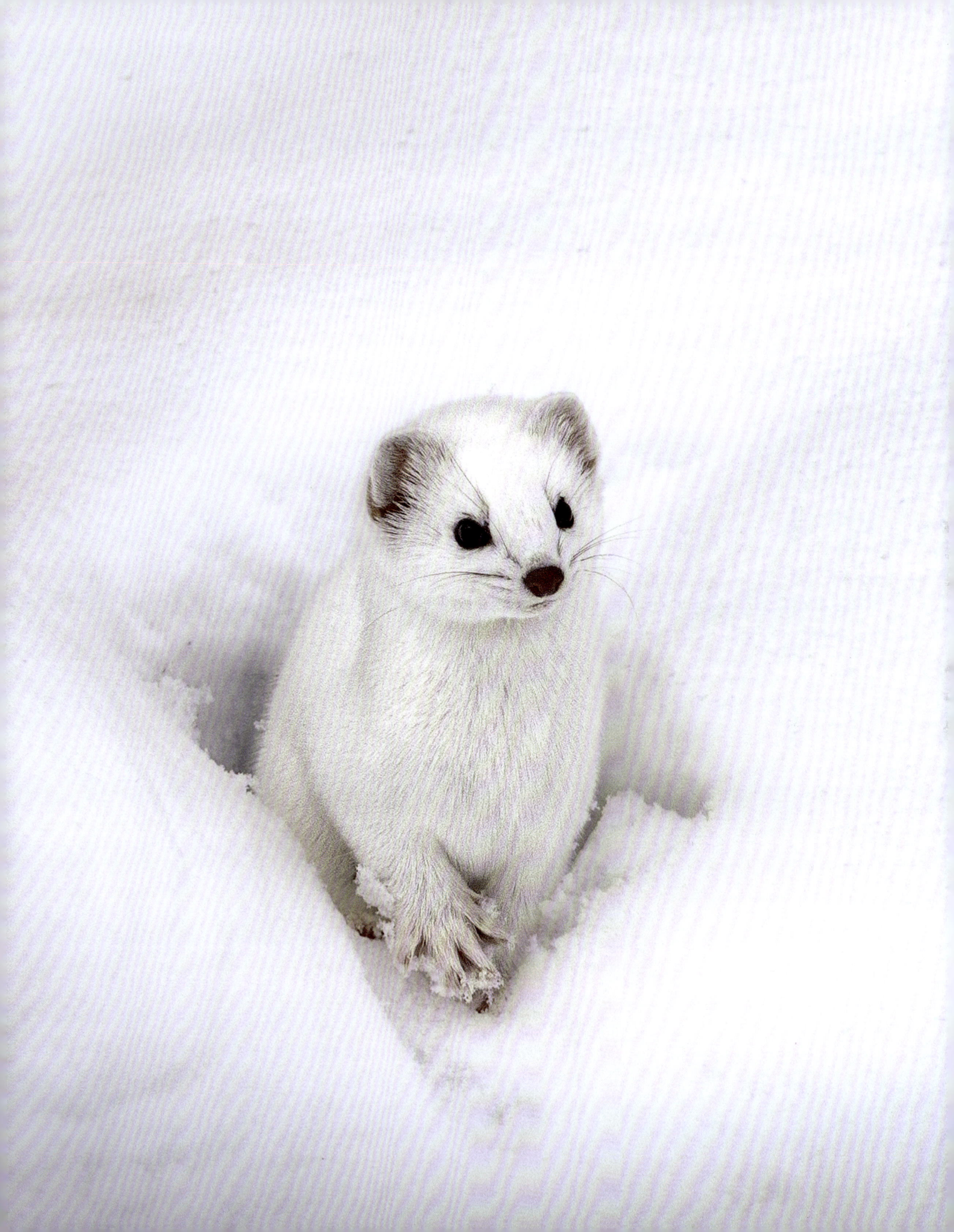

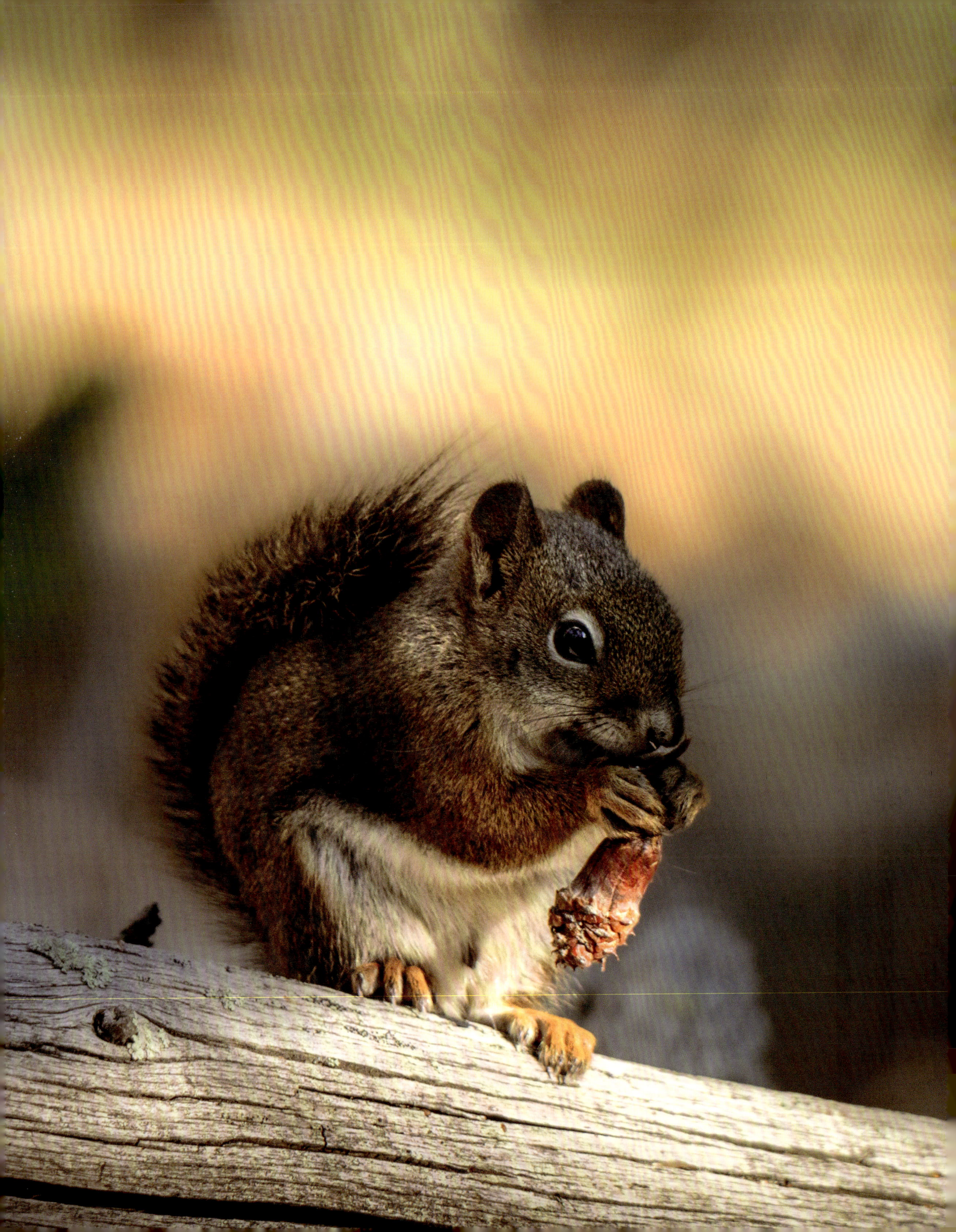

Red Squirrel

Red squirrels are one of the most common animals in Yellowstone, found almost anywhere in pine, spruce, and fir forests including near picnic areas and along hiking trails. With their quick and energetic demeanor, squirrels can often be seen darting across logs, climbing trees, and leaping from branch to branch. A squirrel's large, bushy tail helps it balance while quickly navigating the forest canopy. Red squirrels are not always red but can be grayish-brown to a rusty red color. Often squirrels are heard before they are seen; their loud and long series of chirps rings through the trees, particularly in the fall as they defend their territory from rivals. Squirrels are surprisingly territorial and will fearlessly fight off rivals to protect their food stores.

A red squirrel's diet consists of a wide variety of foods, including seeds, mushrooms, insects, and occasionally even young birds. Squirrels spend much of their time preparing for winter because they do not hibernate. As a result, squirrels must collect and store food for the long season. Pine cones are a vital source of nourishment for red squirrels, and in the fall, they will collect cones and cache them in a midden, a large pile of food often stored loosely at the base of trees. These middens are used year after year and can become massive. Grizzly bears will often seek out middens to obtain pine nuts.

Outside of the mating season and raising young, red squirrels live independently. Males will leave their territory during the mating season in February in search of a female. Squirrels usually give birth to three to seven kits which weigh a quarter of an ounce at birth. The young squirrels stay with their mothers for about ten to twelve weeks until they disperse to find their own territory and start collecting food for the long winter ahead of them. Squirrels are common prey for coyotes, weasels, foxes, badgers, grizzly bears, hawks, eagles, and owls, but their quick and agile ways can help them evade predators.

◀ A red squirrel pauses on a log to eat a pine cone.

Red squirrels are an animal I hear and see often. Their loud and frankly annoying alarm calls usually echo through the otherwise quiet forests and interrupt a peaceful stroll. Despite regularly encountering squirrels, I very rarely photograph them; I'm always looking for a more interesting animal, although I have learned to appreciate squirrels for their own sake.

During the middle of the day in late October, I decided to take a break from looking for wildlife and simply go for a hike. I debated leaving my camera behind, but ultimately decided to bring it just in case. The trail first led me through a large open meadow. I noticed grizzly tracks in the dried mud underfoot, although they were likely several days old. The sun was surprisingly warm for late fall, and I soon paused to take off a layer of clothing. In the distance I could see the forest's edge and quickened my pace. The tall trees welcomed me with the sweet smell of pine and provided a break from the intense midday sun. Near the trail was a large fallen log inviting me to take a rest.

Swinging my heavy pack off my shoulder, I sat down on the ground and leaned against the log. Somewhere behind me a squirrel called, though it soon fell silent. While enjoying the peaceful moments in nature, movement caught my eye: a squirrel leaping from a nearby branch and darting off into the trees. Soon, the squirrel returned with a mouthful of pine cone. I slowly reached for my pack and grabbed my camera, unable to resist photographing the frantic little creature. The squirrel rested atop a stump for a few moments until it jumped onto a tree trunk. It held a single pine cone in its mouth while racing up the tree with ease. Though the squirrel moved quickly, I was able to capture a few images of it peering around the edge of the trunk before it disappeared into upper branches. Relieved I had brought my camera, I placed it back in my pack and continued down the trail.

▶ A red squirrel gathers a pine cone in the forest to prepare for winter.

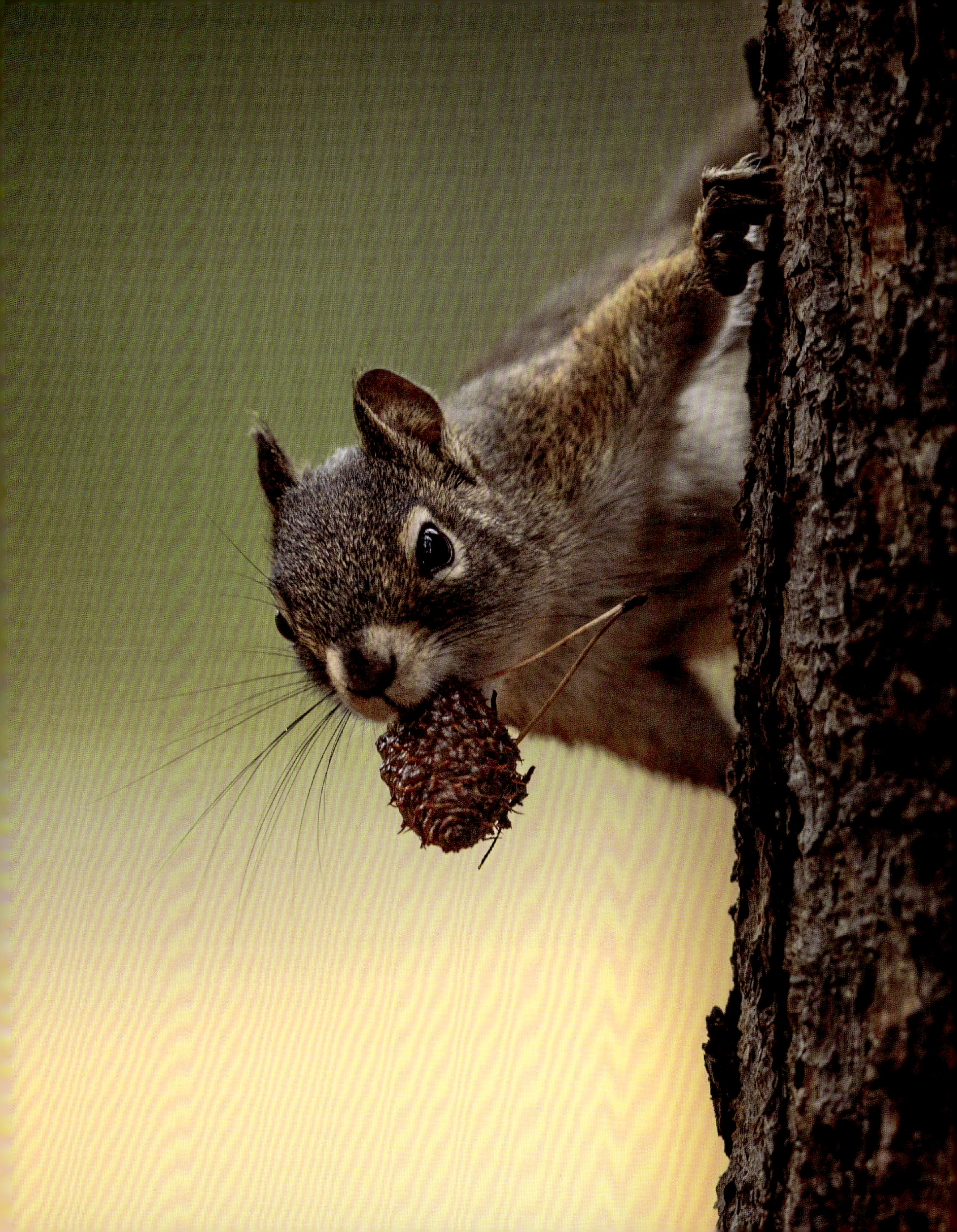

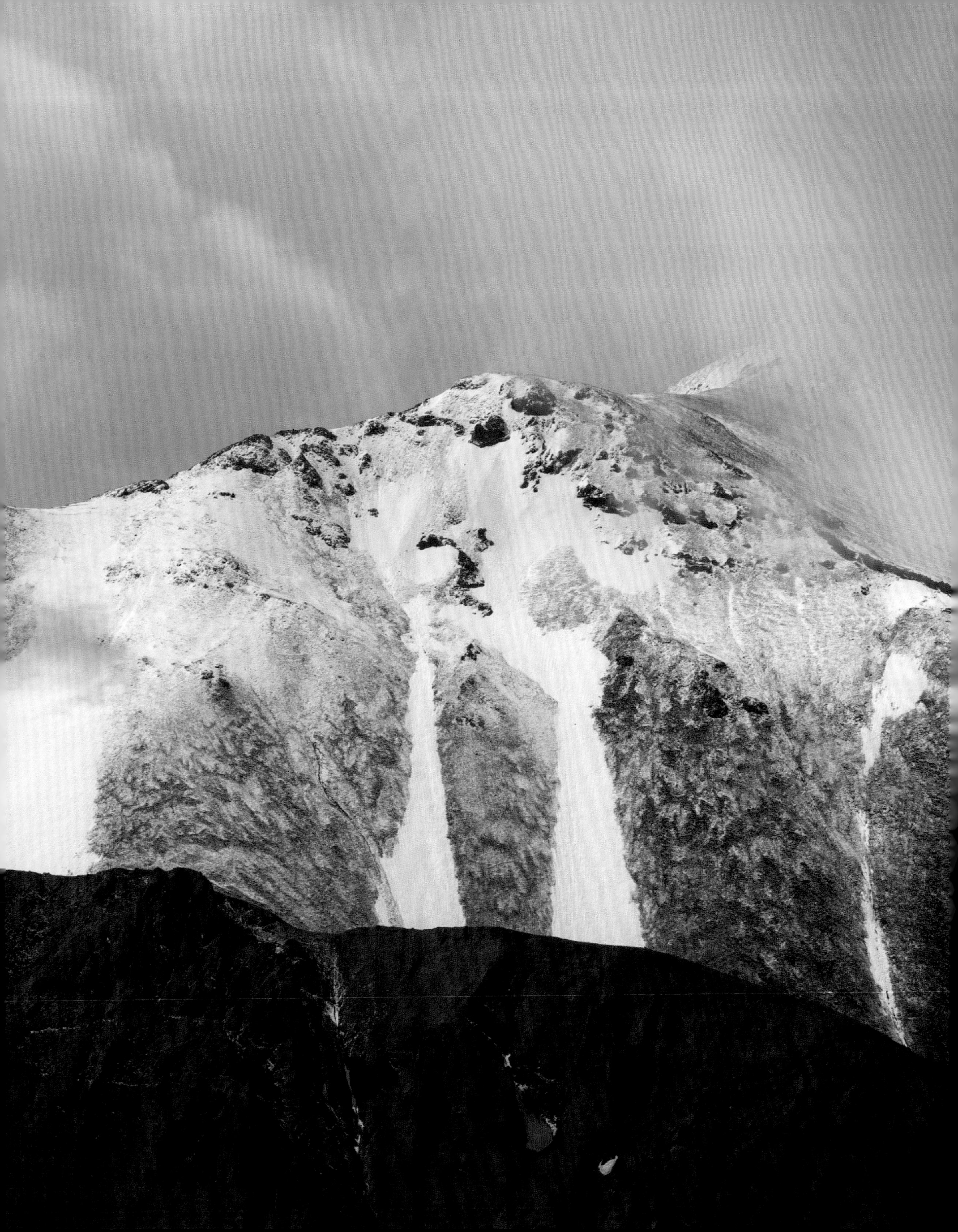

ALPINE REGIONS

The alpine regions may seem like a desolate environment, but the animals here are perfectly adept at surviving even the harshest conditions. These habitats are usually above 9,000 feet (2.7 km) in elevation, where the air is thinner and cooler than in the forests and meadows below. Winter lasts longer here, with snow remaining yearlong in some places. The habitat of the alpine regions begins as the forests thin out and eventually end as you climb above the tree line. The only vegetation above the tree line is small, low-growing plants fed primarily by snowmelt or powerful summer thunderstorms blowing across the peaks. Lichen-covered rocks and boulders dominate the landscape, with steep cliffs and jagged peaks boldly rising toward the sky.

Alpine habitat covers the tops of mountain peaks and ridges, making it a challenging location to explore. However, there are some places in Yellowstone that offer an accessible taste of the alpine regions. The road up Sylvan Pass winds through the forest while gaining elevation to 8,500 feet (2.6 km), where forest and alpine environment collide. Similarly, Dunraven Pass follows the slope of Mount Washburn, providing unique viewpoints and lookouts of the surrounding areas. Outside of Yellowstone's Northeast Entrance is the Beartooth Highway, which rises over 10,000 feet (3 km) in elevation and provides breathtaking panoramic views of the Absaroka Range in both Wyoming and Montana.

While the alpine regions are harsh, they are one of the most beautiful environments to experience. Towering peaks provide a vantage from which to view the forests, meadows, and plains below. The species that thrive in the alpine regions each have their own method of survival, ranging from hibernating for months at a time, like marmots, or bravely enduring the wild winter weather, like bighorn sheep. Welcome to the alpine regions of Yellowstone.

◀ A snowy alpine peak in the Greater Yellowstone Ecosystem.

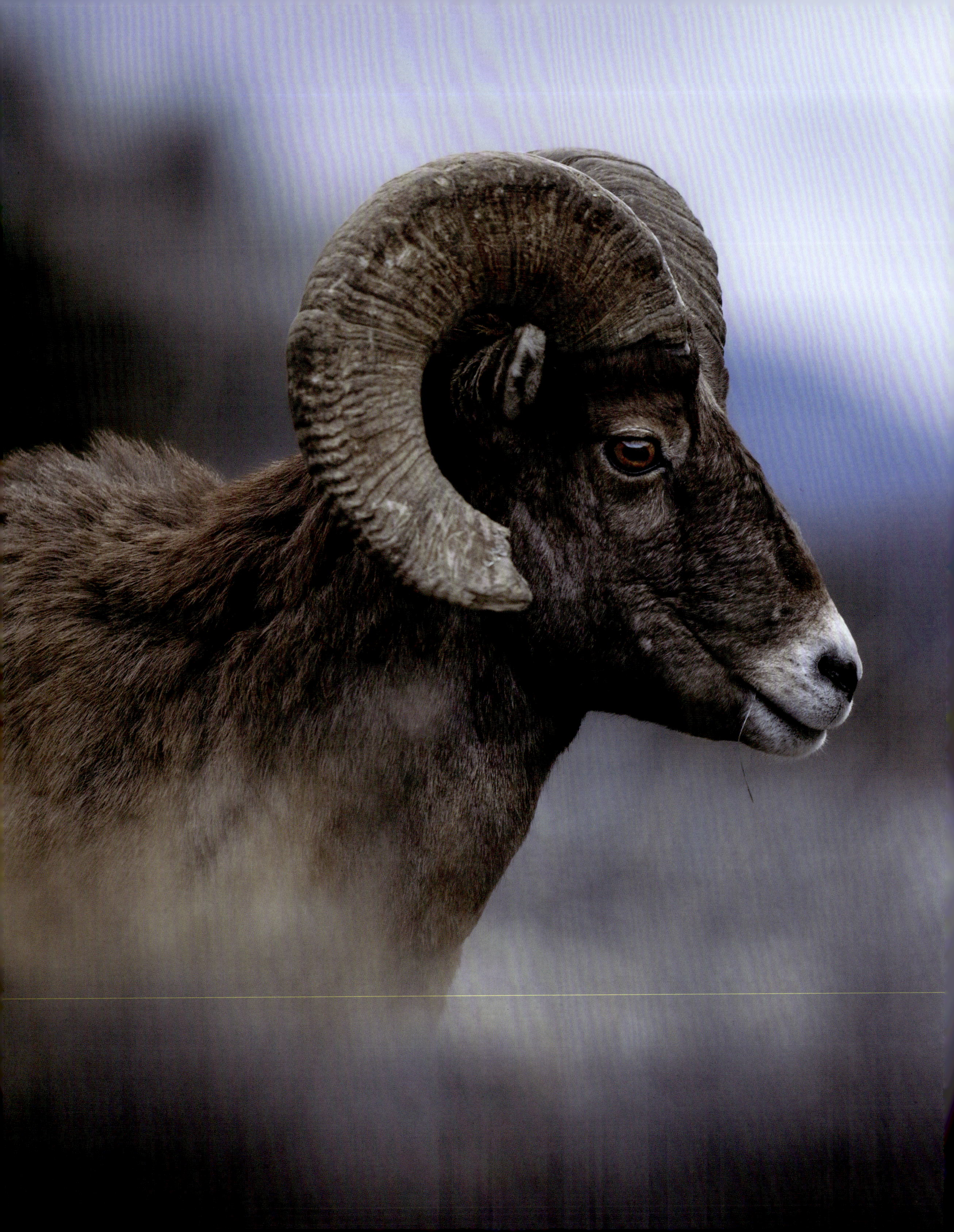

Bighorn Sheep

The aptly named bighorn sheep is an impressive species found on rocky cliffs and steep terrain in high elevation areas of Yellowstone. In the summer months bighorn sheep usually remain high in the mountains, but can be seen near Gardner Canyon, Sylvan Pass, Dunraven Pass, or on cliffs near Tower Fall. When winter arrives, bighorns migrate to lower areas to find vegetation like grasses and shrubs.

Bighorn sheep are grayish-brown in color, with white rumps and muzzles. Their wide-set eyes provide a wide field of vision that allows them to watch for predators, including mountain lions and wolves. Bighorns often scale cliffs to avoid danger, using specially adapted hooves to nimbly climb narrow edges and steep inclines. In addition to predators, diseases like pneumonia spread by domesticated sheep are a major threat to bighorn sheep. Their average lifespan is twelve to fourteen years.

Males, called rams, have large, curved horns that can weigh up to 40 pounds (18 kg). The horns consist of a bony core sheathed in keratin, the same material that makes up our fingernails, and continue growing throughout a ram's life. Horns are important in establishing dominance, with rams violently butting heads during the mating season in the late fall. Rams will charge toward one another before rearing up at the last minute and butting heads until one submits. Though the force of the impact is over sixty times that necessary to crack a human skull, rams have two layers of bone and thick fat above their brain that act as shock absorption to protect against brain damage.

Females, called ewes, also have horns, though they are thinner and smaller. Lambs are born in the spring and are soon able to climb the rocky terrain of their home. Young rams will leave their mothers after about two years, while ewes will usually stay with their herd for life. Ewes, lambs, and young sheep live in herds throughout the summer, while rams join in bachelor herds. Rams and ewes typically only come together during the mating season in the early winter.

◀ A bighorn sheep ram in profile.

Bighorn sheep survive in unforgiving habitats, living on cliff faces and jagged mountain edges. They are a species I usually only photograph in the winter months, when snow in the alpine mountains sends them to the lower meadows where winter's control is lessened. Rams have come to signify winter for me; their return to lower elevation means winter is near.

Late in the fall, with the first snow dusting the landscape, I spotted a group of rams. They were right on time for the return of winter. They meticulously walked across a steep, rocky hillside, never stumbling despite the snow and ice. Hoping to capture a few photographs before dark, I worked my way up the slope in the direction the rams were slowly headed. While the sure-footed rams gracefully navigated the uneven terrain, I was scrambling for solid footing and using my hands for extra balance. Small rocks went sliding down the hill behind me.

Once I decided I had climbed far enough, I sat down awkwardly, bracing myself against a larger rock to avoid slipping down the slope. The rams hadn't moved much, content with the small patch of grass they had found. I scanned the herd, locating the largest ram standing a few steps behind the rest. He was the one I wanted to photograph. The setting sun cast a glow across the opposite mountainside, turning it a beautiful gradient from blue to orange. Given the unique and picturesque background, I willed the rams to lift their heads.

Eventually the rams began walking farther up the hillside—all but the largest. He remained, staring steadily across the surrounding mountains from his rocky perch. I watched as he looked first toward the far slope where the sun still illuminated the peak, then to the river and meadow far below. Finally, he turned and looked directly at me, his golden eyes matching the golden rays of the evening sun, before he too climbed the hillside and eventually disappeared into the forest above. I stayed, staring across the mountains just as the ram had done and watching as the last light faded to the blue shadows of dusk.

▶ A bighorn sheep ram surveys the mountain range around him.

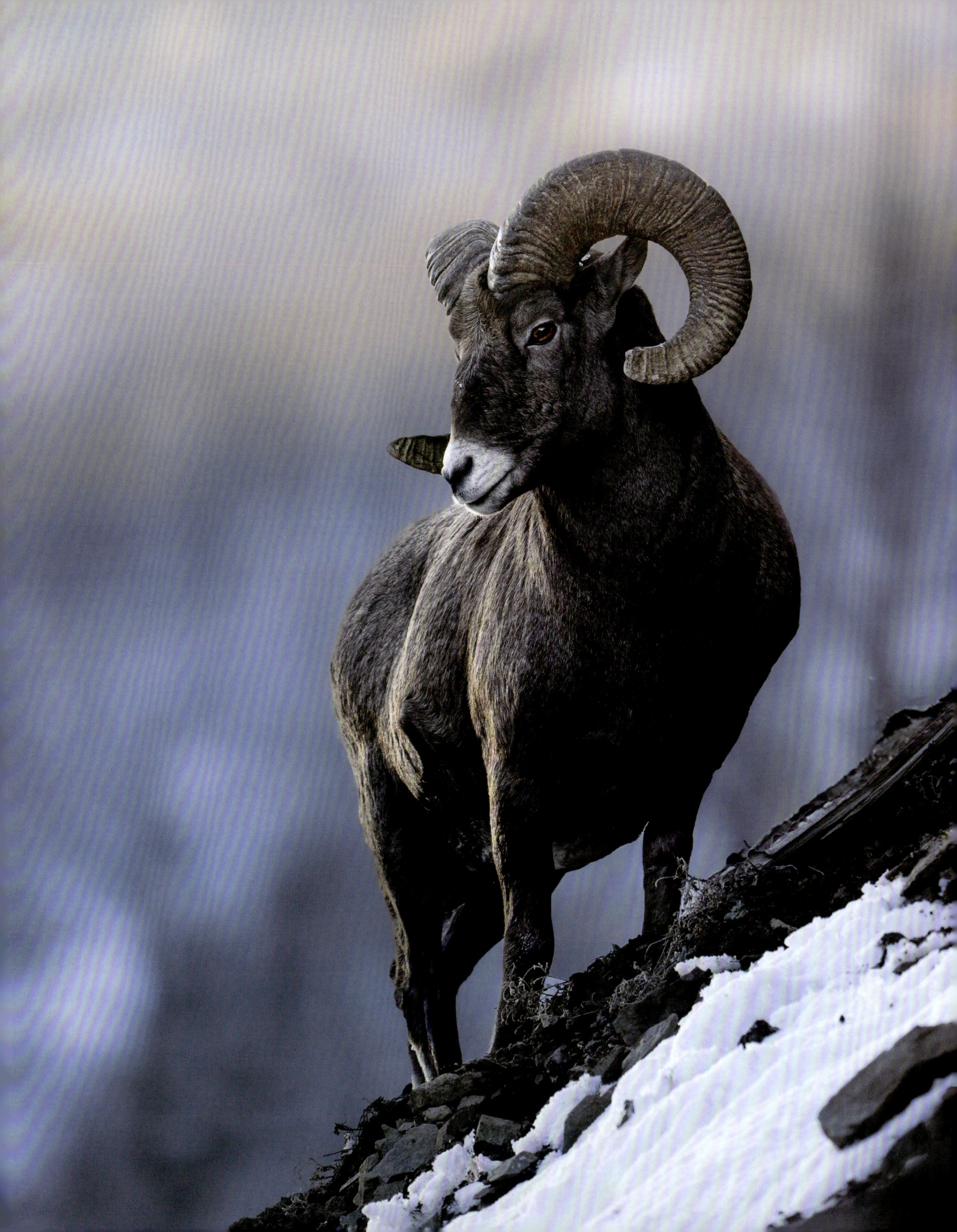

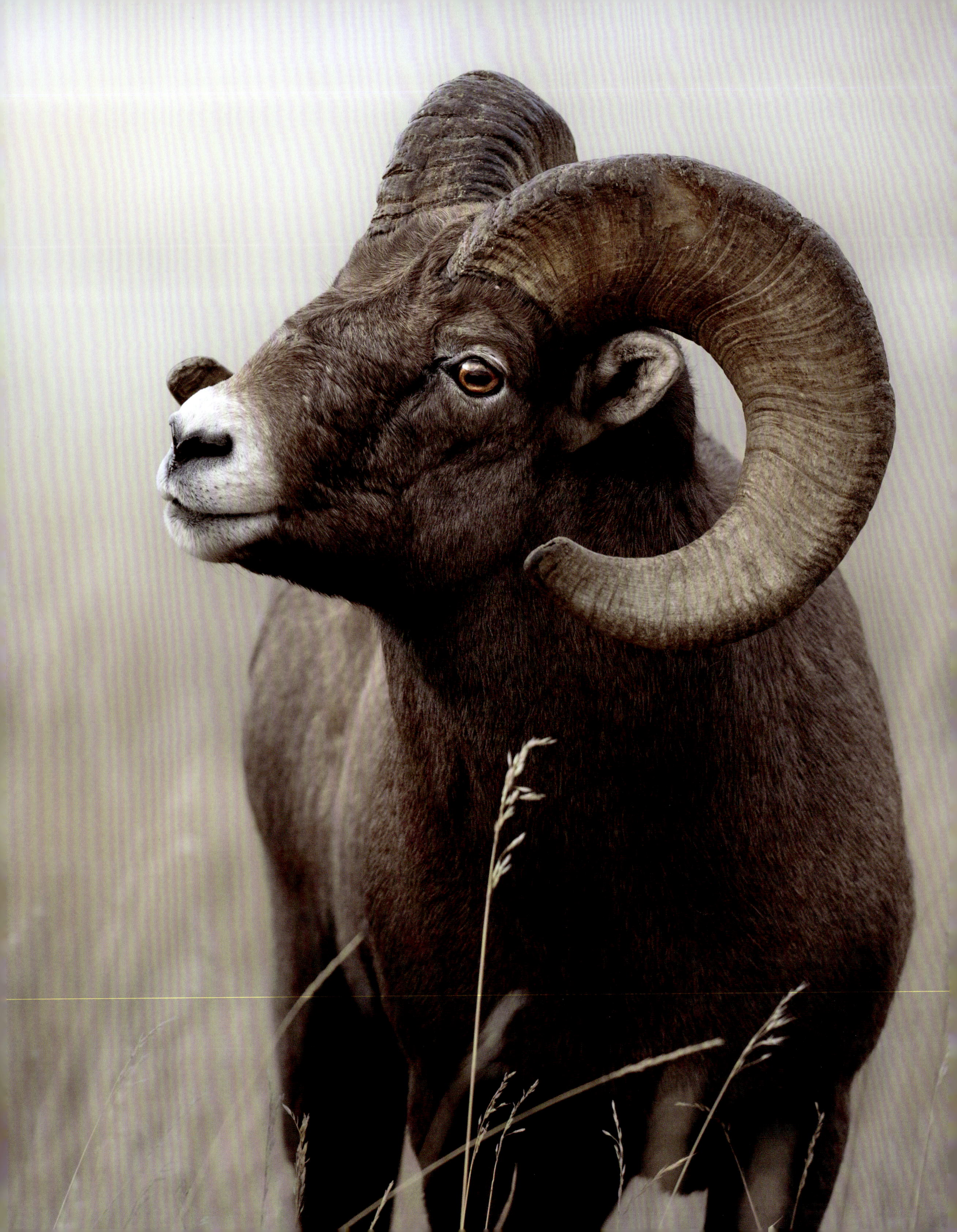

Bighorn sheep rams, especially mature rams, are imposing and move with wild confidence during the rut. They are headstrong, strong-willed, and stubborn. Fully consumed by their desire to mate, rams challenge and chase one another before butting heads in an ancient duel. By the end of the rut, rams have run themselves ragged, going to any lengths necessary to establish dominance over other rams.

While photographing a herd of nearly a dozen ewes and a solitary ram, a bachelor herd emerged from the trees and sauntered into the meadow with bold arrogance. The dominant ram immediately detected the challengers' presence and sent an intimidating stare in their direction while anxiously pacing and awaiting their move. The bachelor herd moved toward the ewes, vying for mating rights. But with his head low and cocked to the side in a threatening stance, the dominant ram was able to intimidate three young rams into backing down with just a glare, leaving only one mature ram as a serious contender.

The two rams circled one another, each waiting for the other to act. The defending champion lowered his head once again and charged the challenger, who stepped out of the way and made a counterattack. With a deafening bang easily mistakable for a gunshot, the rams collided, their muscles rippling from the force of impact. With each too stubborn to surrender, the fight continued while the ewes grazed, clearly unimpressed.

After relentless chasing and butting, the challenger finally backed off and slowly retreated. The dominant ram, once again proving his strength, stared boldly after his defeated opponent, his head held high with regal pride. Giving a snort and a shake, he strolled confidently back to his herd of ewes to recover in peace before the next inevitable challenge.

◀ A dominant ram prepares to fend off challengers during the mating season.

Bighorn sheep are the species I spend the most time with during the late fall and winter. I love how their rugged appearance suits their mountain home. During the middle of winter, I went hiking with hopes of finding sheep, but mostly to enjoy the hush that falls across the landscape at this time of year. Most birds had migrated to warmer skies and by now bears were resting in deep slumber in their dens. Before long I entered a large meadow at the foot of a rocky cliffside. Lacking snow, the meadow appeared mostly colorless except for the last golden grasses of autumn and the ever blue-green sage. At the far end of the meadow lay a herd of sheep, their dull tan color blending with their surroundings.

Noticing a few lambs among the herd, I walked toward a large log and sat down, determined to wait for an opportunity to photograph them. Born in the high mountains during the warm days of spring, bighorn sheep lambs are rarely seen until late fall when they migrate to lower elevation meadows alongside their herds. As the evening sun crept closer to the horizon, the sheep finally rose.

They slowly moved toward me while grazing, and I scanned the herd to look for a potential subject—ideally an individual against a clean background. Noticing a lamb and ewe near the edge of the herd, I shifted my focus to them. When the two were nearly facing my direction, a ram approached them boldly from behind. I assumed my chance at a shot had been ruined. He soon relaxed and placed his head on the ewe's back, resting it there for several seconds. Together, the ram, ewe, and lamb calmy stood among the sagebrush as if posed for a family portrait. They remained for longer than I'd anticipated, but soon turned and vanished as a herd up the rocky hillside.

► A bighorn sheep ram, ewe, and lamb pose together in a winter meadow.

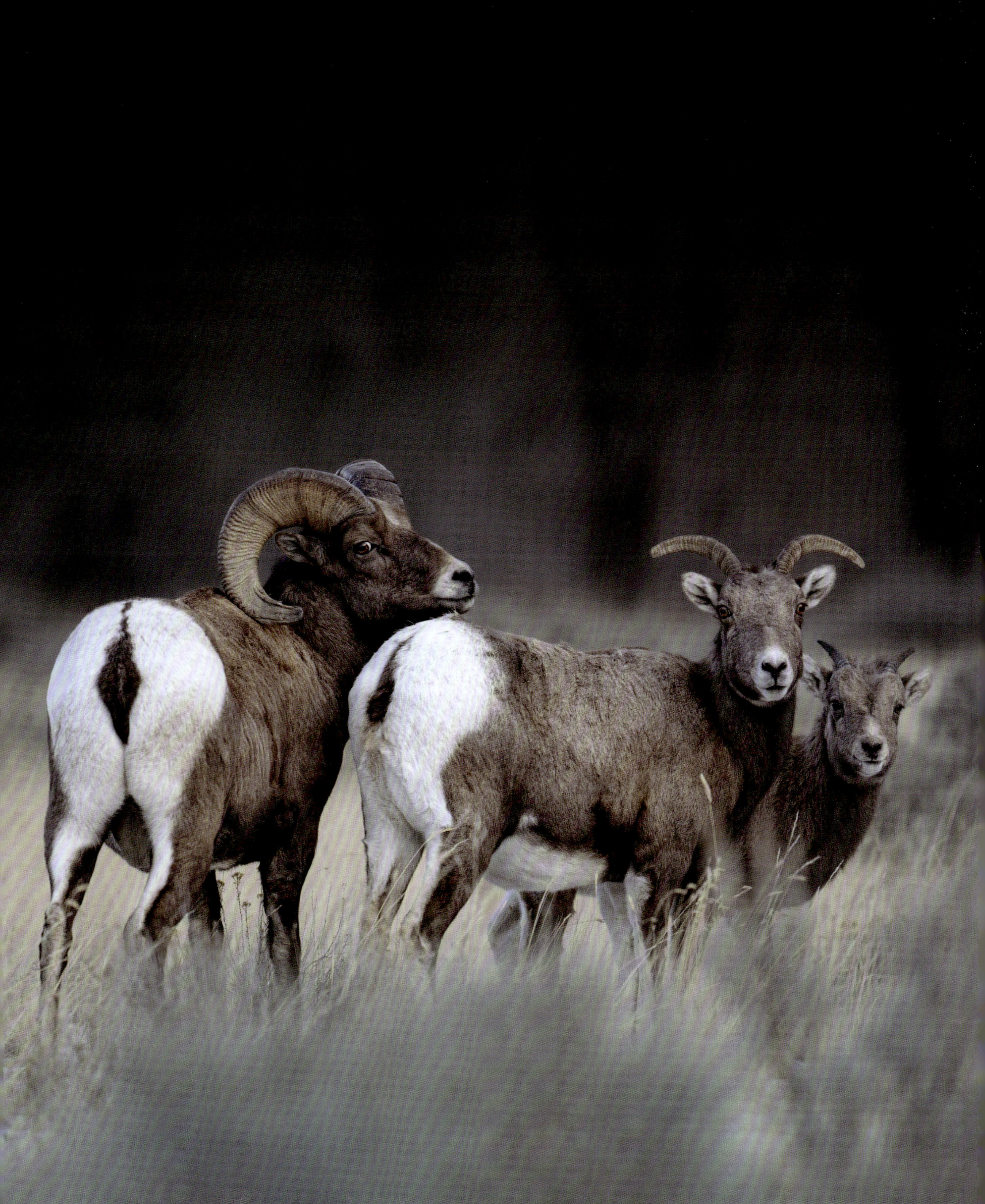

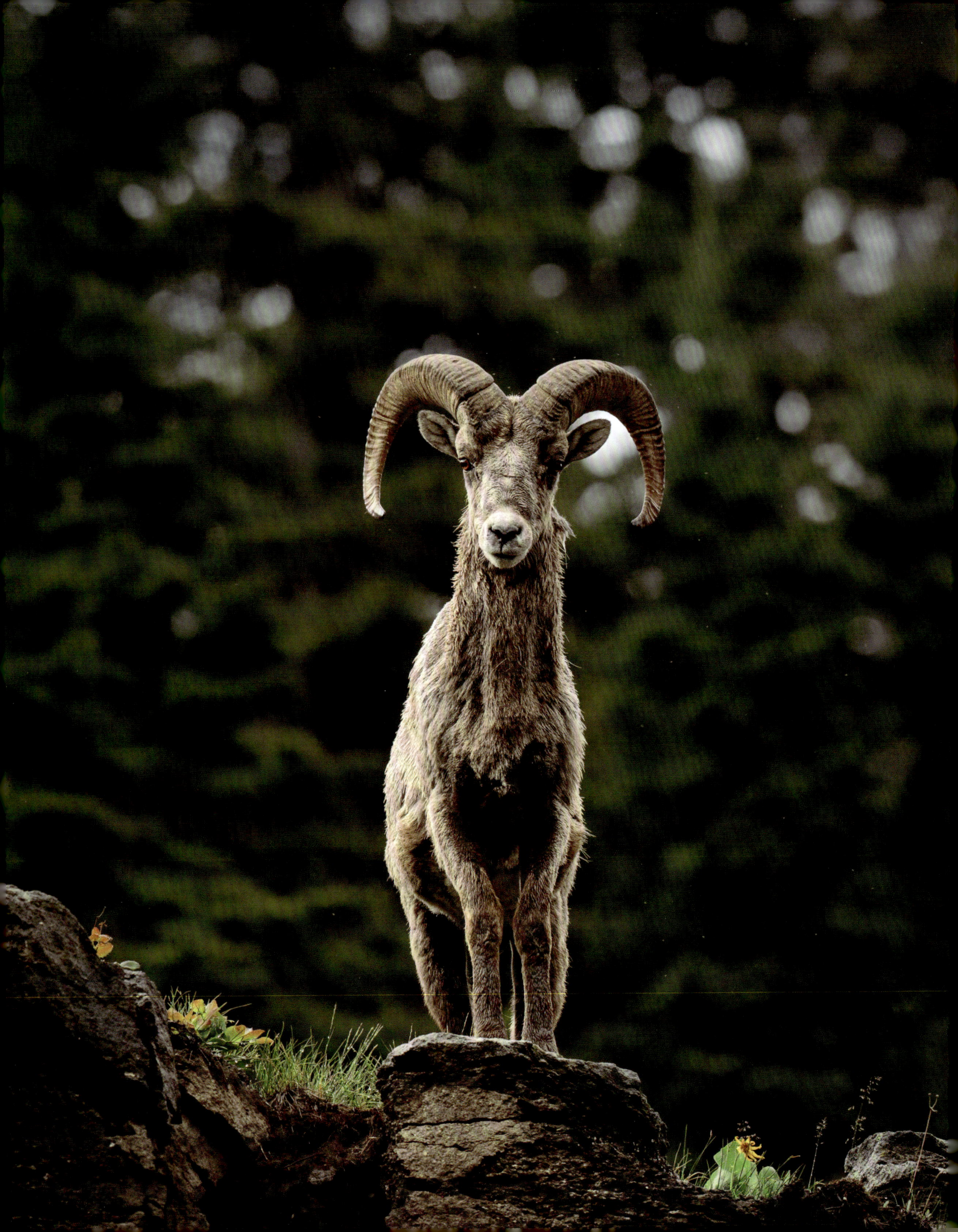

Although rams spend the late fall and early winter challenging each other in violent duels, they unite to form peaceful bachelor herds in the summer months. Together they stay high above the valleys and lowlands that serve as their winter homes and instead roam the rugged cliffs and mountain peaks as a refuge from the heat.

While driving down a mountain pass on my way home after an eventful day, I noticed movement across the top of the cliffside above the road. Pulling over, I scanned the cliff, where I soon spotted the very top of a curved horn. After moving up and down the road trying to find a clear view between the jagged cliffs and boulders, I finally positioned myself at an angle where I could barely see the head and back of a ram and began taking photos.

With a few bold steps, the ram stopped at the very edge of the overhang. Curiously looking below, he remained for quite some time, the pine forest providing a beautiful green background while vivid yellow wildflowers bloomed nearby. His ragged fur was patchy from shedding the remnants of a winter coat, and the mosquitos were adamantly circling him, clearly visible in large swarms even from a distance.

From his vantage point he could undoubtedly see the meadow far below, cut in half by the winding river and eventually giving way to the lodgepole forests and cliffs of the neighboring peaks. Perhaps every inch of the landscape was as familiar to him as the slope he now stood on, a home through the various seasons. I watched him watching the view and felt a sense of jealousy for his intimate knowledge of the mountains—knowledge I will never have the privilege of possessing regardless of how hard I try.

◀ A bighorn sheep ram balances on a cliff edge in summer.

Mountain Goat

Mountain goats, though an iconic species of the northern Rocky Mountains, are not native to the Yellowstone Ecosystem. Instead, they were introduced in the Absaroka Mountains during the 1940s and had established a population within the borders of Yellowstone National Park by the 1990s. Today, roughly two hundred to three hundred goats roam the alpine mountains of Yellowstone and the surrounding areas, where they overlap with bighorn sheep populations. This cohabitation has led to concerns about competition and the spread of diseases such as pneumonia between species. Mountain goats can be seen from afar on peaks such as Barronette Peak but are most commonly observed in the Beartooth Mountains outside of Yellowstone's Northeast Entrance.

Mountain goats have several adaptations that help them navigate their rugged home, including cloven hooves with soft inner pads that allow them to grip rock. Since they remain in the alpine mountains all year without migrating to lower elevations, mountain goats have long white fur to keep them well insulated before they shed for the summer around late June. Goats feed on a variety of vegetation, including flowers, grasses, sedges, moss, and lichen.

Male goats are known as billies while females are called nannies, and they both have characteristic black, curved horns. Billies tend to average around 275 pounds (124.7 kg), though they can weigh over 300 pounds (136 kg), while nannies are smaller, averaging around 175 pounds (79.3 kg). Though their rough and steep habitat provides some protection from predators like bears and mountain lions, mountain goats have been documented attacking and fending off grizzly bears using their horns.

Billies also use their horns during the breeding season to fight one another for breeding rights. Breeding occurs in the late fall, with kids born in late May or early June. Nannies will form nursery herds to raise offspring, usually only having one kid at a time. Mountain goats can live up to fifteen years, with risks like starvation in winter, avalanches, falls from cliffs, and predators all posing threats. Though their home is certainly hostile and harsh, mountain goats have found a way to thrive.

► A mountain goat poised on a rocky alpine cliff.

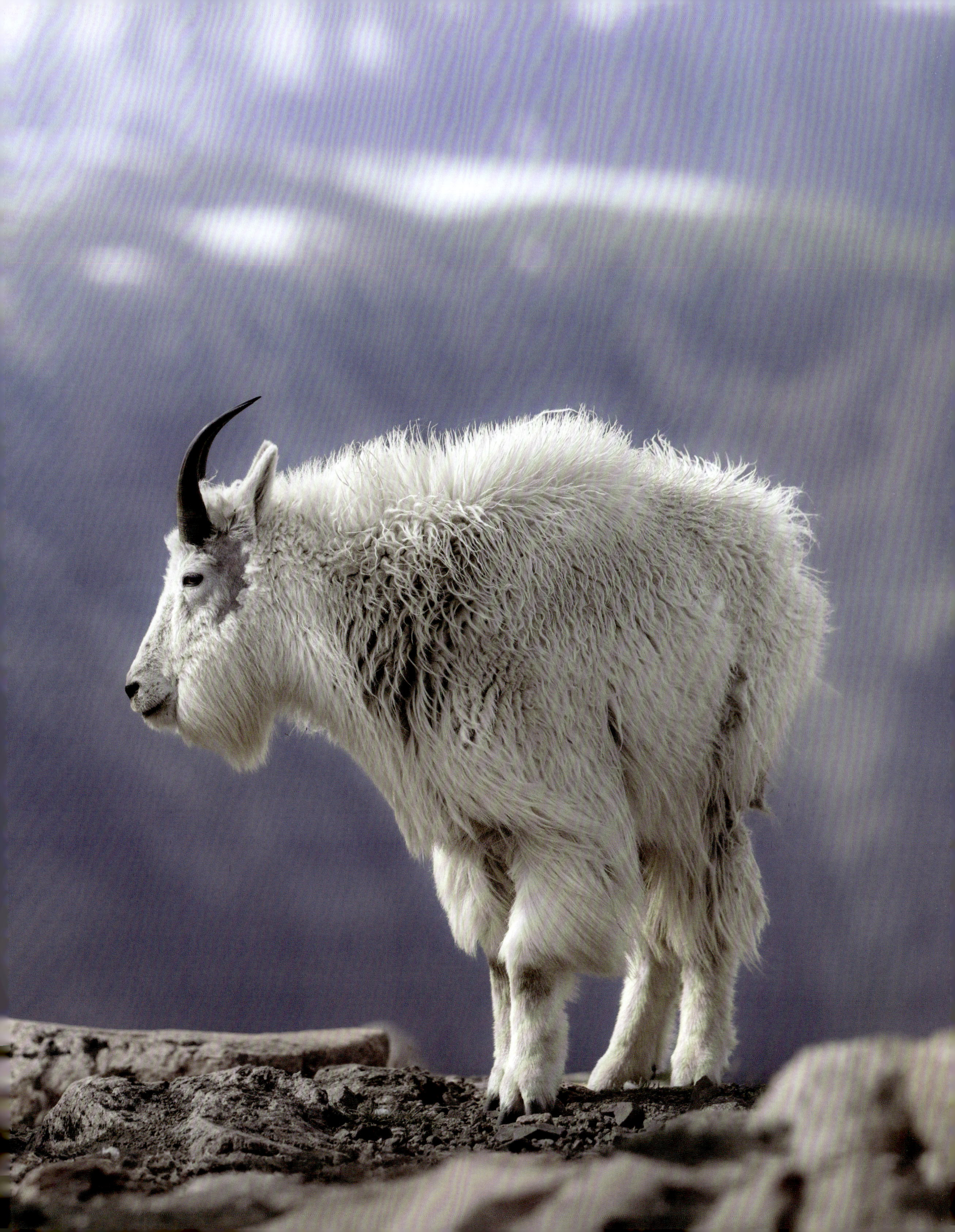

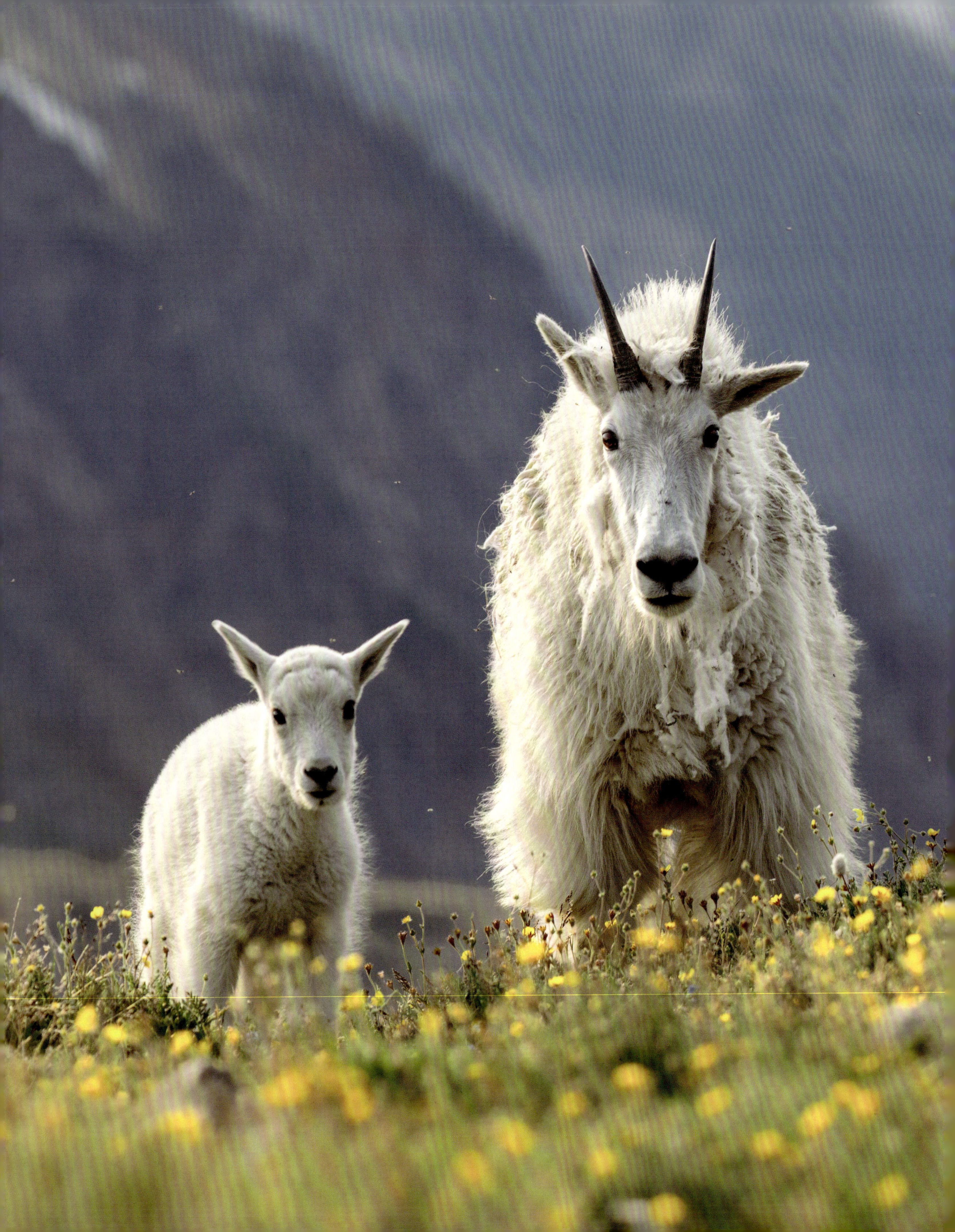

Mountain goats are among my favorite species to photograph. I first fell in love with them on a summer day in July, when the alpine environment provided a retreat from the heat of lower elevations. A cool breeze blew, following the contours of the mountainsides over cliffs and meadows alike. While admiring the view from a scenic overlook, I noticed two fluffy white shapes on the slope below me; it was a mountain goat nanny with a kid. I immediately grabbed my camera and started traversing the steep hillside toward the pair.

Moving slowly along a curved path to avoid approaching them head-on, I carefully watched the goats' body language for any signs of stress. After noticing a large boulder slightly uphill from the goats, likely dropped there at the end of the last Ice Age by receding glaciers, I kneeled behind it to give the goats their space and appear as nonthreatening as possible. Raising my camera, I began photographing the two while they calmly grazed.

Vibrant yellow wildflowers fed by the snowmelt bloomed across the entire mountainside, contrasting with the subtle blue of distant mountains across the valley floor. The nanny continued to graze while the kid playfully frolicked through the flowers and occasionally chased butterflies, though it never ventured far from mom's side. Golden rays of sunlight filtered through the light cloud cover, illuminating the goats' fur and turning the flowers even more colorful. Suddenly, a loud chirp sounded behind me: the annoying alarm call from a marmot that grabbed not only my attention but the goats'. Both mother and kid raised their heads, looking toward me and the call. For a moment, the two were posed perfectly among the yellow flowers, backdropped by the never-ending mountains of their alpine home. The nanny resumed grazing seconds later, while the kid was already once again bouncing across the slope with wild energy. Still in awe of the beautiful scene, I leaned against the boulder and lowered my camera, deciding instead to simply enjoy the moment.

◀ A nanny and kid mountain goat graze on a flower-covered mountain slope in July.

Winter doesn't have a clear end in the alpine regions; it lingers even into summer months, with some snow patches never surrendering. Mountain goats spend much of the summer at the cusp of seasons, their long winter fur remaining well into July, even as they thrive on the vibrant vegetation fed by snowmelt.

While photographing a group of nannies and kids as they traversed the treacherous cliffsides across from the slope I sat on, I hadn't noticed a lone billy slowly working his way down the green hillside behind me. He moved steadily yet unhurriedly, his head swinging from side to side while grazing through the variety of low-lying, hardy plants that flourish in the tough and rocky terrain. With the other group of goats having disappeared completely down the sheer cliff face, I shifted my focus to the billy, deciding to wait and hopefully photograph him as he moved nearer.

Soon, however, the billy disappeared too, behind a small rise that blocked my view. Assuming he was still happily grazing just on the other side, I didn't dare move. A few moments later, the billy reappeared. The goat's head was now held high, his ears alert as he climbed to the top of the rise with even and determined steps. He knew I was there. His long, wispy fur moved gently with the soft breeze, which pulled several clumps loose and carried them away across the alpine tundra before they snagged on a rock. His warm brown eyes stared severely into mine as he continued down the slope. He never broke eye contact until he had sufficiently passed me, as if telling me this was his mountain. Taking his message, I finally stood and began the trek back uphill, the billy watching as I left before he too turned and continued on his way.

▶ A billy goat, just starting to shed his long winter coat, traverses a cliffside in summer.

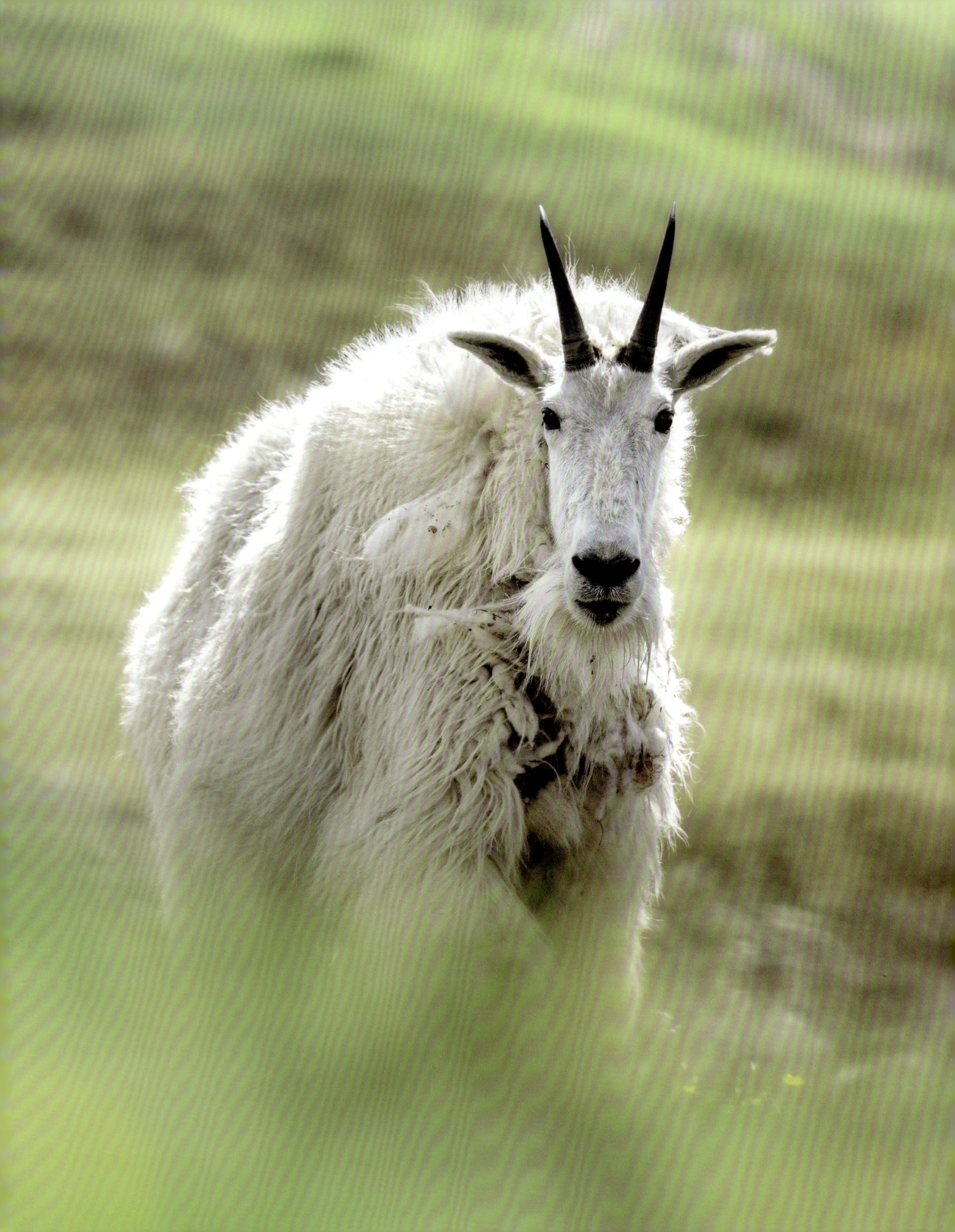

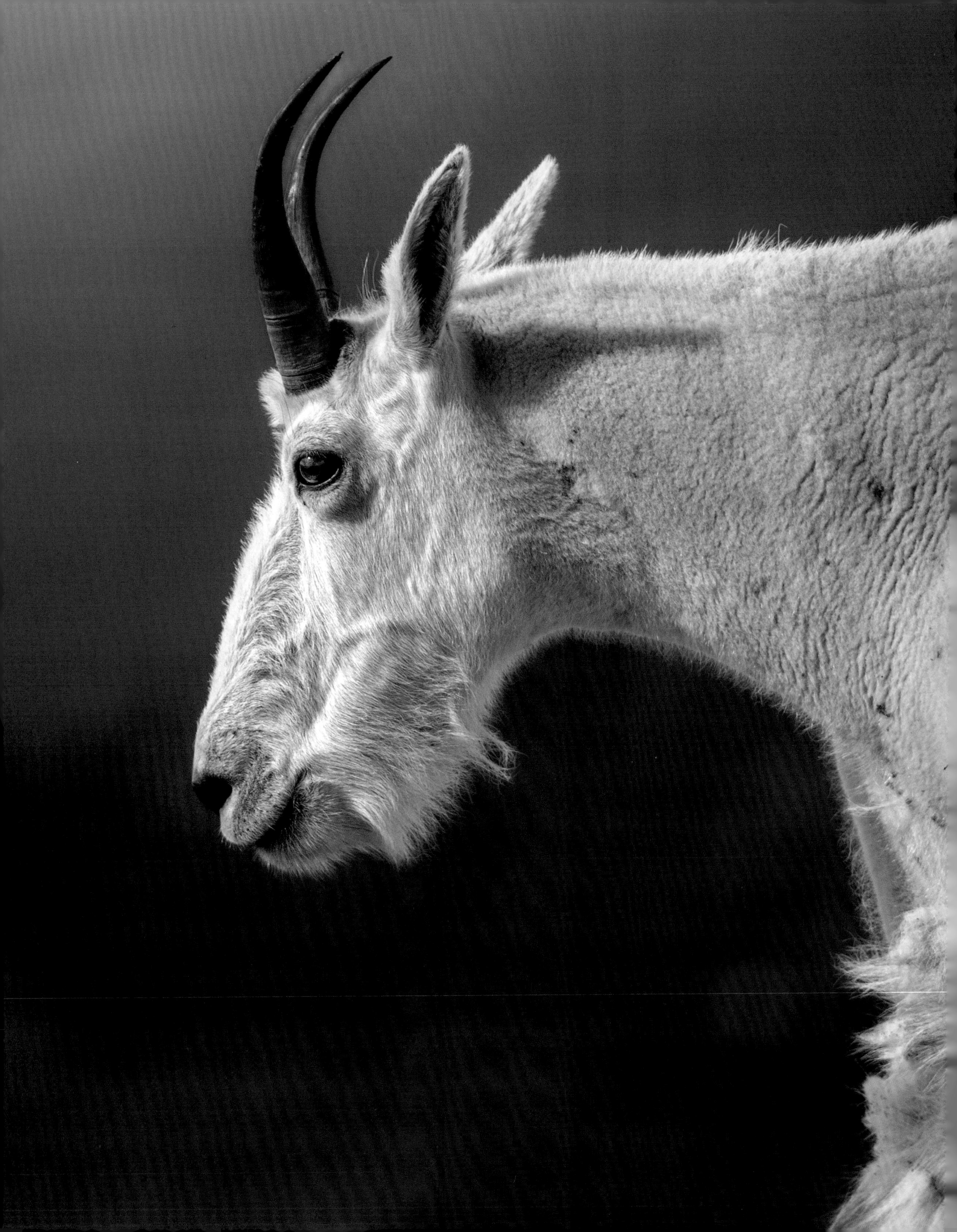

Mountain goats seem to enjoy the relief the short summer in the alpine regions brings, especially when their wooly winter coats are shed, leaving them with a short and sleek appearance.

In July I drove up the familiar and brutally windy road into the Beartooth Mountains during an exceptionally hot day. With my window rolled down I could feel the temperature gradually dropping as I drove higher up the mountain, the trees eventually thinning out and giving way to the alpine tundra. I stopped and hiked to the edge of an overhang to scan the green meadows for any white dots, but I didn't find any goats. I sat down with my back against a nearby rock to relax and enjoy the view instead.

The mountains spanned in all directions with jagged crags and narrow ridgelines adding a wild ruggedness to the view. Snow lingered atop most of the peaks, while the alpine lakes in the ravines far below were nearly completely thawed, exposing the intense blue water beneath. Though the tundra meadows were green, when looking across the distant mountains they all faded to infinite shades of blue.

The midafternoon sun was intense as it warmed my back, nearly soothing me to sleep—at least until I heard rocks shift on the cliff below. Suddenly a goat crested the steep ledge with grace and ease. It briefly stared at me, a surprised and whimsical expression on its face, before walking past me along the cliff edge. With its winter coat gone, the goat had a smooth appearance. Its thin black horns and ears cast shadows across its neck while its eyes reflected the summer sunshine. The endless slate-blue mountain peaks provided a gorgeous backdrop for the summer goat as it hurried on, clearly on the way to graze the lush alpine tundra of summer while it lasted.

◀ A mountain goat with a sleek summer coat.

Of any species I have photographed, mountain goats without a doubt inhabit the most treacherous terrain. Often I am left scrambling up steep slopes, standing atop cliffsides, and out of breath from walking on rocks while trying to photograph goats; however, they are also one of the most rewarding species to photograph.

Shortly after sunrise following a night of solo camping in the alpine mountains, I found a group of roughly a dozen mountain goats a good distance away from where I stood while scanning the slopes below. I quickly planned a route that would take me parallel to the steep cliffside and put me in the perfect location if the goats decided to climb down the cliff. After hiking down the hill I sat down at the cliff's edge to catch my breath, just in time to watch the goats slowly leave their green meadow and walk toward the precipice. In a single file line, the goats stepped onto the rugged granite cliff and disappeared down the other side of a ridge.

A yearling goat brought up the rear, lagging slightly behind the rest of the herd. With an energetic leap the young goat confidently landed atop a lichen-covered boulder, its nimble hooves providing an excellent grip on the rough rock face. Peering beyond its perch, the goat watched as the herd continued downhill. The occasional sound of pebbles cascading down the mountain revealed the goats' location. For a few minutes the young goat stood atop the ridge, the first rays of the morning sun illuminating its white fur in stark contrast to the surrounding shadowy blue cliffs. After what seemed like a moment of peaceful admiration for its mountain home, the young goat leaped from the boulder and disappeared. A soft clatter echoed up the ridge—clearly the result of the goat kicking small rocks down the mountain as it descended to rejoin the herd in the golden light of sunrise.

► A young mountain goat descends a daunting cliff face.

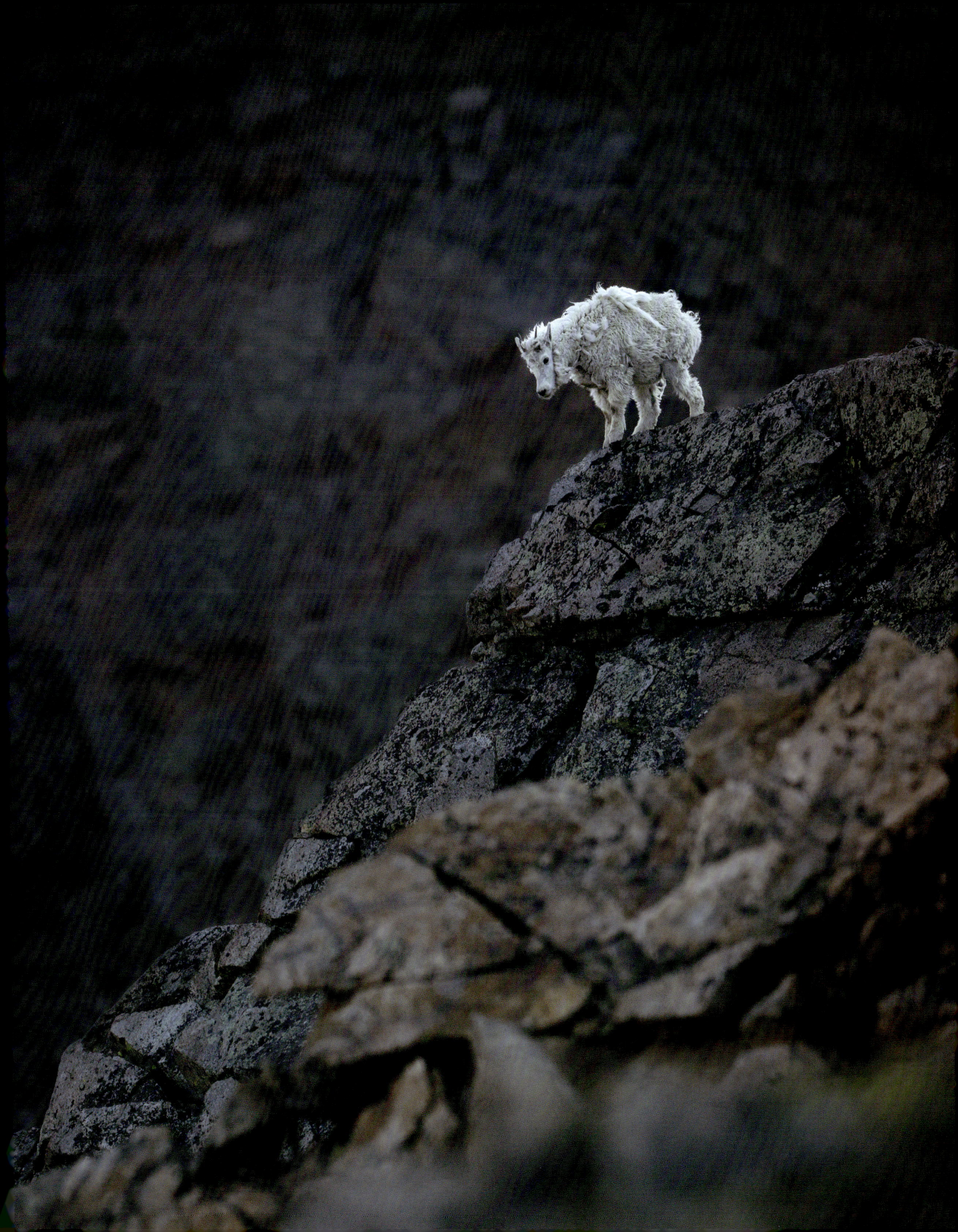

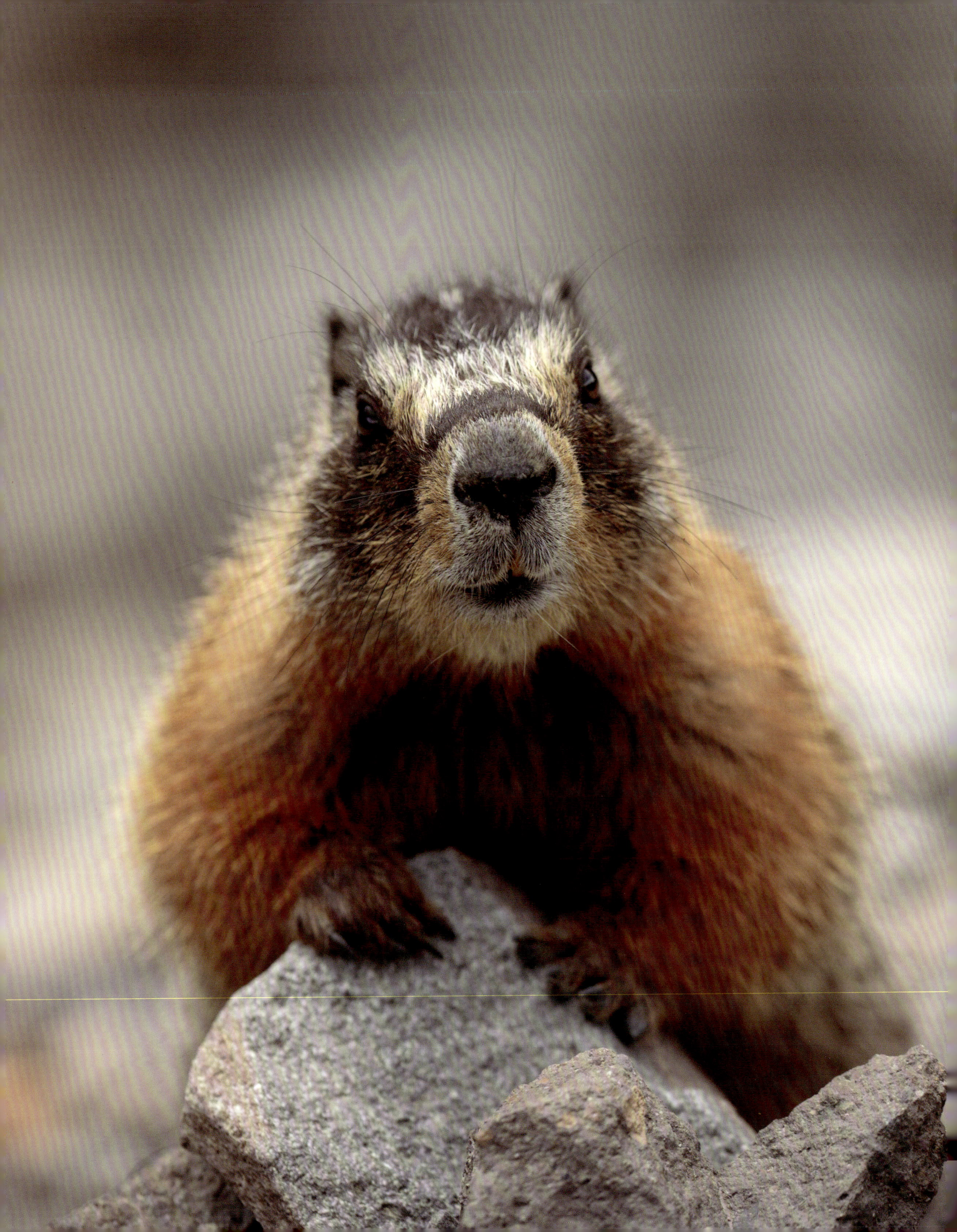

Yellow-bellied Marmot

The yellow-bellied marmot is known by many other names, including groundhog, whistle-pig, and rockchuck. Almost always found near large rocks, often lying on them in the sun, marmots range from lower elevation meadows to the alpine tundra almost anywhere in Yellowstone, including Sylvan Pass, Dunraven Pass, Craig Pass, Sheepeater Cliff, the side of Lake Butte, near Tower Fall, and various other rocky outcrops.

Like the name implies, yellow-bellied marmots have reddish-brown fur with a yellow underside. They can range in size anywhere between 4 and 11 pounds (1.8 and 4.9 kg), feeding on grasses, wildflowers, and seeds throughout the summer and fall seasons. Marmots hibernate longer than any other mammal in Yellowstone, spending on average eight months of the year in the den to avoid the harsh winters. Dens are usually dug into the soil beneath boulders; marmots that fail to dig a deep enough den are at risk of not surviving the winter. With such a lengthy hibernation, marmots spend most of the summer and fall seasons eating as much as possible to gain weight in preparation for winter. During hibernation, marmots may lose half their summer weight, while their metabolism and heart rate slow to preserve resources.

Marmots live in colonies consisting of a dominant male, several females, and their young. Litters of marmots usually consist of three to five pups, which are weaned within the first month of life. Alarm calls are used to communicate danger to other individuals, alerting them and giving the signal to seek shelter. Predators include a wide range of animals like coyotes, foxes, grizzly bears, hawks, and eagles. Some marmots will live as long as fifteen years; their long hibernation is thought to be the key to their longevity.

◀ A yellow-bellied marmot curiously looks up from a rock ledge.

Marmots are an underrated subject to photograph, and I'll admit I have spotted them hundreds of times without ever raising my camera: They are often seen but rarely appreciated. On a slow afternoon in Yellowstone, I decided to entertain myself by photographing marmots, a species I can always rely on finding.

Along the side of a steep and rocky slope, I located several marmots outstretched while sunning in the midday heat. Two of them quickly retreated into the safety of their den, while one marmot remained, watching curiously as I sat atop a large boulder. Soon it dove behind a rock. A few moments later the marmot reappeared, slowly and inquisitively creeping forward, its small hands tightly gripping the rough granite rock. I slowly raised my camera, mimicking the marmot's gradual pace to avoid startling it. Once again, the marmot ducked behind its rock.

This pattern continued, the marmot venturing toward me before losing its nerve and taking shelter. I captured a few photos of the marmot peering over the edge of the rock each time, its orangish-red fur contrasting with the greens of the distant pine slope across the ravine. It became like a game, awaiting its cautious approach and inevitable disappearance. Eventually, the marmot seemed more comfortable with my company and inched even farther away from its hiding spot.

I couldn't help but smile at the comically beady eyes and buck teeth staring back at me. I wondered what thoughts were drifting through the marmot's mind, if any at all. Surely thoughts of survival and instincts to prepare for the seemingly far off winter occupied a decent portion of the marmot's brain, even on a hot summer day. Winter is never far off, and marmots have the luxury of hibernating through its entirety. While contemplating the inner workings of a marmot brain, I was surprised when the marmot leapt off its familiar rock and ran across the hillside, sending pebbles rolling downhill as it went, leaving me alone with my own thoughts on the rocky slope.

► A curious marmot cautiously emerges from behind a boulder.

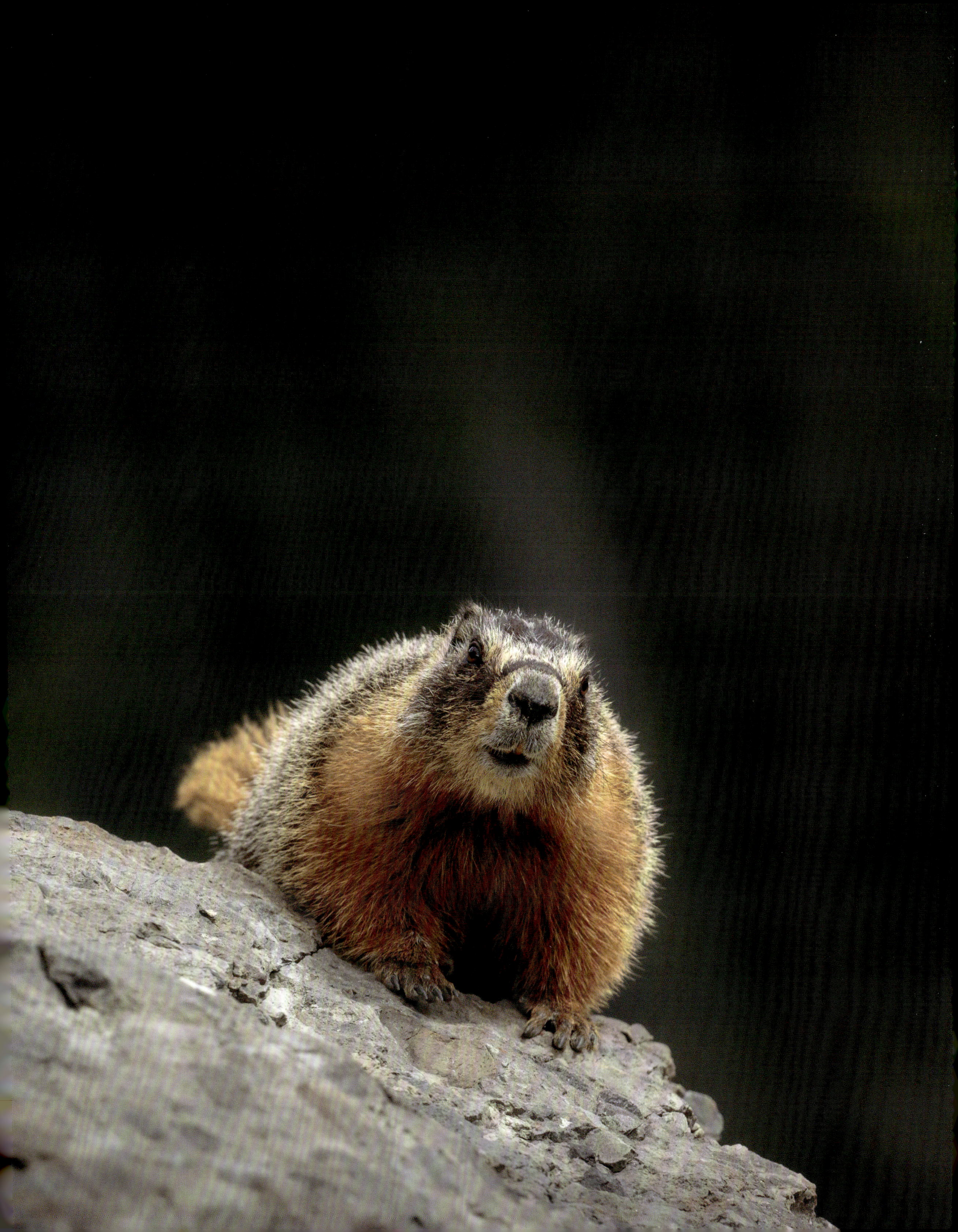

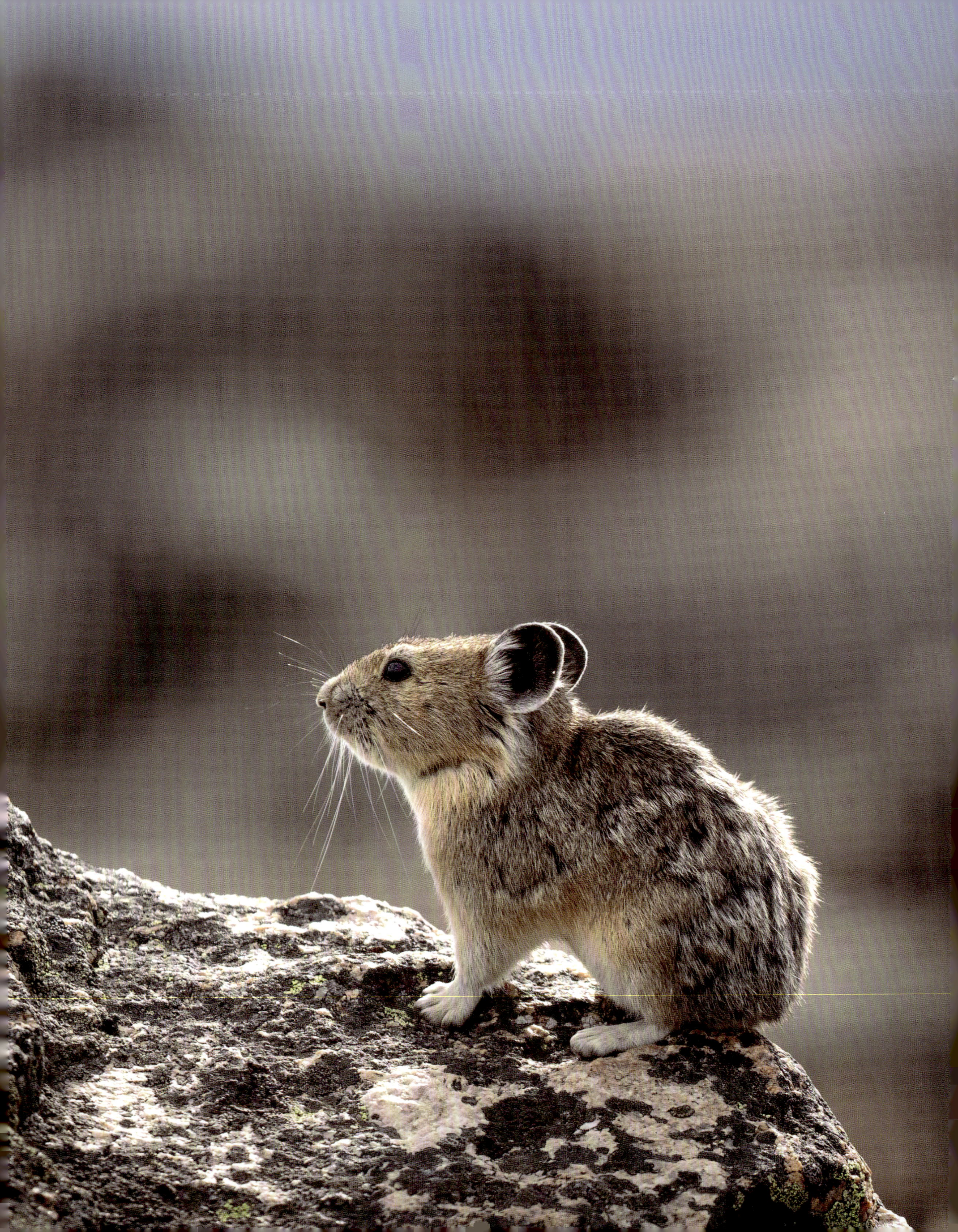

Pika

The pika is a fascinating species and one that easily goes unnoticed. Inhabiting alpine and subalpine areas of Yellowstone, pika prefer talus slopes comprised of loose, large rocks and boulder fields. They can be found in rocky areas across the park, including near Mammoth and Tower-Roosevelt, and on the steep slopes of Sylvan Pass.

Pika have small round ears and round tailless bodies, and though they resemble rodents, they are closely related to rabbits. With grayish-brown fur, they easily camouflage among rocks, which, when combined with their speed and small size, can make them difficult to spot. When pika are seen, they are often darting between rocks or carrying bundles of grass and other vegetation in piles known as haystacks. Pika collect various grasses, sedges, wildflowers, and weeds which they dry in the sun before storing in piles for winter. Pika remain active all year long, burrowing in snow tunnels during the winter months and surviving off their stored food.

For protection, pika live in groups. Pika will alert each other of danger through a distinctive shrill alarm call, allowing them to seek safety. However, pika are also incredibly territorial, particularly over their dens and food stores, and will defend their territory against others. Breeding twice a year, first in the spring and then again in the summer, each pika litter ranges in size between two and six young. Young pika are weaned after a month and can live for six or seven years.

Because they rely heavily on their alpine environment, pika have become an indicator of the ecological impact of climate change. Pika numbers are declining in response to increased warming reducing the number of suitable habitats, especially in areas lower in elevation than Yellowstone. Pika are very sensitive to temperatures above seventy-eight degrees and are often the most active during the early morning and late evening when it is cooler. Other threats to pika include predators like coyotes, foxes, weasels, and birds of prey such as hawks.

◀ A pika blends into its rocky environment.

With their small size and incredible speed, pika are one of the most challenging animals to photograph. However, they are incredibly fun to watch as they dart between boulders and scamper over rocks. On a slow afternoon while camping in the alpine regions, I sat down at the edge of a rock field in search of pika. Their iconic chirps rang out, each one coming from a different direction as I searched the rocks for any movement.

Several pika darted past before I was even able to raise my camera. With dappled gray and tan fur, they blended into the granite boulders, making them nearly invisible when still. After noticing a pika following a clear path from the steep rock pile to the edge of the open tundra, I positioned myself behind a nearby boulder in hopes of photographing the pika on its desperate dash to safety after collecting a haystack. Pika are busy creatures, always preparing for hibernation in an almost frantic and anxious manner.

The pika ran past several more times, but my reflexes were always too slow for a photo, even if my camera was already raised. Like a blur across the rocks, the pika raced here and there, never stopping for more than a few seconds to give a loud chirp before hurrying off again. Most of the photos I'd taken were unsuccessful, either blurry or missing the pika altogether. The pika were winning.

Then, without warning, a pika leapt atop a nearby boulder, almost startling me. Moving slowly to avoid scaring it, I raised my camera and snapped a few photos, amazed that the animal remained still for even a few seconds. I held my breath, waiting for the pika to dart away at any moment. Instead, it simply rested on the edge of the rock. The pika's long whiskers twitched furiously up and down. Its ears were perked for any sign of danger, and its dark eyes were wide and alert. From such a close distance I could even see the pika's delicate flank rise and fall with each small breath of fresh mountain air. I blinked, and it was gone.

▶ A pika takes a rare moment to pause on a boulder.

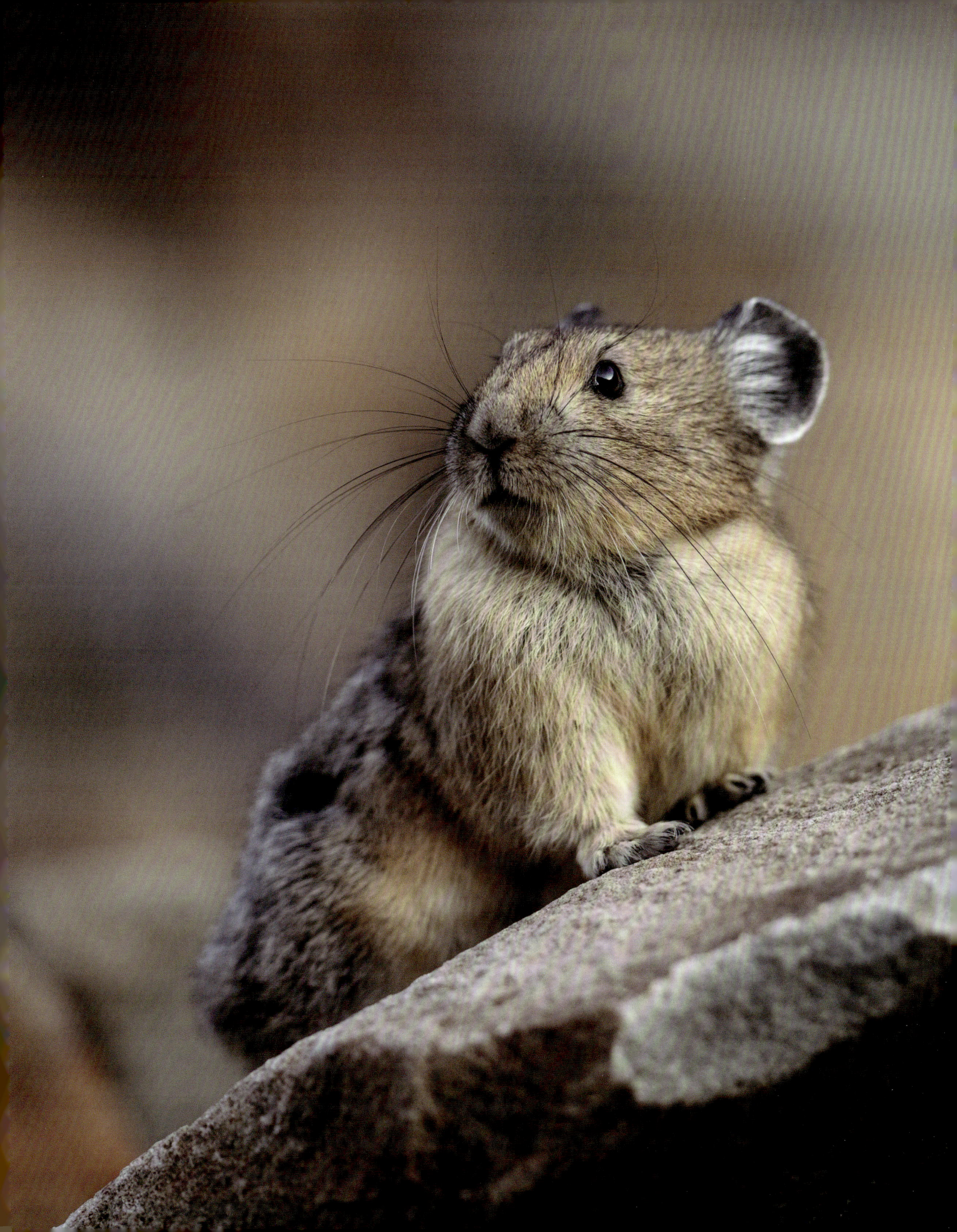

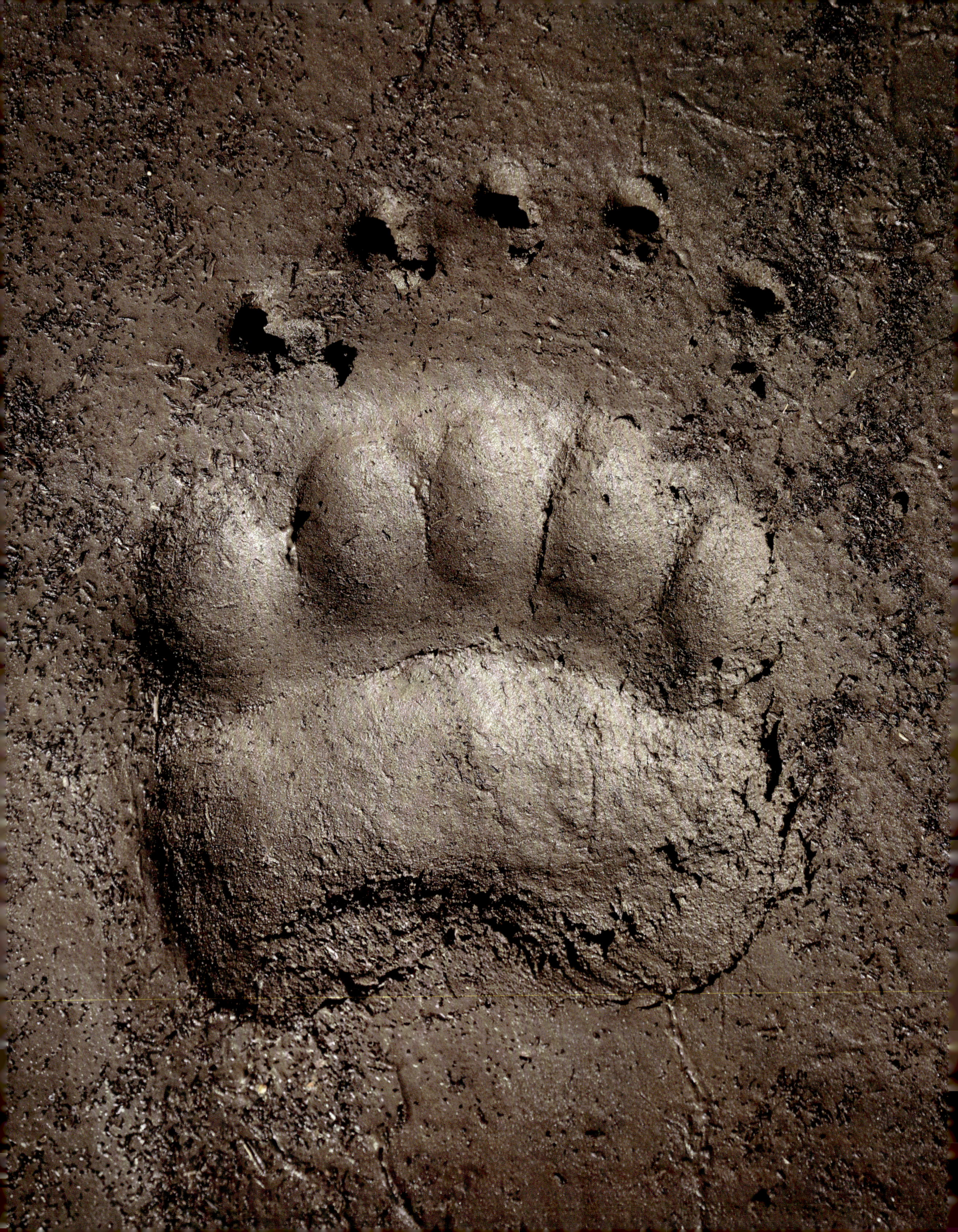

Elusive Animals

Wildlife photography is incredibly unpredictable. I often go days without photographing a single animal. While it can be frustrating, the erratic nature of wildlife constantly inspires me and keeps me returning to the mountains, camera in hand, ready for anything.

I never know when an unforgettable encounter may occur—something I was powerfully reminded of on a spring afternoon when I crossed paths with Yellowstone's most elusive species: the wolverine. The sighting lasted only a matter of seconds as the wolverine loped across the road in front of me and disappeared into the shadowy forest, but it serves as a reminder that in Yellowstone anything can happen at any given moment. I have never felt such a sheer rush of awe and shock. More importantly, the wolverine taught me that the value of an encounter goes beyond the images I am able to create; instead, the true value is in spending time in the presence of a wild animal.

There are many species that inhabit Yellowstone that I have not had the pleasure of crossing paths with or been lucky enough to photograph. While their images have not been included in the previous pages, I wanted to acknowledge their presence in the ecosystem and the excitement the mere thought of photographing them brings me. Some are rarely seen due to their nature, either because they're nocturnal or favor remote areas of the ecosystem. Other species simply have smaller populations, making every individual a rarity. Camouflage or small size helps conceal some species, allowing them to completely fade from view.

Yellowstone's more elusive species are the pine marten, mink, fisher, wolverine, mountain lion, bobcat, lynx, porcupine, snowshoe hare, numerous species of small rodents, and several bats. Still, they are not completely hidden away. They leave signs of their presence in their tracks and scat, and occasionally reveal themselves, even if for a few seconds, to anyone lucky enough to be at the right place at the right time.

Perhaps the next time I cross paths with a wolverine (if there is a next time), I will be lucky enough to walk away with a photograph. Until then, I will continue to spend as much time as I can in the presence of wild animals.

◀ A grizzly track in the mud; tracks are often the only indication an animal has been in the area.

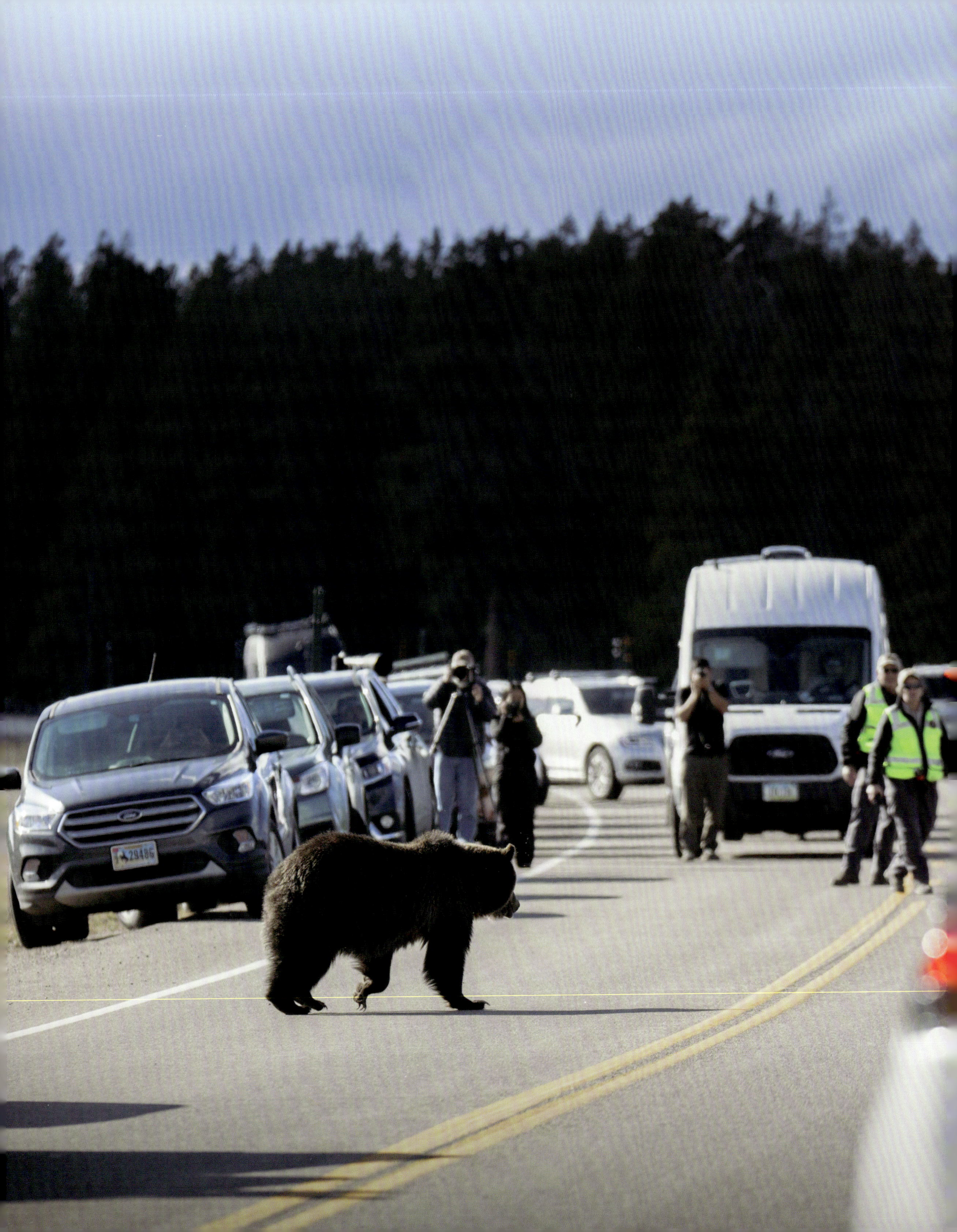

Yellowstone of the Future

In 2024, 4,744,352 people visited Yellowstone. It was the second busiest year on record behind 2021. Projections show even more visitors will enter Yellowstone's gate in future years, all coming to enjoy the area's natural beauty, wildlife, and various outdoor recreation opportunities. I have seen this shift firsthand in my lifetime as busy places in the park only become busier and once-quiet spots grow crowded. With visitation numbers almost doubling in just the last twenty-five years, it brings concerns about balance and long-term effects on the park's ecosystem and resources. Many other national parks, including Glacier, Zion, and Rocky Mountain, have started limiting the number of daily visitors through a timed-entry reservation system designed to reduce the daily impact on natural resources. Though Yellowstone has not followed suit yet, I believe it is only a matter of time. For now, Yellowstone is trying to better accommodate large numbers of visitors by focusing more on increased education and an ongoing infrastructure improvement plan to widen and strengthen roads.

More than anything, visitors need to be aware of their own personal impact on Yellowstone. Following all regulations—including remaining on boardwalks and trails, keeping a safe distance from wildlife, and properly storing food—is important not only for a visitor's personal safety, but for the well-being of the entire Yellowstone Ecosystem. Wildlife is especially sensitive to the impacts of irresponsible tourism. Every year, numerous animals fall victim to human-wildlife conflicts like vehicle collisions and management removal after being fed. As people who recreate in the outdoors, we have a responsibility to protect and preserve our wildlife and public lands for future generations.

Despite potential pressures from visitation, the wildlife of Yellowstone continues to thrive. Yellowstone remains one of the last and largest intact ecosystems in the lower forty-eight states. It is a place where bison and wolves roam without borders and grizzlies and elk have free range of the vast mountains. Thermal features bubble with forceful energy from deep under the surface. Rivers continue to carve canyons and plummet over falls. Few places on Earth rival Yellowstone's pure and undeniable wildness. Regardless of what the future holds, one thing is certain: Yellowstone has been and always will be purely wild in the best ways imaginable.

◀ Visitors look on and stop traffic as a grizzly bear crosses the road.
▼ *Following:* A bull elk bugles in a fall meadow during the elk rut.

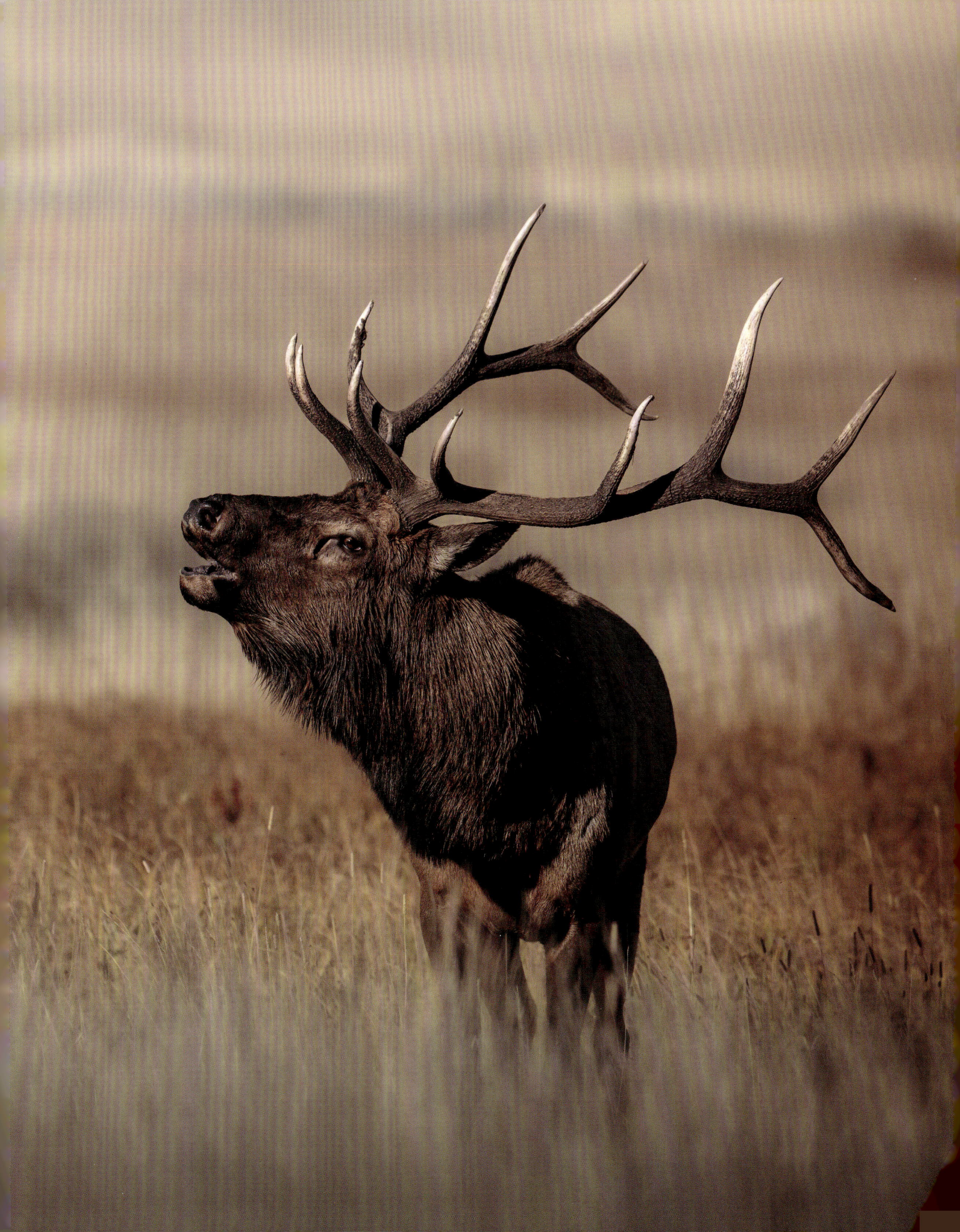

Index

Page numbers in **bold** type indicate photographs.

C

D

E

S

T

U

W

Y

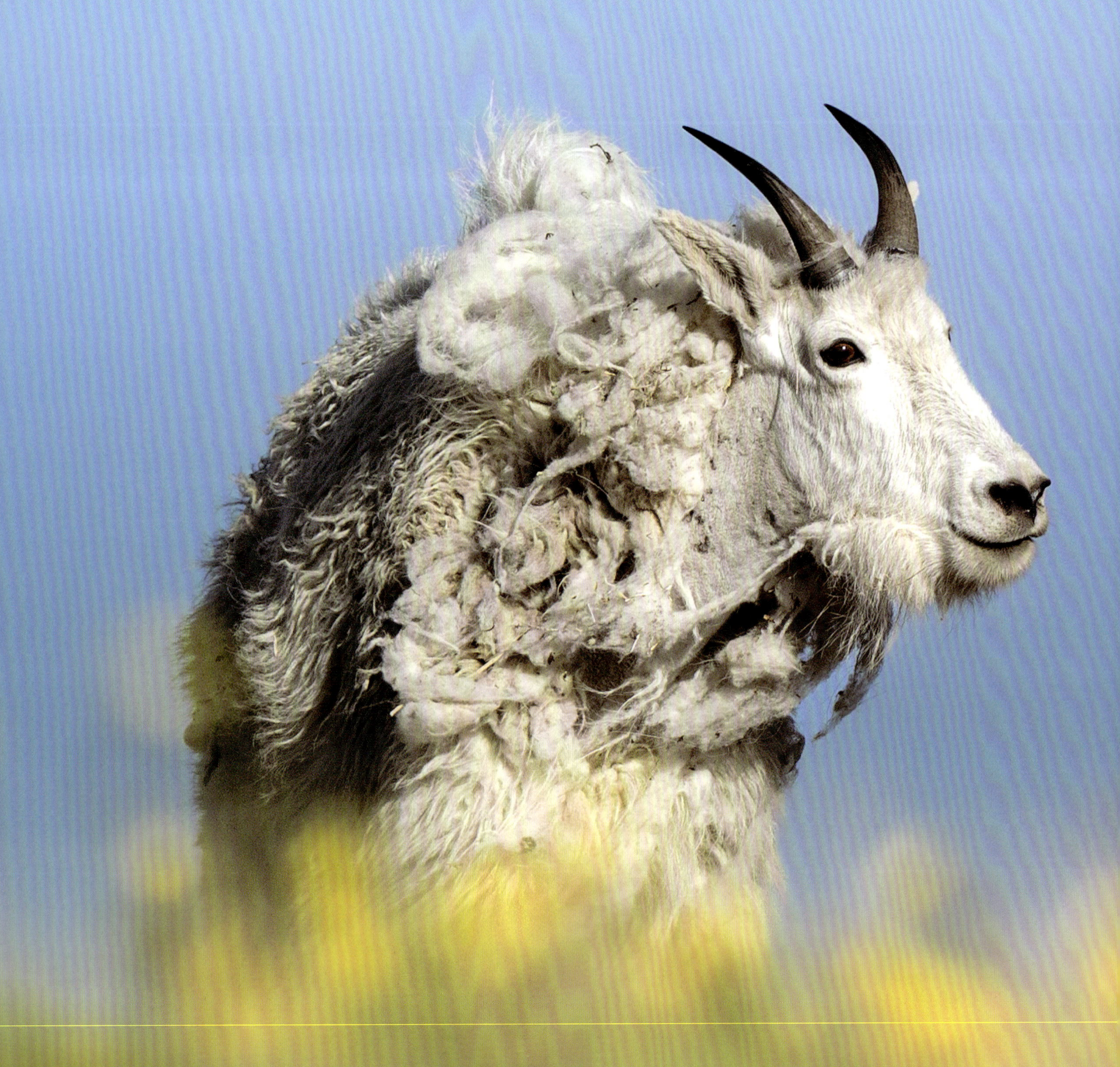

Acknowledgments

First and foremost, I would like to thank my parents for fostering my love of nature from an early age and for everything they have done to support me. Mom, thank you for encouraging my creativity and seeing value in the arts. I would also like to thank my brother, Trevor, for constantly being an inspiring role model and a creative person to share ideas with. Additionally, his beautifully written foreword serves as the perfect introduction to the Yellowstone we both grew up sharing.

To two special labs—first my sweet Beach and now Sylvan—thank you for your unwavering companionship through many long days in the field.

Tanner Haver, thank you for loving grizzly bears and Yellowstone as much as I do and for constantly pushing me to be a better photographer and storyteller. Here's to many more days spent together in pursuit of wild places and, most importantly, grizzlies.

There have been many friends I have met solely through photography, all of whom I thank for the wonderful sense of community and for the countless hours spent in conversation while waiting for wildlife.

Thank you to Amy Gerber for nurturing my love of science and wildlife—first as a teacher, but most of all as a friend. Your inspiration has helped guide me to where I am today.

I would like to acknowledge the diligent work of the National Park Service for protecting and preserving Yellowstone and its wildlife. Yellowstone would not be the same without each and every ranger who educates visitors, enforces regulations, and manages wildlife; the importance of your work cannot be overstated.

I owe a deep and sincere thank-you to everyone at The Quarto Group who made this book possible and for giving me a way to share the amazing wildlife of Yellowstone with others.

Lastly, I'd like to thank every wild animal I have ever crossed paths with, especially those whose images appear in this book.

► A grizzly bear leads her two cubs along the shore of Yellowstone Lake.
▲ *Previous:* A shaggy mountain goat walks through wildflowers.

About the Author

Julia Cook is a wildlife photographer and conservationist based in the Greater Yellowstone Ecosystem of Wyoming. Growing up in Cody, Wyoming, less than an hour from Yellowstone National Park, Julia developed a love for nature at an early age, which eventually led her to pick up wildlife photography as a creative outlet. Julia graduated from the University of Wyoming in 2023 with a BS in environment and natural resources and a BA in history, with human-wildlife conflicts and the history of conservation practices in Yellowstone being a particular area of focus throughout her studies. Now working full time as a wildlife photographer, Julia spends most of her free time in the field photographing various species of wildlife, though grizzly bears are a favorite. Other hobbies include drawing, hiking, fishing, camping, and spending time with friends and family. Julia's overall goal in photography is to capture impactful images of native wildlife to promote wildlife conservation while inspiring others to spend meaningful time in nature.

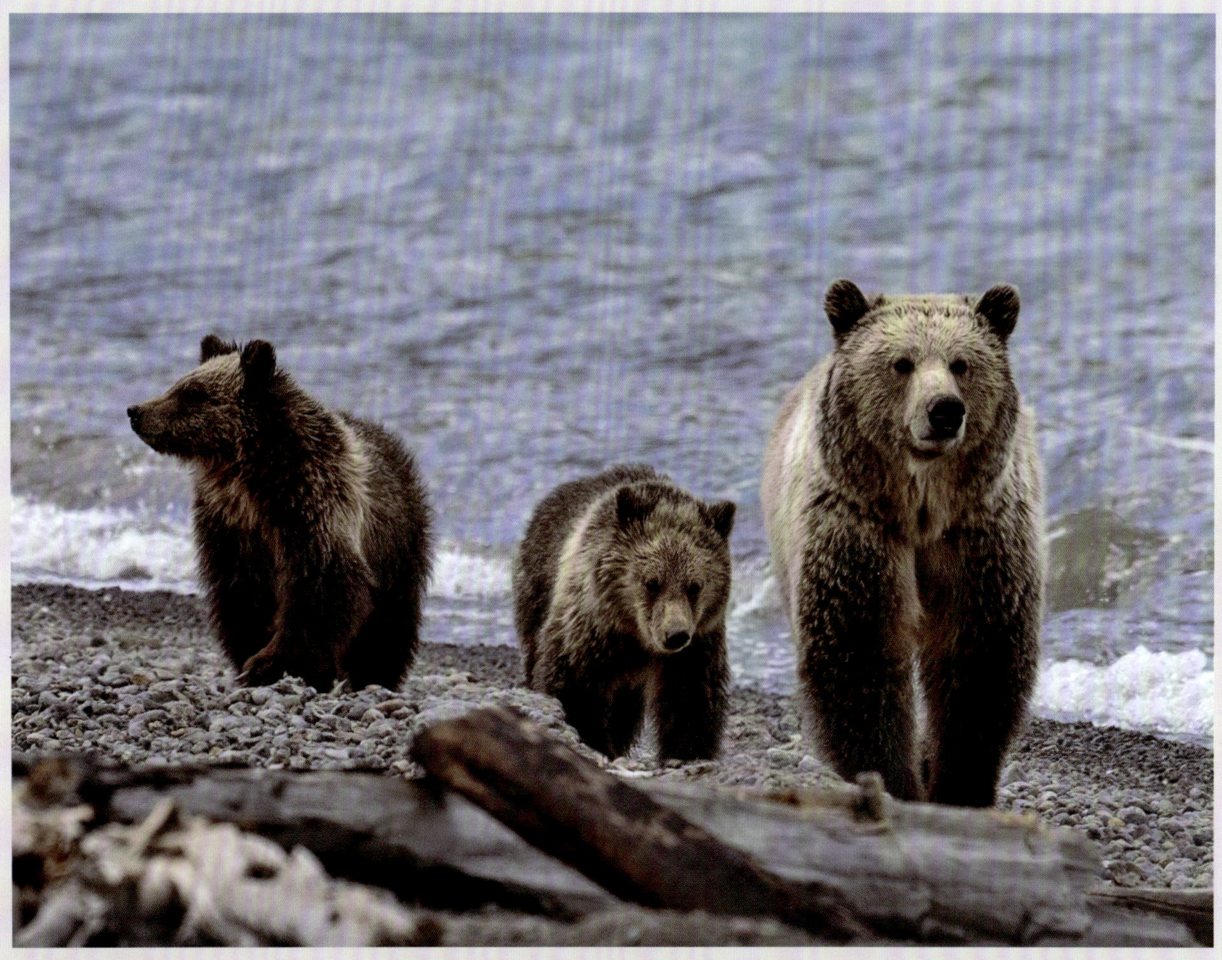

First published in 2025 by Epic Ink,
an imprint of The Quarto Group,
142 West 36th Street, 4th Floor,
New York, NY 10018, USA
(212) 779-4972
www.Quarto.com

Epic Ink titles are also available at discount for retail, wholesale, promotional, and bulk purchase. For details, contact the Special Sales Manager by email at specialsales@quarto.com or by mail at The Quarto Group, Attn: Special Sales Manager, 100 Cummings Center Suite 265D, Beverly, MA 01915 USA.

10 9 8 7 6 5 4 3 2 1

ISBN: 978-0-7603-9408-3

Digital edition published in 2025
eISBN: 978-0-7603-9409-0

Library of Congress Control Number: 2025934138

Group Publisher: Rage Kindelsperger
Creative Director: Laura Drew
Managing Editor: Cara Donaldson
Editors: Katie McGuire and Flannery Wiest
Interior Design: Kim Winscher
Cover Design: Laura Drew
Cartography: Julie Witmer Custom Map Design

Printed in China